Sharing, Privacy and Trust in Our Networked World

A Report to the OCLC Membership

OCLC

Sharing, Privacy and Trust in Our Networked World

A Report to the OCLC Membership

Principal contributors
Cathy De Rosa, MBA, Vice President for the Americas and Global Vice President of Marketing
Joanne Cantrell, Marketing Analyst
Andy Havens, Manager, Creative Services
Janet Hawk, MBA, Director, Market Research & Analysis
Lillie Jenkins, PhD, MSIS, Market Research Support Specialist

Graphics, layout and editing
Brad Gauder, Creative Services Writer
Rick Limes, Art Director

Contributors
Diane Cellentani, MBA, Market Research Consultant to OCLC
Tam Dalrymple, MLS, Senior Information Specialist
Larry Olszewski, PhD, MLS, Director, OCLC Library
Sam Smith, Art Director
Tom Storey, Editor

OCLC
Dublin, Ohio USA

Cataloged in WorldCat on September 11, 2007
OCLC Control Number: 170923242

ISBN: 1-55653-370-5

        12 11 10 09 08 07   1 2 3 4 5 6

Table of Contents

Introduction   **vii**
    Methodology   xi

Our Digital Lives   **1-1**

Our Social Spaces   **2-1**

Privacy, Security and Trust   **3-1**

U.S. Library Directors   **4-1**

Libraries and Social Networking   **5-1**

Beyond the Numbers   **6-1**

Report Highlights   **7-1**

Conclusion   **8-1**

Appendices   **9-1**
    A: College Students in Our Networked World   A-1
    B: Glossary   B-1
    C: People Consulted   C-1
    D: Readings and Other Sources   D-1
    E: About OCLC   E-1
    F: Comparative Timeline   F-1

Introduction

The new Web is a very different thing. It is a tool for bringing together the small contributions of millions of people and making them matter.

—From *Time*, "Time's Person of the Year: You," by Lev Grossman, Dec. 13, 2006

I wrote in the introduction of our last landscape report, *Perceptions of Libraries and Information Resources* (2005), that the report "didn't challenge as much as it confirmed" what we knew about library use, the library brand and the ever-growing appetite for Internet information services. The *Perceptions* study confirmed our belief that "Googling" and Internet search engines had gone from fads to phenomena to infrastructure, and that libraries had to reach out to users on the Internet—not wait, or hope, for users to find the library in the rapidly expanding universe of digital information resources. With "books" as the dominant perception (brand) of libraries, users were comfortable with the occasional trip to the library to find a book of interest, but were more than comfortable substituting a visit to Yahoo! or MSN or Google for a visit to the library to get quick access to digital information. And information consumers were confident that what they found on the Internet was as credible and as trustworthy as information obtained from a library.

Eighteen months later, the story is in many ways the same. Users remain confident and comfortable with Internet information resources and libraries are still seen primarily as a source of books. No surprise—and no retreat.

But of this report, *Sharing, Privacy and Trust in Our Networked World*, I must say that our research doesn't "confirm as much as it challenges" us to think about the Internet beyond "the search." What comes next? What will information access and library services look like on an Internet that has moved beyond simple search, beyond corporate Web sites, past the library Web site, and beyond the blog? What is it that motivates, even inspires, millions of users to spend hours online, not searching for information, but creating information, building content and establishing online communities? What drives users to not only contribute information, but to contribute "themselves," creating detailed personal profiles on social sites and sharing that information to establish new relationships with hundreds of new virtual friends? No longer accurately defined as "information consumers," Internet users are becoming "information producers" and will soon be the primary authors, producers and architects of information on the World Wide Web.

In less than 24 months, social sites like MySpace, Mixi, Facebook and YouTube have built a new "social Web," connecting communities of hundreds of millions of users, across much of the industrialized world. In June 2007, the world's top three social sites (YouTube, MySpace, Facebook) attracted more than 350 million people to their Web sites, according to comScore. And, in September 2007, five of Alexa's global top ten Web sites were categorized as "social Web sites," a classification that did not appear in our survey results when we last reviewed the information landscape in 2005.

We know relatively little about what these emerging social Web communities will mean for the future of the Internet or the possibilities they hold for library services on the Internet. So it was an easy decision to select exploration of online social spaces as the primary area of research for this latest scan of the information landscape. What was a bit more challenging was to settle on the relevant aspects of social spaces to study. Much has already been researched and written about the top social sites like YouTube and MySpace, their founders and financiers. And from what we observed on the surface, it appeared that much of what is happening on social sites is unrelated to education or to library services. Many information professionals I spoke with about our plans to study social networking saw little merit, educational or otherwise, in what is happening on these sites. This piqued our interest. So we decided to construct a study that explored the social networking attitudes and habits of both end users and librarians.

Our study explores four primary areas:

1) User practices and preferences on their favorite social spaces

2) User attitudes about sharing and receiving information on social spaces, commercial sites and library sites

3) Information privacy; what matters and what doesn't

4) Librarian social networking practices and preferences; their views on privacy, policy and the potential of social networks for libraries

We were pleased to again partner with Harris Interactive to conduct our online surveys. We surveyed over 6,100 users, ages 14 to 84 from Canada, France, Germany, Japan, the United Kingdom and the United States. While we surveyed users in Canada, the United Kingdom and the United States for previous reports, we were excited to expand our studies and learn more about online attitudes and practices in Germany, France and Japan for the first time. We conducted these surveys in German, French and Japanese. We also polled 382 U.S. library directors. Unfortunately, the lack of an available online research pool of library directors outside the United States limited our survey to U.S. directors, a shortcoming we hope to reverse in future reports.

The report begins with a review of "Our Digital Lives" in 2007. Use of standard Internet services (e-mail, search, online banking, etc.) is now widespread and strikingly uniform across age groups, geographies and communities (i.e., urban, suburban, rural) in the six countries surveyed. In fact, our findings suggest that it is no longer very interesting to differentiate the habits of experienced (digital natives) and novice (digital immigrants) Internet users. Nearly 90% of Internet users in the geographies surveyed have been online four years or more and a quarter of users have been online for a decade. The Internet is now familiar territory, and users are looking for "what's next."

Today, the term **social networking** *is being used in new ways, but the concepts behind it—sharing content, collaborating with others and creating community—are not new.*

We review the origins of social networking in "Our Social Spaces" and explore the use of social networking and social media sites across the six countries. Twenty-eight percent (28%) of the online population surveyed have used a social networking site in the last 12 months. We review users' top motivations for selecting social sites, what information they share, why they share, who they share with and why they leave.

Much of our research concentrated on learning more about user attitudes regarding privacy and trust online. In "Privacy, Security and Trust," we explore social sites and how user privacy and participation practices on these sites differ from participation on commercial sites and library sites. We report concerns, and lack of concern, about Internet privacy and security in general. What does information privacy mean to users, and are their views changing? What are the implications for library services and the promise of privacy?

In the chapter "U.S. Library Directors," we compare and contrast U.S. librarian online habits and attitudes with habits and attitudes of the U.S. general public. Our survey finds that while librarians are using the same Internet resources as the general online population (often at higher rates), their practices and attitudes about sharing, privacy and trust differ substantially from the populations they serve.

We asked both users and library directors to share their thoughts about the potential of combining the benefits of social spaces with the offerings of their libraries in "Libraries and Social Networking." What could social space(s) tailored for library users, maybe largely built by library users, look like? Can/should the library provide new services via social spaces that foster collaboration, community and trust across the information landscape?

And finally, in-depth interviews with information services professionals across a broad spectrum of the community were conducted to gain personal insights into social networking, trust and privacy online. These early adopters of social networking have been working collaboratively on the Web for many years, and they shared with us both the practical and theoretical issues at stake. Selections from over 200 pages of interviews can be found in "Beyond the Numbers."

So what will come next? What will information access and library services look like on an Internet that has moved beyond simple search, beyond corporate Web sites, beyond the blog and beyond the traditional library Web site? We hope the findings challenge our views of the role of "social" networks in the future of libraries. We also hope that the user viewpoints revealed in the survey guide us as we build policies and practices affecting access, privacy, sharing and participation to serve users who are now both borrowers, and builders, of information in our networked world.

Cathy De Rosa
Vice President for the Americas and
Global Vice President of Marketing
OCLC

Methodology

OCLC commissioned Harris Interactive, Inc. to field a blind study targeting two primary audiences: the general public in six countries and library directors in the United States. Harris drew a sample for the general public survey from the Harris Poll Online (HPOL) panel and from members of online research panels managed by Harris partner vendors. OCLC supplied Harris with a random sample of U.S. library directors.

A total of 6,545 respondents were surveyed between December 7, 2006 and February 7, 2007. Respondents were 14 years or older.

The online survey for the general public was open to panelists in Canada, France, Germany, Japan, the United Kingdom and the United States. The survey was conducted in English in Canada, the United Kingdom and the United States. The survey was conducted in French in France, German in Germany and Japanese in Japan.

Harris used the HPOL for Canada, the United Kingdom and the United States samples and executed samples from vendor partners in France, Germany and Japan. A total of 6,163 members of the general public in the six countries completed the survey. The following table shows the total general public respondents by country, age and gender. Survey respondents were age 14 or older in Canada, Japan, the United Kingdom and the United States. Due to local parental permission laws for surveys in France and Germany, the youngest age of survey participants was 15 years of age.

Total General Public Respondents
By Gender, Age and Country

	Total General Public	Canada	United States	Japan	France	Germany	United Kingdom
Total Respondents	6,163	921	1,801	804	821	846	970
Age							
14/15 to 21	20%	15%	21%	27%	14%	17%	10%
22 to 49	53%	51%	49%	54%	68%	62%	51%
50+	27%	34%	30%	19%	18%	21%	39%
Gender							
Male	51%	48%	49%	54%	53%	52%	55%
Female	49%	52%	51%	46%	47%	48%	45%

Source: *Sharing, Privacy and Trust in Our Networked World*, OCLC, 2007.

Demographics of Survey Respondents

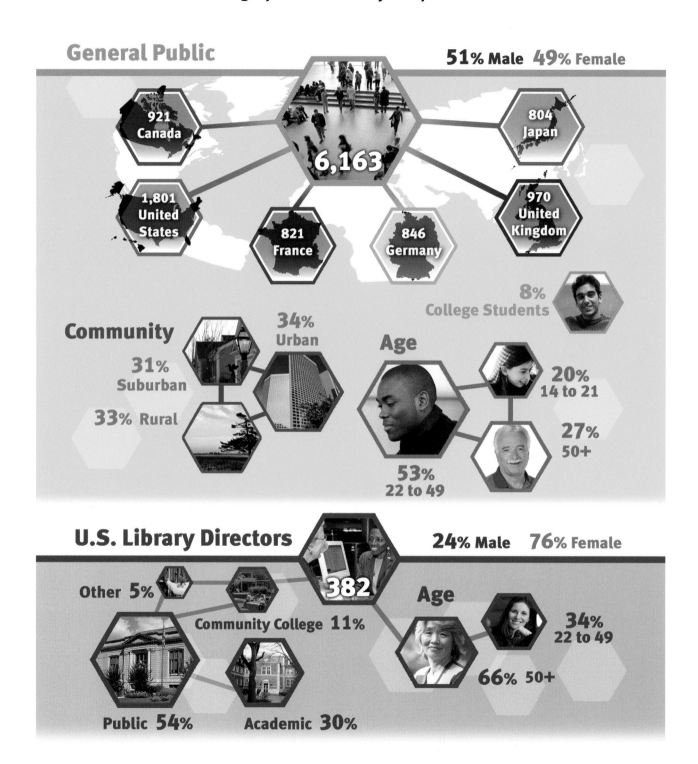

General Public

51% Male 49% Female

921 Canada

804 Japan

6,163

1,801 United States

821 France

846 Germany

970 United Kingdom

8% College Students

Community

31% Suburban

34% Urban

33% Rural

Age

20% 14 to 21

27% 50+

53% 22 to 49

U.S. Library Directors

24% Male 76% Female

Other 5%

382

Community College 11%

Public 54%

Academic 30%

Age

34% 22 to 49

66% 50+

Statistical margin of error +/− 1.3% at the 95% confidence level for the general public survey.
Age, gender, education and income data are representative of the online population for the general public.
Statistical margin of error +/− 5% at the 95% confidence level for the U.S. library director survey.
Library director data have not been weighted.

OCLC surveyed U.S. library directors as a separate sample audience. Harris Interactive mailed 4,000 postcards to U.S. library directors inviting participation in the survey. Each invitation included the online survey URL and unique log-in information to verify each respondent's completion. The online survey consisted of the same questions as administered to the general public with additional questions relevant to library professionals. In total, 382 library directors from academic, public, community college, K–12 school and special libraries completed the survey online.

The collected general public survey data have an overall statistical margin of error of +/– 1.3% at the 95% confidence level for the online population in the countries surveyed. The online population may or may not represent the general population of each country surveyed. The collected librarian survey data have an overall statistical margin of error of +/– 5% at the 95% confidence level for the U.S. online population.

Based on statistics from www.internetworldstats.com, the following table shows the percentage of residents in the countries surveyed who have Internet access (the online population). The table also provides Internet access growth over the last seven years.

Internet Users from Internet World Stats

	Canada	United States	Japan	France	Germany	United Kingdom
Population (2007 est.)	32,440,970	301,967,681	128,644,345	61,350,009	82,509,367	60,363,602
Internet users	22,000,000	210,575,287	86,300,000	32,925,953	50,426,117	37,600,000
Penetration of Internet access in 2007 (% of population)	67.8%	69.7%	67.1%	53.7%	61.1%	62.3%
User growth (2000–2007)	73.2%	120.8%	83.3%	287.4%	110.1%	144.2%

Table content is based on data at www.internetworldstats.com, accessed September 24, 2007 from data last updated June 30, 2007.

The table below details how often respondents visited the library in person or online in the last 12 months. Respondents were then asked to identify the library that they use primarily (e.g., public, college/university, community college, school, corporate, other) and were asked to answer all library-related questions with that library in mind.

Library Visits in the Last 12 Months
By Country

	Total General Public	Canada	United States	Japan	France	Germany	United Kingdom
Daily	1%	2%	2%	2%	0%	0%	1%
Weekly	9%	12%	10%	6%	9%	7%	8%
Monthly	13%	12%	14%	11%	16%	11%	12%
Several times a year	26%	26%	32%	17%	19%	17%	24%
Once a year	7%	7%	7%	6%	4%	7%	9%
I have not been to a library and/or library Web site in the last 12 months but have visited in the past	27%	31%	28%	18%	23%	36%	35%
I have never been to the library and/or library Web site	17%	10%	7%	40%	29%	22%	11%

Source: *Sharing, Privacy and Trust in Our Networked World*, OCLC, 2007, question 855.

All general public survey data were weighted demographically to be representative of each country's online population. Question wording may introduce some error or bias into opinion poll findings.

Percentages in data tables may not total 100 percent due to rounding or question format. Respondents were sometimes asked to select all responses that may apply or were not required to answer the question.

A total of 83 questions were included in the survey. The survey included a series of branching questions such that a participant's response to a question could lead to a series of follow-up questions. The survey also asked open-ended questions to ensure that respondents had the opportunity to provide input in their own words. This report includes samples of the verbatim comments.

The survey results included 29,000 verbatim responses to 19 questions. Over 14,000 survey responses to seven questions were categorized by the OCLC Market Research team and presented in the report as tag clouds. Tag clouds are visual representations of data that present the most frequently expressed opinions in relatively larger font text and less frequently expressed opinions in smaller font text. Verbatim responses from questions are also presented in the margins of selected sections of the report. All verbatim comments are presented as entered by survey respondents, including spelling, grammatical and punctuation errors.

The OCLC market research team analyzed and summarized survey results to produce this report. The team performed correlation and regression analyses on several interrelated questions to elicit additional information from the data.

OCLC market research staff conducted interviews with information professionals and researchers who represent academic, public and special libraries and commercial organizations. OCLC staff also conducted three focus group sessions with graduate and undergraduate university students, and members of the general public. Focus group participants included staff from Rafiel's Signature Salon, a hair salon in Columbus, Ohio, U.S., and undergraduate students and graduate students at McMaster University in Hamilton, Ontario Canada. The participants discussed their use of social networking tools and the roles such tools play in their lives. Their views are incorporated into the report.

Terms

Social Networking Sites: Web sites primarily designed to facilitate interaction between users who share interests, attitudes and activities, such as Facebook, Mixi and MySpace.

Social Media Sites: Web sites that allow individuals to share content they have created, such as YouTube (video sharing) and Flickr (photo sharing). While interaction occurs on social media sites, the primary purpose of the site is to publish and share content.

Commercial Sites: Web sites used for browsing and purchasing goods and services.

Our Digital Lives

... Look at 2006 through a different lens and you'll see another story, one that isn't about conflict or great men. It's a story about community and collaboration on a scale never seen before. It's about the cosmic compendium of knowledge Wikipedia and the million-channel people's network YouTube and the online metropolis MySpace. It's about the many wresting power from the few and helping one another for nothing and how that will not only change the world, but also change the way the world changes.

—From *Time*, "Time's Person of the Year: You," by Lev Grossman, Dec. 13, 2006

Nearly

90%

of the total
general public
**have used the
Internet for four
or more years.**

Over

50%

of the total
general public
**have used the
Internet for
seven years or
more.**

The Internet has come of age.

Distinctions between the attitudes and behaviors of younger people who have grown up with personal computers and Internet technology and those born before the Internet era are no longer easy to classify. The rapid adoption of Internet applications and the duration of Internet use by users of all ages suggest that the time may have arrived when it is no longer fruitful to create comparisons between attitudes and habits of individuals born before personal computers were widespread and those born after.

Scholars, press and librarians have spent a fair amount of time researching differences in behavior, attitudes and skill sets between "digital natives"—mostly children and young adults born after 1980 and raised with access to computer technology and the Internet—and "digital immigrants"—that is, everyone else. Purchasing behaviors, learning styles, work and communication habits have been studied and analyzed between these two groups. Research suggests that these two groups analyze and process information differently. There is nothing in our research to suggest that this conclusion is not valid, nor that age differences in the use and adoption of Internet tools do not exist. Our research and other current studies do suggest, however, that due to the widespread adoption of digital technologies over more than a decade, the behaviors and attitudes of these two technology generations are beginning to converge—that many digital immigrants are now fully indoctrinated into the culture. Since the publication of the OCLC membership report *Perceptions of Libraries and Information Resources* in 2005, usage of many Internet activities has grown substantially in the three countries surveyed in both 2005 and 2007—Canada, the United Kingdom and the United States. Search engine use has gone from 71% to 90%. E-mail use has grown from 73% to an outstanding 97%. And the use of blogs, a newly discovered communication medium for many in 2005, has grown from 16% to 46% in 18 months. The unfortunate exception is the use of library Web sites; usage has dropped from 2005 to 2007.

Internet access is now "standard equipment" for the majority of the general public respondents in the countries surveyed. Respondents in these countries report long-term Internet usage and experience. Nearly 90% of all respondents have used the Internet for four or more years and over half have been using the Internet for seven years or more. And, it is no longer just youth who can be labeled as the experienced Internet users. The clear majority of adults over the age of 50 have experience using the Internet.

OCLC's survey data also found that Internet usage is quite similar across geographies, both by country and by residential community—urban, suburban and rural locales.

These findings prompt our belief that we may have arrived at a tipping point in the digital evolution timeline. A tipping point that may move the focus of Internet activities away from exploration toward creation and mass contribution.

Respondents are moving from Internet visitors to developers, creating their own digital experiences and communities. Respondents reported using a vast array of Internet publishing services, from blogging to building their own Web pages. Online activities considered "emerging services" just a few years ago, such as online banking and instant messaging, are now used by the majority of respondents across most age groups and countries surveyed. For many of all ages, the Internet has moved well beyond a specific tool used for spot reference.

Across the online population in the six countries and within the urban, suburban and rural communities surveyed, Internet usage tenure and types of activities respondents participate in are remarkably similar. Usage and interests across age groups also show interestingly consistent attitudes and behavior. And while usage and activity patterns are generally consistent across the parts of the world surveyed, differences between countries and age groups will be noted.

We begin our report with an update on the digital lives of the general public we surveyed in the six countries, their Internet tenure, activities and country differences.

Perceptions to Sharing ...

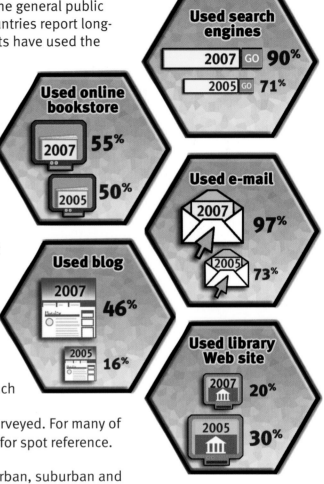

Figures compare data from OCLC's 2005 report, *Perceptions of Libraries and Information Resources* and OCLC's 2007 report, *Sharing, Privacy and Trust in Our Networked World* for the online populations surveyed in Canada, the United Kingdom and the United States.

On Internet Time

The vast majority of the total general public surveyed are not new to the Internet; 89% have used the Internet for four years or more, and nearly a quarter have been online for more than a decade.

Internet use is now well-established among the general public respondents across all countries surveyed. Nearly 90% of respondents have been using the Internet for four years or more. Nearly a third have been online for four to six years and more than a third have been online for seven to 10 years. Nearly a quarter of respondents (23%) have been using the Internet more than a decade.

Length of Time Using the Internet
By Total General Public

Thinking of your overall usage of the Internet, how many years would you estimate you have been using the Internet?

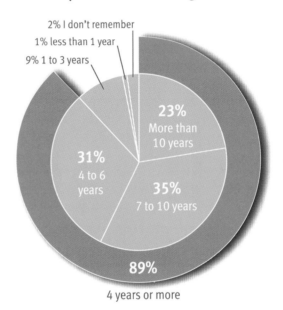

Source: *Sharing, Privacy and Trust in Our Networked World*, OCLC, 2007, question 525.

Tenure on the Internet was generally consistent among respondents across all countries surveyed. Eighty percent (80%) or more of respondents in each country have used the Internet for four years or more. The respondents in Canada and the U.S. represent the most experienced group of Internet users, with more than a quarter who have been online for more than 10 years.

Length of Time Using the Internet
By Country

Thinking of your overall usage of the Internet, how many years would you estimate you have been using the Internet?

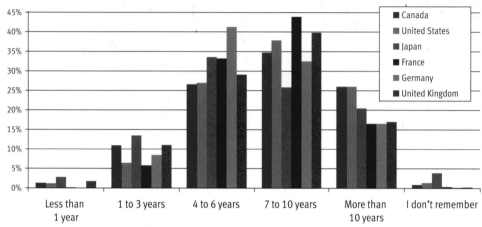

Source: *Sharing, Privacy and Trust in Our Networked World*, OCLC, 2007, question 525.

The results indicate that Internet tenure is not driven by just urban and suburban use. There is little difference in the Internet tenure among the general public respondents in urban, suburban and rural communities across the six countries surveyed. Over 50% of respondents in all communities have seven years or more experience. Slightly fewer respondents in rural communities report having been online for more than 10 years.

Length of Time Using the Internet
By Community

Thinking of your overall usage of the Internet, how many years would you estimate you have been using the Internet?

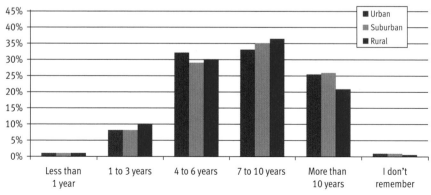

Source: *Sharing, Privacy and Trust in Our Networked World*, OCLC, 2007, question 525.

Exploring Internet tenure by age of respondent provided interesting results, perhaps different than what might be expected. The most tenured group of Internet users surveyed are those age 50+. Nearly a third (30%) of the most senior Internet users have been online for more than a decade.

While a quarter (25%) of the general public respondents ages 22–49 have been online more than a decade, the vast majority of this age group (91%) have been online for four years or more, and nearly two-thirds have seven years or more years of experience.

The youngest respondents surveyed (ages 14/15–21) are logically the least tenured Internet users, yet over 75% have also been online for four years or more. For many in this age category, this equates to living about a quarter of their lives online.

The data reveal the online population has very few novice Internet users; less than 3%, across all age groups and geographies surveyed, have been using the Internet less than a year.

30%
of respondents
age 50+ have been online for more than a decade.

Length of Time Using the Internet
By Age

Thinking of your overall usage of the Internet, how many years would you estimate you have been using the Internet?

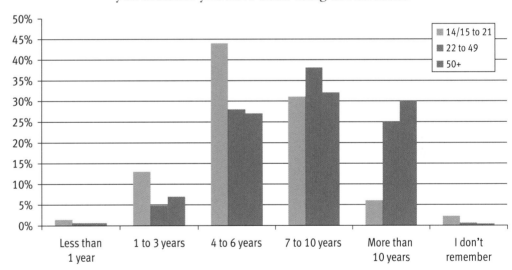

Source: *Sharing, Privacy and Trust in Our Networked World*, OCLC, 2007, question 525.

Today's Internet users are experienced users, who are becoming increasingly familiar and comfortable on the Web. The Internet is not used only by the technologically savvy, the youth or the urban population. And as tenure and familiarity grow, life online is beginning to take a new shape.

Life on the Internet

Searching for information, banking/investing, purchasing items, e-mailing and instant messaging are now standard online activities conducted by more than half of the total general public surveyed. Life online is moving beyond browsing and searching to interacting, creating, collaborating and community.

Life online incorporates a wide variety of activities. We asked respondents to indicate which of 18 online activities they have performed in the last 12 months. These activities were grouped into three categories: **Browsing/purchasing, Interacting** and **Creating**.

Browsing/purchasing activities: Activities considered as emerging several years ago, such as online banking, have been used by more than half of the total general public respondents. Over 40% of respondents have read someone's blog, while the majority have browsed for information and used e-commerce sites in the last year, a substantial increase in activity as seen in 2005. While commercial and searching activities have surged in the past two years, the use of the library Web site has declined from our 2005 study.

Interacting activities: The majority of the respondents have sent or received an e-mail and over half have sent or received an instant message. Twenty percent (20%) or more of respondents have participated in social networking and used chat rooms.

Creating activities: Twenty percent (20%) or more of respondents have used a social media site and have created and/or contributed to others' Web pages; 17% have blogged or written an online diary/journal.

31%

of respondents
age 50+ have read blogs;

40%

have used instant messaging.

Online Activities
By Total General Public

What types of online activities have you done or participated in during the last 12 months? Please select all that apply.

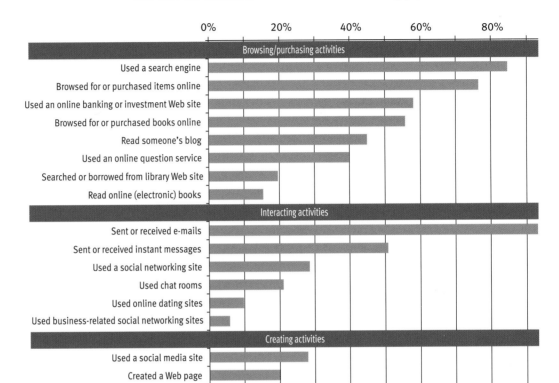

Source: *Sharing, Privacy and Trust in Our Networked World*, OCLC, 2007, question 530.

37%

of American respondents
have used a social networking site,

the highest rate of any country surveyed.

While usage among general public respondents across all countries surveyed was generally consistent, there were also some interesting differences.

The Japanese respondents showed the largest variation in online activity usage when compared to the other countries' respondents. Overall, Japanese respondents were least likely to have used most of the online activities evaluated, including e-mail and search engines, and significantly fewer have used library Web sites in the last 12 months, at 12%. Their online activity exceeded the other five countries' respondents in three of the four "creating categories": created a Web page, contributed to others' Web pages, and blogged or wrote an online diary/journal.

The general public respondents in the U.S. had the highest usage (37%) of only one online activity: social networking. Tied with France, the U.S. general public showed the lowest propensity to have created a Web page, at 18%.

The Canadian respondents reported the highest usage of a library Web site and the lowest usage of browsing for or purchasing books online.

The German respondents were more likely to have used chat rooms and online question services, and to have browsed for or purchased books online, while significantly less likely to have read a blog. German and French respondents were among the least likely to have used a social networking site during the last 12 months, at 13% and 10%, respectively.

Most respondents have not used an online dating service; overall usage was less than 10%. The highest usage of online dating sites was among the French general public, at 17%.

The French and the Canadian general public respondents were the most likely to have sent or received instant messages. The lowest level of use of social networking and social media sites was among the French general public at 10% and 19%, respectively.

The U.K. general public respondents reported the highest levels of e-mail and search engine use. They also had the greatest propensity to have browsed for or purchased items online and used online banking/investment sites.

Downloaded Music

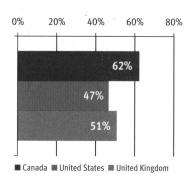

Source: *Sharing, Privacy and Trust in Our Networked World,* OCLC, 2007, question 1220. This question was directed to the Harris HPOL only, so respondents in Japan, France and Germany were not asked.

26%

of Japanese respondents have

contributed to others' Web pages,

the highest rate of any country surveyed.

69%

have used

search engines,

th lowest of any country.

Online Activities—Country Highlights

What types of online activities have you done or participated in during
the last 12 months? Please select all that apply.

■ Canada ■ United States ■ Japan ■ France ■ Germany ■ United Kingdom

34%
of U.K.
respondents
used a social
media site,
the highest rate of any
country surveyed.

Online banking

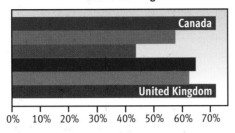

The U.K. (72%) and Canadian (71%) general public
respondents were most likely to have used online
banking or investment services. (Total=58%)

Browsed for or purchased books

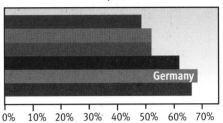

The German general public were the most likely to
have browsed for or purchased books online (69%).
(Total=56%)

Sent or received instant messages

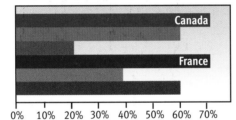

The Canadian and French respondents were the
most likely to have sent or received an instant
message, at 71% each. (Total=51%)

Used a social networking site

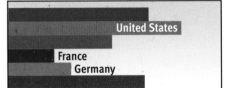

The American general public were most likely to
have used a social networking site (37%); France
(10%) and Germany (13%) were least likely.
(Total=28%)

Created a Web page

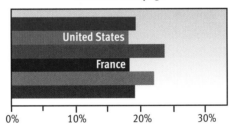

The general public respondents in the U.S.
(18%) and France (18%) were the least likely to
have created Web pages. (Total=20%)

Used a library Web site

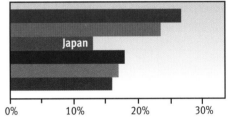

Japan's general public were significantly less
likely to have borrowed items or searched on a
library Web site (12%). (Total=20%)

71%
of French and
Canadian
respondents have
sent or
received instant
messages.

Browsed for or purchased items online

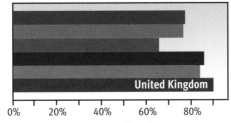

The general public in the U.K. (90%) were most
likely to have browsed for or purchased items
online. (Total=77%)

Read someone's blog

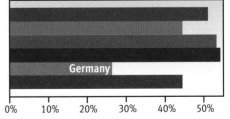

The general public in Germany were
significantly less likely to have read
someone's blog (26%). (Total=45%)

Source: *Sharing, Privacy and Trust in Our Networked World*, OCLC, 2007, question 530.

Online Activities
By Country

What types of online activities have you done or participated in during
the last 12 months? Please select all that apply.

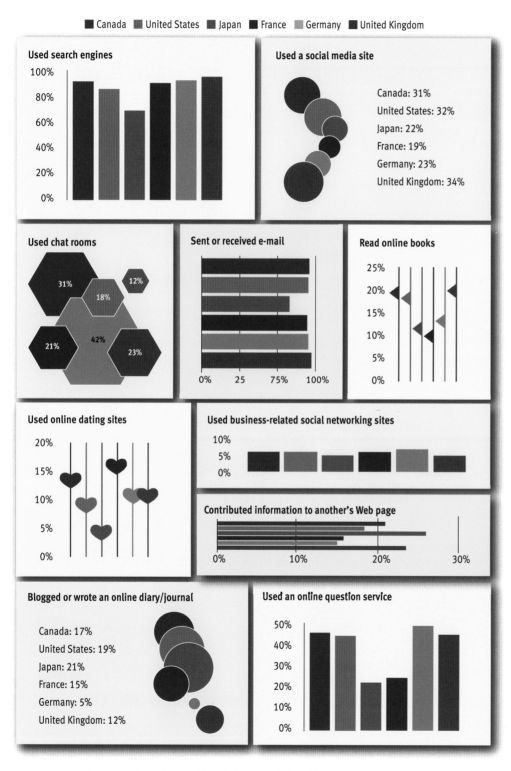

German respondents were most likely to have **used chat rooms** *and least likely to have blogged.*

At **27%,** *Canadian respondents* *reported the highest use of a library Web site.*

Source: *Sharing, Privacy and Trust in Our Networked World*, OCLC, 2007, question 530.

When comparing online activity by geographic community, we saw remarkable consistency among the general public respondents across the urban, suburban and rural online population.

Usage of online activities is
remarkably similar
by the general public respondents across urban, suburban and rural communities.

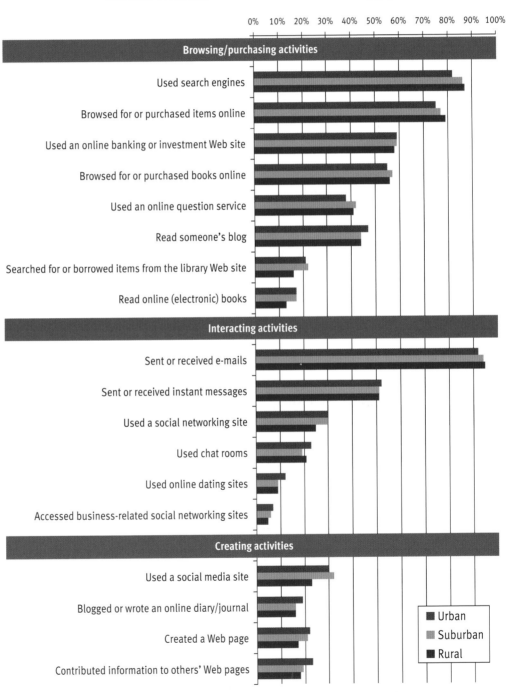

Online Activities
By Community

What types of online activities have you done or participated in during the last 12 months? Please select all that apply.

Browsing/purchasing activities
- Used search engines
- Browsed for or purchased items online
- Used an online banking or investment Web site
- Browsed for or purchased books online
- Used an online question service
- Read someone's blog
- Searched for or borrowed items from the library Web site
- Read online (electronic) books

Interacting activities
- Sent or received e-mails
- Sent or received instant messages
- Used a social networking site
- Used chat rooms
- Used online dating sites
- Accessed business-related social networking sites

Creating activities
- Used a social media site
- Blogged or wrote an online diary/journal
- Created a Web page
- Contributed information to others' Web pages

Legend:
■ Urban
▨ Suburban
■ Rural

Source: *Sharing, Privacy and Trust in Our Networked World*, OCLC, 2007, question 530.

Online activities can no longer be characterized by just searching or browsing. Usage is evolving to interacting, and quickly to creating and sharing content. In the first years of the Internet, posting online content was done by a Webmaster. Creating a Web page required a certain knowledge of complex technological concepts and tools. Services today have made it possible for almost any Internet user to post a blog entry or to build a Web page or engage in a social networking community; the composition of online activities is changing.

Creating Web Pages

The top reason for creating a Web page is to communicate with friends and family.

It is estimated that there are over 22 billion Web pages on the Internet today. And more and more, these Web pages are being built by end users and their primary motives are not commercial, but communication.

To communicate with friends and family (37%) is the top reason among the total general public for creating a Web page. *To write a blog and/or diary/journal* (28%), *to share photos* (27%), *to promote and sell products* (21%) and *to publish writing or music* (19%) are also key motivations. Personal Web sites often combine aspects of social networking (to write diaries and share photos and music), social media (to share photos and music) and commercial (to promote or sell products) sites.

Respondents are sharing content using multiple avenues. Of the total general public surveyed who have used a social networking site (28%), 47% have also created a Web page.

20% *of the total general public* **have created a Web page.**

As we compare the general public respondents across the six countries surveyed, we see many similarities as well as some interesting variances as to why they created a Web page.

Half of the respondents in Canada and Germany created a Web page *to communicate with friends and family,* the highest rate among respondents in the countries surveyed. The Canadian respondents were also the most likely to have created a Web page *to share photos.*

Over half of the Japanese respondents (53%) created a Web page *to write a blog and/or diary/journal,* a rate significantly higher than the general public in the other countries surveyed.

The American, Canadian and German respondents were the most likely to have created a Web page *to promote or sell products,* at 26% each.

Reasons for Creating a Web Page
By Country

Earlier you mentioned that you created a Web page(s)/site(s).
Why did you create the Web page(s)/site(s)?

Base: Respondents who have created a Web page/site.

	Total General Public	Canada	United States	Japan	France	Germany	United Kingdom
To communicate with friends and family	37%	50%	36%	28%	43%	51%	33%
To write a blog and/or diary/journal	28%	23%	21%	53%	25%	11%	23%
To share photos	27%	53%	31%	13%	44%	22%	30%
To promote and sell products	21%	26%	26%	11%	11%	26%	18%
To publish my own writing or music	19%	16%	15%	26%	19%	26%	14%
To share information about homework	7%	6%	10%	4%	5%	6%	5%
To share information about online games	7%	9%	3%	11%	17%	7%	5%
To share videos	6%	10%	8%	2%	11%	4%	8%

Source: *Sharing, Privacy and Trust in Our Networked World,* OCLC, 2007, question 820.

Responses by age group highlight interesting motivational differences for creating Web pages. The general public ages 14/15–21 and age 50+ show the largest differences in motivations for creating a Web page.

To communicate with friends and family was the top reason cited by the 14/15–21 and 22–49-year-olds, at 41% and 36%, respectively.

The top reason cited among the 50+ age group was *to promote and sell products* (36%).

Thirty-nine percent (39%) of the 14/15–21-year-olds created a Web page *to write a blog and/or diary/journal,* a rate nearly three times that for age 50+ (14%).

To share photos was among the top three reasons for creating Web pages for each of the age groups surveyed. Nearly a quarter of the respondents surveyed ages 14/15–21 created a Web page *to publish their own writing or music.*

Reasons for Creating a Web Page
By Age

Earlier you mentioned that you created a Web page(s)/site(s).
Why did you create the Web page(s)/site(s)?

Base: Respondents who have created a Web page/site.

	Age 14/15 to 21	Age 22 to 49	Age 50+
To communicate with friends and family	41%	36%	34%
To write a blog and/or diary/journal	39%	26%	14%
To share photos	29%	29%	18%
To promote and sell products	3%	25%	36%
To publish my own writing or music	24%	17%	16%
To share information about homework	9%	7%	5%
To share information about online games	12%	6%	1%
To share videos	11%	5%	4%

Source: *Sharing, Privacy and Trust in Our Networked World,* OCLC, 2007, question 820.

Collaborating and sharing of content online is expanding from e-mail and instant messaging to include the creation of Web pages and other social sites.

Online Addresses

Most Internet users surveyed have multiple online addresses, at least one instant messaging account and between two and four e-mail accounts.

The individuals in the online community surveyed have multiple digital addresses. Approximately three-quarters of the total general public surveyed (72%) who have sent or received an e-mail have more than one e-mail address; most have between two and four and 12% have five or more. The general public respondents in France and Germany are more likely than those in the other countries surveyed to have five or more e-mail addresses.

Half of the total general public who indicated they have sent or received an instant message have at least one instant messaging (IM) account. More than a third have multiple IM accounts. The German general public are significantly more likely to have more than one IM account.

Most respondents **have multiple e-mail accounts** *and at least one instant messaging account.*

Online Addresses
By Country

How many e-mail addresses do you have?
How many IM (instant messaging) accounts do you have?

Base: Respondents who have sent or received an e-mail and/or instant message.

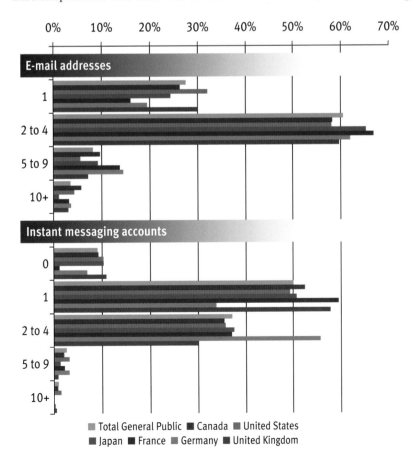

■ Total General Public ■ Canada ■ United States
■ Japan ■ France ■ Germany ■ United Kingdom

Source: *Sharing, Privacy and Trust in Our Networked World*, OCLC, 2007, questions 535 and 540.

The more tenured the Internet user, the more likely he or she is to have multiple e-mail accounts. Over 60% of the general public surveyed who have used the Internet for four years or longer have two to four e-mail addresses; those who have been using the Internet for longer than 10 years are more likely to have five to nine e-mail accounts.

Number of E-Mail Accounts and Internet Tenure
By Total General Public

Thinking of your overall usage of the Internet, how many years would you estimate you have been using the Internet? How many e-mail addresses do you have?

Base: Respondents who have sent or received an e-mail.

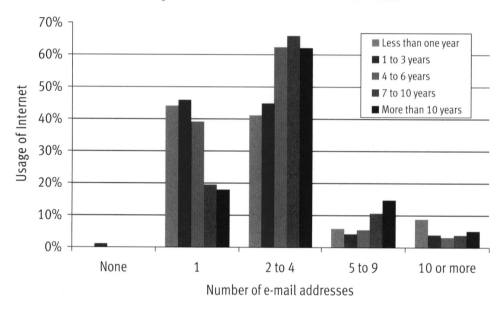

Source: *Sharing, Privacy and Trust in Our Networked World,* OCLC, 2007, questions 525 and 535.

Cell Phone Usage

The majority of the general public surveyed have cell phones and more than three-quarters use them for more than just talking.

For many, cell phones have become as important a digital communication and content transmission device as the personal computer. According to the International Telecommunications Union (ITU), the ownership of cell phones is strong in all countries represented in our study, and in some instances has approached or exceeded one cell phone per user.

Our survey data on the online population show similar usage rates. Eighty-nine percent (89%) of the general public surveyed have cell phones. The German general public have the highest penetration of cell phone ownership, at 96%, and Canadian respondents have the lowest, at 78%, which is significantly less.

More than three-quarters of the general public respondents use their cell phones for more than just placing calls. Over half are "texting," using text messaging services, and over a third use their phones *to take or send photos*. About a quarter of all respondents have *downloaded or used ringtones*.

While the ownership of cell phones is high among the total general public respondents in all six countries surveyed, those in Japan are significantly more likely to use multiple services available on their cell phones. The Japanese general public use their cell phones for many of the services that were once considered the domain of the personal computer, including *text messaging* (68%), *sending e-mails* (55%), *searching the Internet* (40%) and *recording or downloading music* (20%). As noted earlier in this report, while the Japanese general public were less likely to have participated in several of the online activities evaluated, they are using the cell phone for some of the same digital services.

15%
of the total
general public
use cell phones to search the Internet.

40%
of Japanese respondents
use cell phones to search the Internet.

Cell Phone Feature Usage

Which of the following functions/features do you use on your cell phone? Please select all that apply.

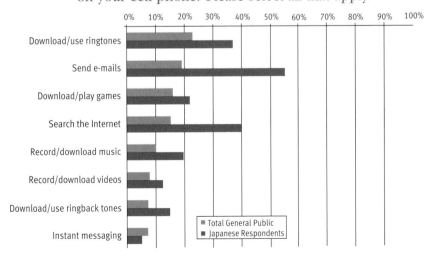

Source: *Sharing, Privacy and Trust in Our Networked World*, OCLC, 2007, question 945.

The American and Canadian respondents report the lowest use of cell phone features and are the most likely to use their cell phones *only to make and receive calls.*

Text messaging on cell phones is highest among the U.K. and German respondents, at 78% and 73%, respectively.

Cell Phone Use
By Country

Which of the following functions/features do you use on your cell phone?
Please select all that apply.

Source: *Sharing, Privacy and Trust in Our Networked World,* OCLC, 2007, question 945.

Reading—Print and Online

The general public respondents have read more in the last year. Twenty-eight percent (28%) of the total general public spend over 10 hours per week reading online and/or print materials. Thirty-five percent (35%) read 11 or more books per year.

While it is evident respondents are spending time online and engaging in many activities on the Web, they are still reading. Whether online or in print format, respondents read and indicate that they are reading more.

U.S. reading rates have increased in the past 50 years. A 27-month study conducted by the Social Science Research Council in 1948 found that about half (48%) of the U.S. population indicated that they read no books per year. Another 18% read just one to four books per year. Our 2007 survey results show increased reading levels among respondents in the U.S. Forty-one percent (41%) read two to ten books a year.

Forty-three percent (43%) of Japanese respondents have read 11 or more books during the past 12 months, tied with the U.K. as the highest rate among respondents across the countries surveyed. Thirty-one percent (31%) of the U.S. general public surveyed have read 11 or more books in the past 12 months.

Number of Books Read Annually
By Country

Approximately how many books have you read or listened to in the past 12 months (e.g., print books, electronic books, electronic audiobooks, books on tape, etc.)?

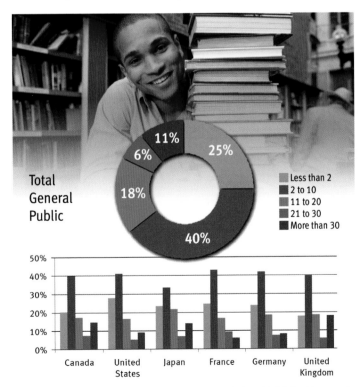

Source: *Sharing, Privacy and Trust in Our Networked World*, OCLC, 2007, question 510.

Respondents are reading books, magazines and digital content on the Web. More than a quarter of the total general public surveyed (28%) read 11 or more hours a week.

More than a third of the general public in Canada and the U.K. read 11 or more hours per week, the highest rates among respondents in the countries surveyed. The majority of the general public in Japan and France spend 10 hours or less a week reading, the lowest rates among respondents in the countries surveyed.

Time Spent Reading Per Week
By Country

Overall, how much time do you estimate you spend reading on a weekly basis (including books, magazines, online Web sites, blogs, etc.)?

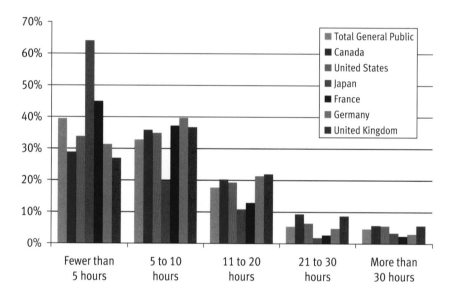

Source: *Sharing, Privacy and Trust in Our Networked World*, OCLC, 2007, question 515.

The general public are reading more compared to a year ago. Approximately a quarter of the total general public surveyed reported the time they have spent reading, in any format, print or digital, has increased in the last 12 months. This increase was fairly consistent across all countries, with more general public in Canada reporting an increase in reading (26%), and the respondents in Germany reporting the lowest increase, at 19%.

In no country did the general public report larger decreases in reading than increases; only Japanese respondents reported no growth in reading.

The online population surveyed are **reading more.**

Change in Reading
By Country

During the last 12 months, has the amount you have read in any format increased, decreased or remained the same?

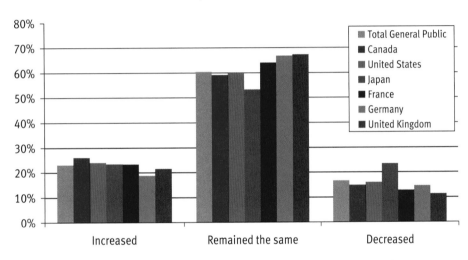

Source: *Sharing, Privacy and Trust in Our Networked World,* OCLC, 2007, question 520.

Our results also show those who use social sites spend more time reading than non-social site users. Nearly seventy percent of the general public who use social sites read five hours or more per week compared to 55% of the general public who do not use these sites.

Time Spent Reading
By Total General Public

Overall, how much time do you estimate you spend reading on a weekly basis (including books, magazines, online Web sites, blogs, etc.)?

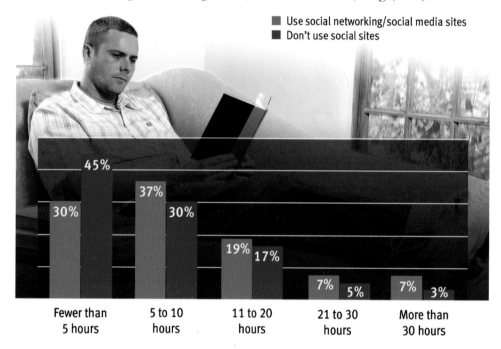

■ Use social networking/social media sites
■ Don't use social sites

Fewer than 5 hours	5 to 10 hours	11 to 20 hours	21 to 30 hours	More than 30 hours
30% / 45%	37% / 30%	19% / 17%	7% / 5%	7% / 3%

Source: *Sharing, Privacy and Trust in Our Networked World*, OCLC, 2007, question 515.

Summary

Respondents are participating in a variety of Internet activities: browsing/purchasing, interacting and creating content.

The majority are experienced Web users; most have been online for four years or more. The activities are expanding as they move from browsing to borrowing to creating Web content. These digital activities are largely PC-based today, but the use of cell phones for sharing and creating digital content is on the rise.

Respondents read and indicate that the amount they are reading has increased. Digital activities are not replacements for reading but perhaps increase the options for expanding communication and sharing content.

Our Social Spaces

"Who knows ... that a day may not come when the dissemination of knowledge, which is the vital function of libraries, will be realised by libraries even by means other than those of the printed book?"

—S. R. Ranganathan, *The Five Laws of Library Science*, 1931

Social Networking History and Background

The practice of using social communities to establish and enhance relationships based on some common ground—shared interests, related skills or a common geographic location—is as old as human culture. As early as the time of Plato in 400 B.C., scholars and philosophers studied and analyzed the formation and interaction of groups of people.

Wikipedia defines a social network as "a social structure made of nodes (which are generally individuals or organizations) that are tied by one or more specific types of relations, such as values, visions, idea[s], financial exchange, friends ..."

Today, the term social networking is being used in new ways, but the concepts behind it—sharing content, collaborating with others and creating community—are not new. What is different is simply the availability of the digital medium, which makes contributing materials and connecting with other people faster, easier and more accessible to a wider population than ever before.

What do we mean by social sites?

Social networks are Web sites "designed to allow multiple users to publish content themselves," according to the *Free On-line Dictionary of Computing* as linked from Dictionary.com. The published information may be on any subject and may be for consumption by a select number of friends, employers, employees, etc., or for general consumption by anyone on the Web. Social networking sites "typically allow users to create ... 'profile[s]' describing themselves and to exchange public or private messages and list users or groups they are connected to in some way."

Wikipedia provides a more social, less utilitarian definition: "A social network service focuses on the building and verifying of online social networks for communities of people who share interests and activities, or who are interested in exploring the interests and activities of others, and which necessitates the use of software. Social network services are primarily Web-based and provide a collection of various ways for users to interact, such as chat, messaging, e-mail, video, voice chat, file sharing, blogging, discussion groups and so on." Cell phone technologies are also enabling the creators of social networking. Social networks include commercially published content or editorial content, or may be entirely user driven. Content is text, images, video or any other media.

Social sites on the Web are a natural extension of mailing lists (listservs) and bulletin boards, and are similar to wikis—a type of site whose content can be edited by anyone with access. Social sites often allow users to publish comments on others' submissions.

Different social sites have different emphases. For example, Classmates.com—one of the first social networking sites—focuses on listing former acquaintances and reuniting them; MySpace began as a music-oriented site; LinkedIn aims to connect business professionals; and del.icio.us, StumbleUpon and Digg are used to exchange links to favorite Web sites. According to the Wharton School's online business journal *Knowledge@Wharton*, there were over 300 social networking sites in 2006.

Social connections or social networking often are not the central function of a site, but a side-effect of bringing together people with shared interests. For example, Slashdot is a site devoted to information technology news but has built a strong social connection across users. In other instances, the community aspect of a site can become more important than the original purpose. Flickr, which began as a utility for an online game, morphed into a photo-sharing and management site.

In this report we will review two types of social sites, social networking and social media sites. We use the term "social networking" to describe sites primarily designed to facilitate interaction between users who share interests, attitudes and activities, such as Facebook and MySpace. We use "social media" to refer to sites that allow individuals to share content they have created, such as YouTube (video sharing) and Flickr (photo sharing). While interaction occurs on social media sites, the primary purpose of the site is to publish and share content.

Social sites do not just have various social features; their essence is social. Their central value as a platform, their functions are social and they enable personal and group connections at levels never before seen in the history of telecommunications. There is no MySpace without the individual contributions of millions with their personal home pages and walls of messages, photos and personal profiles. There is no YouTube without users' contributed videos. There is no Wikipedia without its thousands of authors and editors.

Social Web sites are online bazaars where large numbers of people connect, communicate and share content and build community through the use of social software technology.

A social network service focuses on the building and verifying of online social networks for communities of people who share interests and activities, or who are interested in exploring the interests and activities of others, and which necessitates the use of software.

Wikipedia

Social Sites—Their Growth and Influence

Created in 1995, Classmates.com is often considered the first social networking site, and had approximately 40 million members in June 2007, according to the Classmates.com site. Other social sites quickly followed, including Facebook, eHarmony, Snapfish, LinkedIn and Friendster to name just a few. MySpace was launched in 2003, Facebook and Mixi in 2004 and YouTube in 2005.

According to Alexa, YouTube, MySpace, Orkut, Wikipedia and Facebook—all social sites—rank in the top 10 global Web sites.

Alexa Top 10 Global Web Sites

Traffic Rank	Name: url	% of global users who visit site	Page views per user
1	Yahoo: www.yahoo.com	25.9	13.8
2	MSN: www.msn.com	24.4	6.9
3	Google: www.google.com	24.2	6.1
4	YouTube: www.youtube.com	12.9	12.4
5	Windows Live: www.live.com	17.8	5.9
6	MySpace: www.myspace.com	4.9	36.0
7	Orkut: www.orkut.com	2.9	33.1
8	Baidu: www.baidu.com	4.5	12.8
9	Wikipedia: www.wikipedia.org	6.6	5.2
10	Facebook: www.facebook.com	2.6	32.0

Source: Alexa, September 9, 2007. Traffic rank is based on three months of aggregated historical traffic data from millions of Alexa Toolbar users and is a combined measure of page views and users (reach). Page views per user presented are Alexa's three-month average.

Social sites are among the top 10 most trafficked Web sites across all countries surveyed.

Alexa Top 10 Web Sites
By Surveyed Country

Canada		United States		Japan	
Facebook	**facebook.com**	**Yahoo!**	**yahoo.com**	**Yahoo! Japan**	**yahoo.co.jp**
Google Canada	google.ca	Google	google.com	Google Japan	google.co.jp
Yahoo!	yahoo.com	MySpace	myspace.com	FC2	fc2.com
Google	google.com	YouTube	youtube.com	Mixi	mixi.jp
MSN	msn.com	Facebook	facebook.com	YouTube	youtube.com
YouTube	youtube.com	MSN	msn.com	Rakuten	rakuten.co.jp
Windows Live	live.com	eBay	ebay.com	Livedoor	livedoor.com
Wikipedia	wikipedia.org	Windows Live	live.com	Nicovideo	nicovideo.jp
MySpace	myspace.com	Wikipedia	wikipedia.org	Google	google.com
MSN Canada	msn.ca	Craigslist	craigslist.org	Goo	goo.ne.jp
France		**Germany**		**United Kingdom**	
Google France	**google.fr**	**Google Germany**	**google.de**	**Google UK**	**google.co.uk**
Skyrock	skyrock.com	eBay Germany	ebay.de	Yahoo!	yahoo.com
MSN	msn.com	Google	google.com	Facebook	facebook.com
Yahoo!	yahoo.com	Yahoo!	yahoo.com	Google	google.com
Windows Live	live.com	YouTube	youtube.com	MSN	msn.com
Free	free.fr	Wikipedia	wikipedia.org	eBay UK	ebay.co.uk
Google	google.com	GMX	gmx.net	BBC Newsline Ticker	bbc.co.uk
Dailymotion	dailymotion.com	Studiverzeichnis	studiverzeichnis.com	YouTube	youtube.com
YouTube	youtube.com	MySpace	myspace.com	MySpace	myspace.com
eBay France	ebay.fr	MSN	msn.com	Windows Live	live.com

Source: Alexa, September 9, 2007. Traffic rank is based on three months of aggregated historical traffic data from millions of Alexa Toolbar users and is a combined measure of page views and users (reach). Page views per user presented are Alexa's three-month average.

According to HitWise, social sites now capture one out of every 20 Web visits. In just a few short years, social sites have gone from niche to mainstream—a part of everyday life for millions of Internet users. And momentum continues to build as more people gather online to meet like-minded folks, pushing usage of social sites closer and closer to the use rates of major Internet portals and commercial sites. While marquee Internet properties such as Google, Microsoft and Amazon are growing, social sites like Facebook, Flickr, MySpace, YouTube and Wikipedia are experiencing tremendous traffic growth.

comScore Top Search Engines and Social Sites
By Growth

Note: Unique visitors (in 000s), sorted by growth rate.

	Unique Visitors		
	Jun-06	Jun-07	Growth rate
YouTube	49,371	188,981	282.8%
Facebook	14,083	52,167	270.4%
Flickr	15,893	29,861	87.9%
Photobucket	18,162	33,587	84.9%
MySpace	66,401	114,117	71.9%
Wikipedia	127,982	208,120	62.6%
Google	453,963	544,783	20.0%
Amazon	129,320	145,947	12.9%
eBay	186,462	207,376	11.2%
Microsoft	499,540	529,156	6.0%
Yahoo!	480,933	471,924	-2.0%

Source: comScore World Metrix, June 2007.

Our Favorite Sites

Over three-quarters of Internet users surveyed report having used a commercial Internet site in the past year. Amazon, eBay and Rakuten are among the most used commercial sites. Over a quarter of Internet users have used a social site, with YouTube, MySpace and Mixi among the favorites. Most favorites are common across countries and age groups.

Commercial sites have been available on the Internet for close to a decade and are now regularly used by millions of shoppers worldwide. A review of the most frequently used commercial sites provides insights into usage and preference of commercial and social sites.

While the social networking and media sites are relatively new, these sites command a significant, and growing, portion of Internet activity and account for some of the most popular sites on the Web. The following section reviews the use, attraction, familiarity of and sharing occurring on commercial sites and social sites.

Commercial Sites

More than three-quarters of the total general public surveyed (77%) have browsed for or purchased items on a commercial site in the last 12 months. A few commercial sites dominated among these respondents. Amazon and eBay were the most used commercial sites among the total general public surveyed, at 51% and 50%, respectively. In France, Canada, the U.S., Germany and the U.K., Amazon and eBay were also the top two commercial sites used by the majority of the shoppers. Usage of Amazon and eBay was particularly high among shoppers in Germany and the U.K. Unique among the Japanese respondents was the usage of Rakuten; it was the most used commercial site, followed closely by Amazon.

iTunes was used by shoppers in all six countries surveyed, ranging from 5% in Japan to 19% in the U.S. and 22% in the U.K. Library Web site usage was reported at rates ranging from 6% in France to a high of 16% among Canadian respondents. While relatively low, usage exceeded visits to many major corporate sites.

Commercial site usage was split across vendors for shoppers in Canada, Japan and the U.S., where six or more vendors were used by 10% of respondents. Walmart.com was used by a large number of respondents in Canada (25%) and the U.S. (41%); Yahoo! Auction and Yahoo! Shopping were used by nearly a third or more of the Japanese respondents but did not make the list in any other country.

Favorite Commercial Sites
By Total General Public

Below is a list of Web sites commonly used to browse for and/or purchase music, movies, books and other retail items (e.g., clothing, electronics, etc.). Please select all the Web sites you have used in the past 12 months.

Base: Respondents who have used a commercial site and/or the library Web site.

Total General Public	
Amazon	51%
eBay	50%
Walmart.com	22%
iTunes	16%
Barnesandnoble.com	13%
Rakuten	11%
A library Web site[1]	11%
Amazon.jp	10%
Netflix	9%
Blockbuster.com	7%

Note: The chart shows the top 10 sites.
[1]Library Web site was grouped with commercial sites to provide a view of relative usage.

Source: *Sharing, Privacy and Trust in Our Networked World*, OCLC, 2007, question 770.

Favorite Commercial Sites
By Country

Below is a list of Web sites commonly used to browse for and/or purchase music, movies, books and other retail items (e.g., clothing, electronics, etc.). Please select all the Web sites you have used in the past 12 months.

Base: Respondents who have used a commercial site and/or the library Web site.

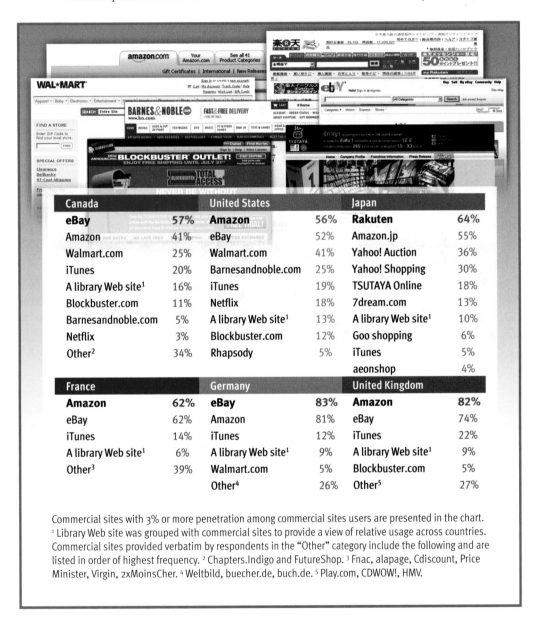

Canada		United States		Japan	
eBay	57%	Amazon	56%	Rakuten	64%
Amazon	41%	eBay	52%	Amazon.jp	55%
Walmart.com	25%	Walmart.com	41%	Yahoo! Auction	36%
iTunes	20%	Barnesandnoble.com	25%	Yahoo! Shopping	30%
A library Web site[1]	16%	iTunes	19%	TSUTAYA Online	18%
Blockbuster.com	11%	Netflix	18%	7dream.com	13%
Barnesandnoble.com	5%	A library Web site[1]	13%	A library Web site[1]	10%
Netflix	3%	Blockbuster.com	12%	Goo shopping	6%
Other[2]	34%	Rhapsody	5%	iTunes	5%
				aeonshop	4%

France		Germany		United Kingdom	
Amazon	62%	eBay	83%	Amazon	82%
eBay	62%	Amazon	81%	eBay	74%
iTunes	14%	iTunes	12%	iTunes	22%
A library Web site[1]	6%	A library Web site[1]	9%	A library Web site[1]	9%
Other[3]	39%	Walmart.com	5%	Blockbuster.com	5%
		Other[4]	26%	Other[5]	27%

Commercial sites with 3% or more penetration among commercial sites users are presented in the chart.
[1] Library Web site was grouped with commercial sites to provide a view of relative usage across countries. Commercial sites provided verbatim by respondents in the "Other" category include the following and are listed in order of highest frequency. [2] Chapters.Indigo and FutureShop. [3] Fnac, alapage, Cdiscount, Price Minister, Virgin, 2xMoinsCher. [4] Weltbild, buecher.de, buch.de. [5] Play.com, CDWOW!, HMV.

Source: *Sharing, Privacy and Trust in Our Networked World,* OCLC, 2007, question 770.

Amazon and eBay were the top used commercial sites among shoppers across geographies, as well as among the three age groups. iTunes ranked third among the 14/15–21-year-olds.

Favorite Commercial Sites
By Age

Below is a list of Web sites commonly used to browse for and/or purchase music, movies, books and other retail items (e.g., clothing, electronics, etc.). Please select all the Web sites you have used in the past 12 months.

Base: Respondents who have used a commercial site and/or the library Web site.

Age 14/15 to 21		Age 22 to 49		Age 50+	
Amazon	57%	Amazon	65%	Amazon	56%
eBay	40%	eBay	53%	eBay	49%
iTunes	23%	Walmart.com	23%	Walmart.com	25%
Walmart.com	15%	iTunes	16%	Barnesandnoble.com	14%
Library Web site[1]	13%	Rakuten	13%	iTunes	10%
Barnesandnoble.com	11%	Library Web site[1]	12%	Library Web site[1]	9%
Rakuten	10%	Barnesandnoble.com	12%	Netflix	9%
Netflix	7%	Netflix	9%	Rakuten	9%
Blockbuster.com	6%	Blockbuster.com	8%	Blockbuster.com	7%
Yahoo! Auction	5%	Yahoo! Auction	8%	Yahoo! Shopping	5%

Note: The chart shows the top 10 sites.

[1]Library Web site was grouped with commercial sites to provide a view of relative usage across age groups.

Source: *Sharing, Privacy and Trust in Our Networked World*, OCLC, 2007, question 770.

Usage by age is very similar for the most frequently used commercial sites. The majority of Amazon and eBay use is from users ages 22–49. More than half of Amazon users are ages 22–49 (58%), a quarter are 50+ (26%) and 16% are ages 14/15–21; 58% of eBay users are ages 22–49, 27% are 50+ and 15% are ages 14/15–21.

Similar to Amazon and eBay, more than half (51%) of library Web site users are ages 22–49, but more of the younger age group (ages 14/15–21) (27%) and less of the of the 50+ age group (22%) make up its usage base.

Amazon Users
By Age

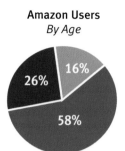

■ 14/15 to 21 ■ 22 to 49 ■ 50+

Source: *Sharing, Privacy and Trust in Our Networked World*, OCLC, 2007, question 770.

eBay Users
By Age

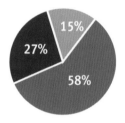

■ 14/15 to 21 ■ 22 to 49 ■ 50+

Source: *Sharing, Privacy and Trust in Our Networked World*, OCLC, 2007, question 770.

Library Users
By Age

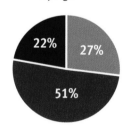

■ 14/15 to 21 ■ 22 to 49 ■ 50+

Source: *Sharing, Privacy and Trust in Our Networked World*, OCLC, 2007, question 770.

Social Networking Sites

A significant portion of this study is aimed at providing a deeper understanding of social sites and their similarities to and differences from other Web sites. We explored two categories of social sites: social networking sites—sites primarily created to allow users to interact while also publishing content, and social media sites—sites that allow users to publish and share content. While interaction often occurs on social media sites, the central function of the site is to share content.

MySpace is the most used social networking site (Alexa, September 2007) and was also cited as the most used site among the total general public surveyed who have used a social networking site, at 61%. Classmates.com came in a distant second, at 24%.

More than half *of social networking users use* *MySpace.*

Favorite Social Networking Sites

By Total General Public

Below is a list of social networking Web sites. Please select all the Web sites you have used in the past 12 months.

Base: Respondents who have used a social networking site.

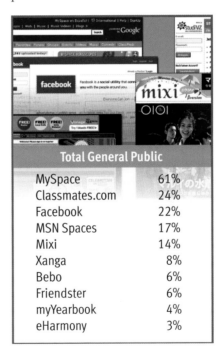

Total General Public	
MySpace	61%
Classmates.com	24%
Facebook	22%
MSN Spaces	17%
Mixi	14%
Xanga	8%
Bebo	6%
Friendster	6%
myYearbook	4%
eHarmony	3%

Note: The chart shows the top 10 sites.
Source: *Sharing, Privacy and Trust in Our Networked World,* OCLC, 2007, question 605.

More than half of the social networking users surveyed had used MySpace in the past 12 months in all countries except Japan. Mixi was the most used social networking site in Japan, where it was used by 91% of the Japanese social networking users.

While MySpace was overall the most used social networking site, respondents have also used a variety of other sites. MSN Spaces had a usage penetration rate of nearly a third or more among social networking users in all countries surveyed, except for the U.S. and Japan. Facebook and Classmates.com were popular sites among social networking users in Canada and the U.S., while these sites were lightly used in France, Germany and the U.K. Just as Yahoo! Auction and Yahoo! Shopping were popular commercial sites in Japan, Yahoo! Days also was used by Japanese social networking users (14%).

Usage of Social Networking Sites
By Country

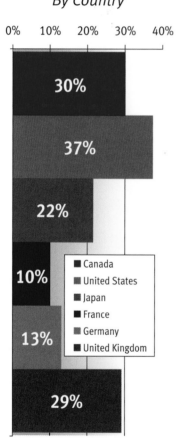

| Canada |
| United States |
| Japan |
| France |
| Germany |
| United Kingdom |

28%

of the total general public surveyed **have used a social networking site.**

Source: *Sharing, Privacy and Trust in Our Networked World,* OCLC, 2007, question 530, "What types of online activities have you done or participated in during the last 12 months? Please select all that apply."

Favorite Social Networking Sites
By Country

Below is a list of social networking Web sites. Please select all the
Web sites you have used in the past 12 months.

Base: Respondents who have used a social networking site.

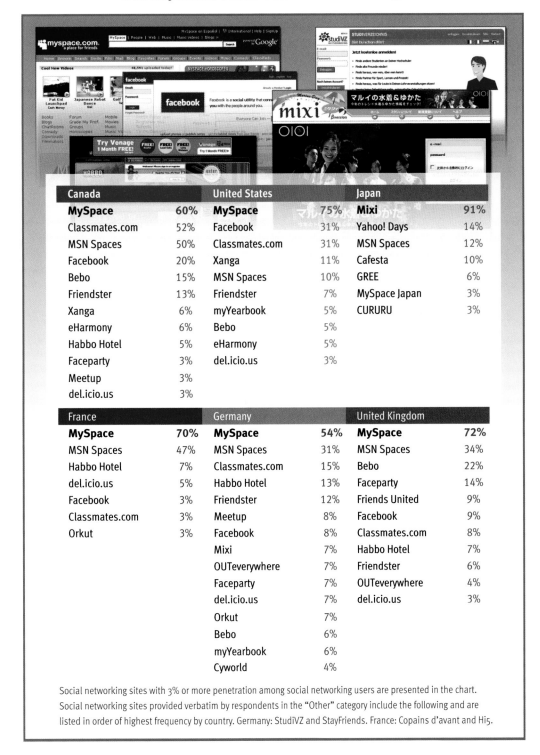

Canada		United States		Japan	
MySpace	60%	**MySpace**	75%	**Mixi**	91%
Classmates.com	52%	Facebook	31%	Yahoo! Days	14%
MSN Spaces	50%	Classmates.com	31%	MSN Spaces	12%
Facebook	20%	Xanga	11%	Cafesta	10%
Bebo	15%	MSN Spaces	10%	GREE	6%
Friendster	13%	Friendster	7%	MySpace Japan	3%
Xanga	6%	myYearbook	5%	CURURU	3%
eHarmony	6%	Bebo	5%		
Habbo Hotel	5%	eHarmony	5%		
Faceparty	3%	del.icio.us	3%		
Meetup	3%				
del.icio.us	3%				

France		Germany		United Kingdom	
MySpace	70%	**MySpace**	54%	**MySpace**	72%
MSN Spaces	47%	MSN Spaces	31%	MSN Spaces	34%
Habbo Hotel	7%	Classmates.com	15%	Bebo	22%
del.icio.us	5%	Habbo Hotel	13%	Faceparty	14%
Facebook	3%	Friendster	12%	Friends United	9%
Classmates.com	3%	Meetup	8%	Facebook	9%
Orkut	3%	Facebook	8%	Classmates.com	8%
		Mixi	7%	Habbo Hotel	7%
		OUTeverywhere	7%	Friendster	6%
		Faceparty	7%	OUTeverywhere	4%
		del.icio.us	7%	del.icio.us	3%
		Orkut	7%		
		Bebo	6%		
		myYearbook	6%		
		Cyworld	4%		

Social networking sites with 3% or more penetration among social networking users are presented in the chart.
Social networking sites provided verbatim by respondents in the "Other" category include the following and are
listed in order of highest frequency by country. Germany: StudiVZ and StayFriends. France: Copains d'avant and Hi5.

Source: *Sharing, Privacy and Trust in Our Networked World*, OCLC, 2007, question 605.

MySpace was the most used social networking site among social networking users ages 14/15–21 and 22–49, while Classmates.com was the top used site among the 50+ age group.

Facebook was the second most used site among users ages 14/15–21, at 40%. MySpace (62%) was dominant for respondents ages 22–49; Classmates.com was the second most used site, at 29%.

Favorite Social Networking Sites
By Age

Below is a list of social networking Web sites. Please select all the Web sites you have used in the past 12 months.

Base: Respondents who have used a social networking site.

Age 14/15 to 21		Age 22 to 49		Age 50+	
MySpace	70%	MySpace	62%	Classmates.com	52%
Facebook	40%	Classmates.com	29%	MySpace	33%
MSN Spaces	18%	Mixi	16%	MSN Spaces	25%
Xanga	17%	MSN Spaces	14%	Mixi	9%
Mixi	13%	Facebook	14%	Yahoo! Days	5%
Bebo	11%	Friendster	8%	eHarmony	3%
Classmates.com	7%	eHarmony	5%	Friendster	3%
Habbo Hotel	5%	Bebo	4%	Bebo	2%
Friendster	4%	del.icio.us	4%	Facebook	2%
myYearbook	4%	Faceparty	3%	del.icio.us	1%

Note: The chart shows the top 10 sites.

Source: *Sharing, Privacy and Trust in Our Networked World*, OCLC, 2007, question 605.

MySpace and Mixi are both used heavily by social networking users under the age of 50 across the countries surveyed but used very little by social networking users over age 50. Only 6% of MySpace users are age 50+. Mixi use is also concentrated in the younger age groups. Only 7% of Mixi users are over the age of 50.

MySpace Users
By Age

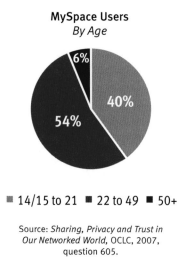

■ 14/15 to 21 ■ 22 to 49 ■ 50+

Source: *Sharing, Privacy and Trust in Our Networked World*, OCLC, 2007, question 605.

Mixi Users
By Age

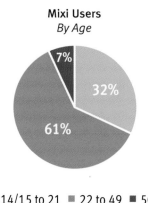

■ 14/15 to 21 ■ 22 to 49 ■ 50+

Source: *Sharing, Privacy and Trust in Our Networked World*, OCLC, 2007, question 605.

Social Media Sites

The most used social media site among the total general public was YouTube; more than three-fourths of social media users have used YouTube in the past 12 months. Yahoo! Photos came in a distant second, at 21%.

Favorite Social Media Sites
By Total General Public

Below is a list of social media Web sites. Please select all the Web sites you have used in the past 12 months.

Base: Respondents who have used a social media site.

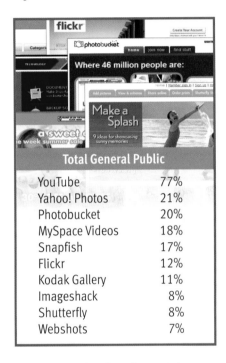

Total General Public	
YouTube	77%
Yahoo! Photos	21%
Photobucket	20%
MySpace Videos	18%
Snapfish	17%
Flickr	12%
Kodak Gallery	11%
Imageshack	8%
Shutterfly	8%
Webshots	7%

Note: The chart shows the top 10 sites.

Source: *Sharing, Privacy and Trust in Our Networked World,* OCLC, 2007, question 710.

The majority of the social media users in all countries surveyed have used YouTube in the past 12 months. Usage was very strong, ranging from 73% to 83% in each country. Usage of all other social media sites was much lower. Yahoo! Photos was the second most used social media site among social media users (21%) and showed usage in all countries surveyed, ranging from 14% in Japan to 26% in Canada. GyaO (44%) was the second most used social media site among users in Japan, behind YouTube (83%).

Unlike social networking sites and commercial sites for which respondents showed concentrated use in a relatively small number of sites, social media users reported a broader use of social media sites. Although YouTube was by far the most used site by users in each of the six countries surveyed, nearly a quarter or more have also used such sites as Yahoo! Photos, Photobucket, Flickr, MySpace Videos and Imageshack. [NOTE: After the survey was conducted, Yahoo! closed Yahoo! Photos in September 2007.]

Favorite Social Media Sites
By Country

Below is a list of social media Web sites. Please select all the
Web sites you have used in the past 12 months.

Base: Respondents who have used a social media site.

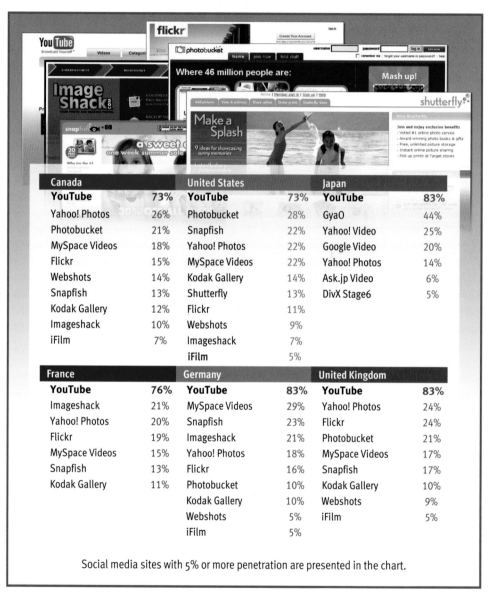

Canada		United States		Japan	
YouTube	**73%**	**YouTube**	**73%**	**YouTube**	**83%**
Yahoo! Photos	26%	Photobucket	28%	GyaO	44%
Photobucket	21%	Snapfish	22%	Yahoo! Video	25%
MySpace Videos	18%	Yahoo! Photos	22%	Google Video	20%
Flickr	15%	MySpace Videos	22%	Yahoo! Photos	14%
Webshots	14%	Kodak Gallery	14%	Ask.jp Video	6%
Snapfish	13%	Shutterfly	13%	DivX Stage6	5%
Kodak Gallery	12%	Flickr	11%		
Imageshack	10%	Webshots	9%		
iFilm	7%	Imageshack	7%		
		iFilm	5%		

France		Germany		United Kingdom	
YouTube	**76%**	**YouTube**	**83%**	**YouTube**	**83%**
Imageshack	21%	MySpace Videos	29%	Yahoo! Photos	24%
Yahoo! Photos	20%	Snapfish	23%	Flickr	24%
Flickr	19%	Imageshack	21%	Photobucket	21%
MySpace Videos	15%	Yahoo! Photos	18%	MySpace Videos	17%
Snapfish	13%	Flickr	16%	Snapfish	17%
Kodak Gallery	11%	Photobucket	10%	Kodak Gallery	10%
		Kodak Gallery	10%	Webshots	9%
		Webshots	5%	iFilm	5%
		iFilm	5%		

Social media sites with 5% or more penetration are presented in the chart.

Source: *Sharing, Privacy and Trust in Our Networked World*, OCLC, 2007, question 710.

28% *of the total general public surveyed used a social media site.*

YouTube was the dominant social media site used among social media users surveyed ages 14/15–21 (87%), 22–49 (74%) and 50+ (58%). The second and third most used social media sites varied between age groups. Among the social media users ages 14/15–21, Photobucket and MySpace Videos are the next two most used social media sites, at 30% and 25%, respectively. Yahoo! Photos and Snapfish are the sites that round out the top three most used sites for users ages 22–49 and 50+.

Usage of Social Media Sites
By Country

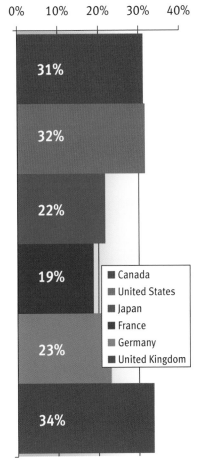

Source: *Sharing, Privacy and Trust in Our Networked World*, OCLC, 2007, question 530, "What types of online activities have you done or participated in during the last 12 months? Please select all that apply."

Favorite Social Media Sites
By Age

Below is a list of social media Web sites. Please select all the Web sites you have used in the past 12 months.

Base: Respondents who have used a social media site.

Age 14/15 to 21		Age 22 to 49		Age 50+	
YouTube	87%	YouTube	74%	YouTube	58%
Photobucket	30%	Yahoo! Photos	20%	Snapfish	27%
MySpace Videos	25%	Snapfish	20%	Yahoo! Photos	26%
Yahoo! Photos	13%	MySpace Videos	16%	Kodak Gallery	19%
Imageshack	11%	Photobucket	16%	Flickr	12%
Snapfish	9%	Flickr	15%	Webshots	9%
GyaO	8%	Kodak Gallery	12%	Shutterfly	9%
Flickr	6%	Shutterfly	10%	GyaO	9%
Kodak Gallery	6%	Webshots	8%	MySpace Videos	8%
Webshots	5%	Imageshack	7%	Photobucket	4%

Note: The chart shows the top 10 sites.
Source: *Sharing, Privacy and Trust in Our Networked World*, OCLC, 2007, question 710.

The majority of YouTube and Snapfish users are under the age of 50, the same use pattern we see with the top social networking sites, MySpace and Mixi.

YouTube Users
By Age

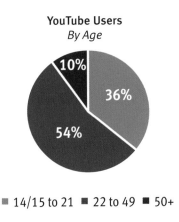

■ 14/15 to 21 ■ 22 to 49 ■ 50+

Source: *Sharing, Privacy and Trust in Our Networked World*, OCLC, 2007, question 710.

Snapfish Users
By Age

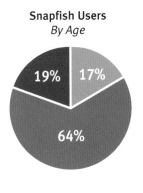

■ 14/15 to 21 ■ 22 to 49 ■ 50+

Source: *Sharing, Privacy and Trust in Our Networked World*, OCLC, 2007, question 710.

The YouTube Phenomenon

YouTube is the most used social media site on the World Wide Web.

Users are contributing a wide variety of videos that, prior to social sites such as YouTube, would likely have been viewed by just a select group of family, friends or co-workers. Many of YouTube's videos are viewed by thousands or hundreds of thousands of people. A September 19, 2007 comScore report revealed that in July 2007, viewers watched 2.4 billion videos on YouTube. The report indicated that 75% of U.S. Internet users watched online videos that month, for a total of 9 billion video streams. Average viewers spent 181 minutes watching online videos during the month.

An analysis of the 100 most viewed YouTube videos (September 2, 2007) provides a snapshot of the types of content being watched, who created them, and from where the videos originate.

25,700 videos on YouTube include *"library," "libraries" or "librarians"* in the title or description.

Source: YouTube, September 13, 2007.

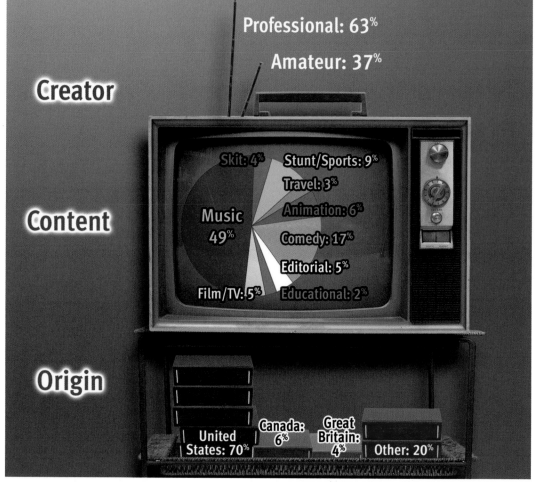

YouTube analysis conducted on September 2, 2007. "Other" category includes countries having one or two videos on the top 100 list: Australia, Brazil, Cuba, France, Germany, Greece, Hong Kong, India, Israel, Kazakhstan, the Netherlands, South Africa, Spain and Turkey. Alexa ranked YouTube as the fourth most used global Web site in September 2007.

Why We Use Social Sites

Maintaining current relationships with friends and family, building new relationships and sharing content or diaries are among the main reasons cited for participating in social networking and social media sites.

Our study findings suggest that much of what takes place on social spaces is motivated by a desire to connect. Most users are using social sites to interact with their friends, to build new relationships and to share and create content about their lives and experiences. Across countries, Internet users surveyed are using many of the same social networking and social media sites, and, in large part, their top motivations for using the sites are the same. Similarly, the sites selected across age groups are consistent, and top motivators show similar preference.

Communicating
with friends,
being part of a
community,
meeting new people and
having fun.

Motivations for using social sites

Motivations for Using Social Networking Sites

My friends use the same site, the Web site is fun and *to network or meet new people* are the key motivators for using social networking sites among the total general public surveyed.

More than half of the total general public who use social networking sites do so because their friends use the same site (66%). Forty-two percent (42%) of users of social networking sites use sites that are fun. Also motivating to social networking site users is the ability *to network or meet new people* and *to become part of a group or community.*

Why We Use Social Networking Sites
By Total General Public

Which of the following describe why you use your preferred social
networking Web site(s)? Please select all that apply.

Base: Respondents who have used a social networking site.

Why we use social networking sites	Total General Public
My friends use the same site	66%
The Web site is fun	42%
To network or to meet new people	37%
To be a part of a group or community	28%
The Web site is useful	27%
To document my personal experiences and share with others	22%
To express myself creatively with self-published material	18%
I get regular updates on new features and functionality	9%
I use it as part of my business	4%

Source: *Sharing, Privacy and Trust in Our Networked World*, OCLC, 2007, question 626.

While the same motivators are shared by respondents in all countries surveyed, there are a couple of noteworthy differences. *My friends use the same site* is the top reason cited for using social networking sites among users in all countries except for Germany. Nearly three-quarters of the respondents in Germany (71%) use social networking sites *to network or meet new people*, a rate nearly double that of users in the other countries. Sixty-four percent (64%) of users in Germany also say *my friends use the same site* influences their decision to use social networking sites—a rate similar to users in the other countries surveyed. A site that is fun motivates more German social networking users than respondents from other countries surveyed.

The French social networking users share the same top motivators as users from the other countries, but they were also the most likely to indicate they use social networking sites *to get regular updates on new features and functionality* (29%). MySpace and MSN Spaces are the two top-ranked social networking sites among the French respondents.

It is like a house.
You put everything you like or want in the house
and invite other people to the house.

Source: *Sharing, Privacy and Trust in Our Networked World*, OCLC, 2007, discussion group.

Why We Use Social Networking Sites
By Country

Which of the following describe why you use your preferred social networking Web site(s)? Please select all that apply.

Base: Respondents who have used a social networking site.

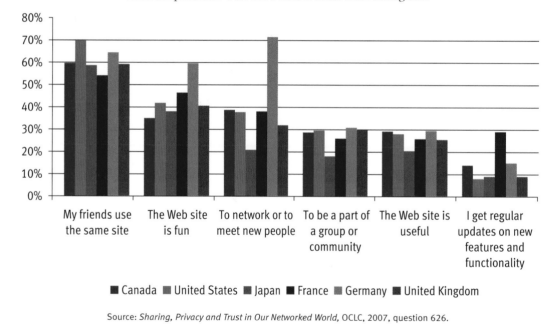

Canada ■ United States ■ Japan ■ France ■ Germany ■ United Kingdom

Source: *Sharing, Privacy and Trust in Our Networked World*, OCLC, 2007, question 626.

Motivations for using social networking sites are the same across the age groups surveyed, but the percentage of those citing each reason varied by age. *My friends use the same site* is by far (80%) the main determinant for using a social networking site among the younger respondents (ages 14/15–21). About a quarter of youth also expressed that documenting personal experiences and expressing themselves through self-published materials on these sites motivates them.

For users ages 22–49, *my friends use the same site* is also the top reason cited for using a social networking site. About 40% of social networking users ages 22–49 say fun and networking to meet people describe why they use their preferred social networking sites.

Users age 50+ were the only group to say that being *part of a group or community* was their top motivator. *My friends use the same site* is also a key motivator for 40% of social networking users age 50 or older, but represents the smallest percentage of any age group surveyed. The third most popular reason for this group was *the Web site is useful*, which was not listed among the top three for users ages 14/15–21 and 22–49 but was cited by roughly the same percentage (26%–32%) of users among all age groups.

Why We Use Social Networking Sites
By Age

Which of the following describe why you use your preferred social networking Web site(s)? Please select all that apply.

Base: Respondents who have used a social networking site.

Why we use social networking sites	Age 14/15 to 21	Age 22 to 49	Age 50+
My friends use the same site	80%	62%	40%
The Web site is fun	49%	40%	26%
To network or to meet new people	36%	39%	25%
To be part of a group or community	28%	25%	42%
The Web site is useful	26%	26%	32%
To document my personal experiences and share with others	24%	21%	19%
To express myself creatively with self-published materials	24%	14%	15%
I get regular updates on new features and functionality	8%	9%	15%

Source: *Sharing, Privacy and Trust in Our Networked World*, OCLC, 2007, question 626.

I have everyone's e-mail on there—like

300 people
that I stay in contact with ...

Source: *Sharing, Privacy and Trust in Our Networked World*, OCLC, 2007, discussion group.

Motivations for Using Social Media Sites

"Fun" describes the top motivation for social media users. *The Web site is fun* was cited as the top reason for using social media sites by about half of users. Being useful is also a motivator; *the Web site is useful* was cited by a third of users. *My friends use the same site* was also cited by nearly a third of users. Users of social media sites are less likely to use their preferred social media sites *to network or to meet new people* (11%) than users of social networking sites (37%).

Even though social media sites are primarily intended to share content, users of social networking sites are more likely to choose *to document personal experiences and share with others* (22%) or *to express themselves creatively and self-publish materials* (18%) on social networking sites compared to users of social media sites, at 15% and 11%, respectively.

Why We Use Social Media Sites
By Total General Public

Which of the following describe why you use your preferred social media Web site(s)? Please select all that apply.

Base: Respondents who have used a social media site.

Why we use social media sites	Total General Public
The Web site(s) is fun	47%
The Web site(s) is useful	33%
My friends use the same site	32%
To document my personal experiences and share with others	15%
To express myself creatively with self-published material	11%
To network or to meet new people	11%
I get regular updates on new features and functionality	10%
To be a part of a group or community	10%
I use it as part of my business	3%

Source: *Sharing, Privacy and Trust in Our Networked World*, OCLC, 2007, question 730.

As with social networking sites, our findings show common motivators for using social media sites across all countries surveyed. *The Web site is fun* is the top reason that describes why social media sites are used among the total general public in all six countries surveyed, ranging from 40% in the U.K. to 64% in Germany.

The Web site is useful is expressed as a top motivator by roughly a third of users in all countries except Germany. The German respondents are significantly more likely than those in the other countries surveyed to use their preferred social media site *to network or to meet new people,* at 29%. Significantly fewer Japanese respondents use their preferred social media site because their friends use the same site. Using a social media site that is fun is the top motivator in Japan.

Why We Use Social Media Sites
By Country

Which of the following describe why you use your preferred social media Web site(s)? Please select all that apply.

Base: Respondents who have used a social media site.

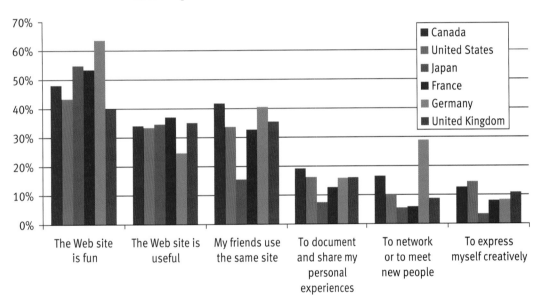

Source: *Sharing, Privacy and Trust in Our Networked World,* OCLC, 2007, question 730.

The Web site is fun is the top reason for using social media sites for well over half of 14/15–21-year-olds surveyed. *The Web site is useful* is substantially lower, at 38%, followed closely by *my friends use the same site* (35%).

The top three reasons for using social media sites among age 50+ general public are fairly evenly distributed; *the Web site is useful* (36%), *the Web site is fun* (34%), and *my friends use the same site* (28%).

Why We Use Social Media Sites
By Age

Which of the following describe why you use your preferred social media Web site(s)? Please select all that apply.

Base: Respondents who have used a social media site.

Why we use social media sites	Age 14/15 to 21	Age 22 to 49	Age 50+
The Web site is fun	60%	43%	34%
The Web site is useful	38%	29%	36%
My friends use the same site	35%	31%	28%
To document my personal experiences and share with others	13%	17%	11%
To express myself creatively with self-published materials	15%	10%	7%
To network or to meet new people	10%	12%	12%
I get regular updates on new features and functionality	12%	9%	9%
To be part of a group or community	10%	10%	11%

Source: *Sharing, Privacy and Trust in Our Networked World,* OCLC, 2007, question 730.

Across the age groups and countries, the online general public surveyed are using the same social networking sites and the same social media sites. Their motivators are clear—to interact with their friends and meet new people on social networking sites and to spend time on social media sites that are fun and useful. Utility and fun are seen as congruent qualities for social media users.

Social Networking Sites Help *Maintain* Current Relationships

Base: Respondents who have used a social networking site.

Canada 38%

United States 44%

Japan 39%

France 38%

Germany 49%

United Kingdom 33%

Source: *Sharing, Privacy and Trust in Our Networked World,* OCLC, 2007, question 971. Note: The chart shows *strongly agree* and *somewhat agree* responses.

Social Networking Sites Help *Build* New Relationships

Base: Respondents who have used a social networking site.

Maintaining and Building Relationships on Social Networking Sites

Users agree that social networking sites help them to both build new relationships and maintain current relationships.

Forty-two percent (42%) of social networking users across countries surveyed *agree* (*strongly agree* or *somewhat agree*) that the sites help **maintain** their current relationships. Users in Germany are most likely to *agree* social networking sites help maintain relationships (49%) while users in the U.K. are least likely to feel this way, at 33%.

The response to *social networking sites help **build** new relationships* yielded an even higher agreement level. The users in the U.S., Canada, the U.K and Japan are slightly more likely to *agree* that social networking sites help build new relationships than to *agree* that they help maintain current relationships. While just a third of users in the U.K. *agree* that social networking sites help maintain current relationships, over half (53%) *agree* they help build new relationships. The social networking users in France are the least likely to *agree* that these sites help build new relationships, at just 30%.

Building and Maintaining Relationships on Social Networking Sites
By Total General Public

Thinking about the social networking Web sites you use, how strongly do you agree or disagree with each of the following statements?

Base: Respondents who have used a social networking site.

Note: The chart shows the *strongly agree* and *somewhat agree* responses.

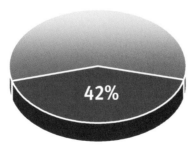 

These sites help maintain current relationships

These sites help build new relationships

Source: *Sharing, Privacy and Trust in Our Networked World*, OCLC, 2007, question 971.

Source: *Sharing, Privacy and Trust in Our Networked World*, OCLC, 2007, question 971. Note: The chart shows *strongly agree* and *somewhat agree* responses.

Spending Time on Commercial and Social Sites

Nearly three-quarters of the total general public log in to their preferred social networking sites at least once weekly; over a third visit daily. Usage of social sites is more frequent than commercial sites, where nearly half visit at least once weekly and 14% visit daily. Usage of social media sites is very similar to commercial sites; half visit weekly.

Internet users surveyed who use commercial sites visit those sites often. Nearly half log onto their preferred commercial sites at least weekly and 14% log in daily. Use of eBay and iTunes was somewhat higher than the average. More than a quarter of eBay users visit the site daily.

Frequency of Amazon Use

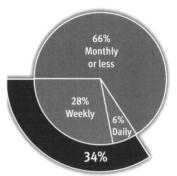

Source: *Sharing, Privacy and Trust in Our Networked World*, OCLC, 2007, question 790.

Frequency of Using Commercial Sites
By Total General Public

Typically, how frequently do you log in to (your preferred commercial site)?

Base: Respondents who have used a commercial and/or library Web site.

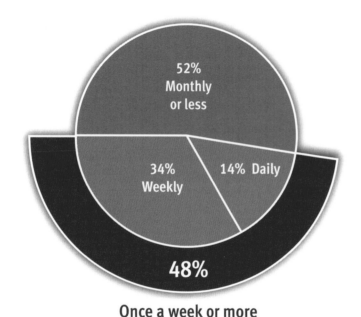

Source: *Sharing, Privacy and Trust in Our Networked World*, OCLC, 2007, question 790.

Frequency of eBay Use

Source: *Sharing, Privacy and Trust in Our Networked World*, OCLC, 2007, question 790.

Frequency of iTunes Use

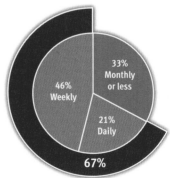

Source: *Sharing, Privacy and Trust in Our Networked World*, OCLC, 2007, question 790.

Users of social networking sites are very active, even more active than commercial site users. More than a third of social networking users (39%) log in at least daily and 73% log in at least weekly to their preferred social networking sites.

Usage was high across the most used social networking sites. Among social networking users who ranked MySpace as their primary social networking site used, 36% log in at least daily (17% several times a day and 19% once a day) and 74% log in weekly or more often. Mixi is the dominant social networking site in Japan. Frequency of use among those who rank Mixi as their primary social networking site used is even greater than the MySpace users; 59% log in at least daily (34% several times a day and 25% once a day) and the majority of users visit Mixi weekly or more often, at 83%.

Frequency of Using Social Networking Sites
By Total General Public

Typically, how frequently do you log in to
(your preferred social networking site)?

Base: Respondents who have used a social networking site.

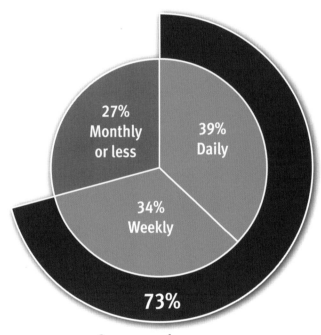

Once a week or more

Source: *Sharing, Privacy and Trust in Our Networked World*, OCLC, 2007, question 635.

Frequency of MySpace Use

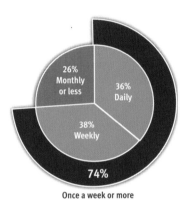

Once a week or more

Source: *Sharing, Privacy and Trust in Our Networked World*, OCLC, 2007, question 635.

Frequency of Mixi Use

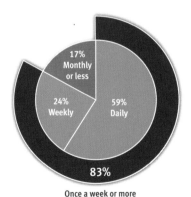

Once a week or more

Source: *Sharing, Privacy and Trust in Our Networked World*, OCLC, 2007, question 635.

Frequency of use of social networking sites differed substantially by age. The youth are the most active users. The younger age group (ages 14/15–21) who ranked MySpace as their primary social networking site used are more than twice as likely than the older age groups to log in several times a day (26% compared to 12% for ages 22–49 and 7% for age 50+).

The younger Mixi users are also logging in more often; 50% of Mixi users ages 14/15–21 log in several times a day compared to 25% of ages 22–49 and 8% for age 50+.

While still very robust, frequency of use on social media sites is less than the use on social networking sites. Just about half (49%) report logging in once a week or more often, with 12% logging on to their favorite social media sites at least daily and 37% at least weekly.

Frequency of Using Social Media Sites
By Total General Public

Typically, how frequently do you log in to (your preferred social media site)?

Base: Respondents who have used a social media site.

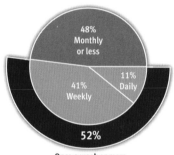

Frequency of YouTube Use

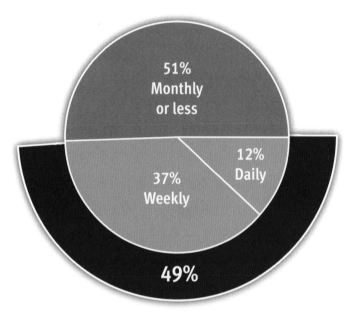

Once a week or more

Source: *Sharing, Privacy and Trust in Our Networked World,* OCLC, 2007, question 740.

Source: *Sharing, Privacy and Trust in Our Networked World,* OCLC, 2007, question 740.

For social media site users who ranked YouTube as their primary social media site used, overall usage very closely matches the total average, with 52% logging in at least once a week or more often—11% log in daily and 41% log in at least once weekly. Social media site users who ranked Snapfish as their primary social media site used frequent the site less often than the total average; 31% log in at least once a week—5% log in daily and 26% log in at least weekly.

As with social networking sites, the younger age group surveyed (ages 14/15–21) log in more often to their top ranked social media sites; 18% log in daily compared to the total average of 12%, and 63% log in at least once weekly compared to 49% of the total average.

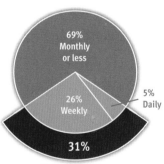

Frequency of Snapfish Use

Once a week or more

Source: *Sharing, Privacy and Trust in Our Networked World,* OCLC, 2007, question 740.

Familiarity with Sites

A third of the general public surveyed across all countries, except Japan, say they are very or extremely familiar with the commercial sites they use. U.S. respondents reported the highest degree of familiarity with social networking sites. Familiarity with social networking sites is approaching levels equal to commercial sites in the U.S. For youth (ages 14/15–21), familiarity of social networking sites exceeds familiarity for commercial sites.

Respondents report the **highest level of familiarity with commercial sites.**

As respondents spend more time online and more time on social sites, familiarity grows. Familiarity of commercial sites is the highest among commercial site users, but the percentage of social networking users who report that they are *extremely* or *very familiar* with social networking sites is not far behind among respondents in some countries. While commercial sites have been in existence longer, familiarity with social networking sites is comparable to commercial sites.

U.S. social networking site users show the highest level of familiarity; more than 40% say they are *extremely* or *very familiar* with social networking sites, a rate close to their familiarity with commercial sites that have been in existence for substantially longer. In fact, 43% of the U.S. general public who ranked MySpace as their most used social networking site are *extremely* or *very familiar* with the site and 43% of those in the U.S. who ranked Amazon as their primary commercial site used are *extremely* or *very familiar* with it.

German and U.K. respondents expressed the highest level of familiarity with commercial sites. Nearly half of the German respondents who use commercial sites are *extremely* or *very familiar* with these sites, which is consistent with their above-average use of commercial sites. More specifically, half of the German general public who ranked eBay and Amazon as their primary sites used are *extremely* or *very familiar* with these sites, 53% and 51%, respectively.

Social site users in France expressed the least familiarity with these sites. Familiarity with social networking and media sites among the French respondents was the lowest, which is consistent with their use; they had the lowest usage of social networking and social media sites among the general public in the six countries surveyed.

Familiarity with Commercial and Social Sites
By Country

How familiar are you with (your preferred social networking,
social media and/or commercial site)?

Base: Respondents who have used a social networking,
social media and/or commercial site.

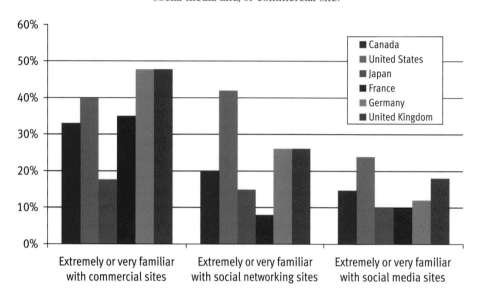

Source: *Sharing, Privacy and Trust in Our Networked World*, OCLC, 2007, questions 640, 745 and 795.

Over
40%
*of U.S. social
networking users are*
*extremely or
very familiar
with social
networking
sites,*
*the highest of any
country surveyed.*

The youngest respondents reported the highest levels of familiarity for both social networking and social media sites. And, familiarity among the 14/15–21-year-olds with commercial sites approximates that of older age groups. Nearly half of the commercial site users ages 14/15–21 (45%) who ranked eBay as their primary commercial site used are *extremely* or *very familiar* with the site compared to 48% of 22–49-year-olds and 35% of those age 50+.

Youth (ages 14/15–21) are by far the most familiar with social networking sites compared to any other age group and also reported the highest level of familiarity with social media sites. Half of all social networking users ages 14/15–21 report being *extremely* or *very familiar* with social networking sites compared to less than a quarter of users ages 22–49 and age 50+.

Well over half of the respondents ages 14/15–21 (61%) who ranked MySpace as their primary social networking site used say they are either *extremely* or *very familiar* with the site; 27% of 22–49-year-olds and 17% of the age 50+ group are *extremely* or *very familiar* with MySpace.

Familiarity with social media sites is the lowest among each age group. About a quarter of users ages 14/15–21 are *extremely* or *very familiar* with social media sites.

YouTube, the top used social media site, follows a similar familiarity pattern among social media users in general; 28% of the 14/15–21-year-olds who ranked YouTube as their primary site used are *extremely* or *very familiar* with the site; 15% of the 22–49-year-olds and 7% of the age 50+ group are *extremely* or *very familiar* with YouTube.

Familiarity with Commercial and Social Sites
By Age

How familiar are you with (preferred social networking, social media and/or commercial site)?

Base: Respondents who have used a social networking, social media and/or commercial site.

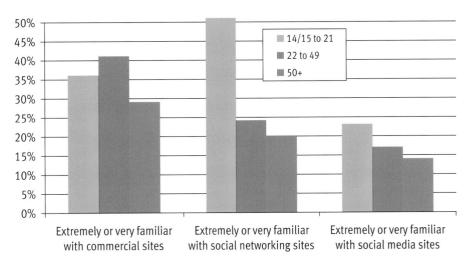

Source: *Sharing, Privacy and Trust in Our Networked World, OCLC,* 2007, questions 640, 745 and 795.

Sharing Our Personal Information Online

Users of commercial sites are likely to share contact information on commercial sites but are generally unwilling to provide individual and interest information. Users of social networking and social media sites are much more likely to share their individual and interest information. Users are often willing to share more than just required information when registering on a site.

The rapid adoption of social networking resources has allowed millions of users to become creators and communicators as well as audience members and customers. In these new roles, users are sharing with each other—and service providers—an increasing amount of feedback and personal information. What information are users willing to share online? Our survey results suggest that it varies by site, the community, and by the information that is expected to be delivered in return.

Most users are willing to share more than just the required information when registering at Web sites. Two-thirds of the total general public indicated that when they initially register on a Web site, they *always, often* or *sometimes* complete the entire registration form, not just the required information—11% *always* complete the entire registration form.

We presented respondents with 22 different types of personal information and asked which, if any, they have provided on social networking, social media or commercial sites. Information provided was grouped into three general categories: **contact information**, including information such as name, address, e-mail and phone; **individual information**, including marital status, personality attributes, sexual preference, physical attributes and birthday; and **interest information** such as subjects of interest, books read and association affiliations.

Users of commercial sites are the most likely to have provided **contact information** on commercial sites. Users of social networking sites are most likely to have shared **individual** and **interest information** on these social sites. Approximately three-quarters of the total general public who have used a commercial site have supplied their *given/first name, surname/last name, e-mail* and *street address*. About half of users have provided their *phone number, birthday* and *credit/debit card information*.

Information sharing on social networking sites is different. Users of social networking sites were less likely to have provided **contact information** compared to users of commercial sites. While half or more of commercial site users have provided their *surname/family name* (73%) or *telephone number* (50%) on a commercial site, just 46% of social networking site users have provided their *surname/last name* and only 12% have provided their *telephone number* on a social networking site. While less likely to have shared traditional **contact information**, users of social networking sites were more likely to have shared their **interest information** on a social networking site than commercial site users do on commercial sites. Seventy percent (70%) of social networking site users have provided their *subjects of interest* on these sites compared to just 28% of commercial site users who have provided the same information.

There are interesting differences between **individual** and **interest information** shared on social networking sites compared to social media sites by their respective users. Fewer social media site users were likely to have shared **individual** and **interest information** on social media sites than commercial and social networking site users

Complete Entire Web Registration Form

Source: *Sharing, Privacy and Trust in Our Networked World*, OCLC, 2007, question 836, by total general public, "In general, when registering at any Web site, how often do you: fill out the complete form, not just the required information?"

do on commercial and social networking sites. Users were also less willing to share **contact information** on social media sites than users do on either commercial or social networking sites.

More than half (57%) of social networking users have provided *photos/videos* on social networking sites compared to just 30% of social media users on social media sites, which are specifically designed to share content. While a quarter or more of social media users have provided *photos/videos, subjects of interest* and *birthday* on a social media site, they report having shared very little additional **interest** and **individual information**. These results suggest that many social media users are likely more engaged in browsing than authoring or sharing on social media sites and that more robust sharing of personal content is taking place on social networking sites.

Information Shared on Commercial and Social Sites
By Total General Public

Which of the following types of information have you ever supplied about yourself on [commercial, social networking and/or social media sites]?

Base: Respondents who have used a commercial, social networking and/or social media site.

Source: *Sharing, Privacy and Trust in Our Networked World*, OCLC, 2007, questions 725, 765 and 625.

Information Shared on Commercial Sites—Country Comparisons

The survey results revealed varying sharing patterns on commercial sites by the general public in the six countries surveyed. While our review of favorite Web sites indicates that survey respondents use many of the same commercial sites, the data sharing practices are different among respondents in varying countries.

U.K. respondents were significantly more likely to have provided *credit card information* on a commercial site. The French and German commercial site users were significantly more likely than those in Canada, the U.S., the U.K. and Japan to have provided their *birthday*. Users of commercial sites in Canada were the most likely to have provided their *income* (17%) on these sites, while the German users were least likely (6%). The Japanese commercial site users were significantly more likely to have provided a *telephone number* (65%) on a commercial site.

Information Shared on Commercial Sites
By Country

Which of the following types of information have you ever supplied about yourself when you were browsing for and/or purchasing music, movies, books and other retail items?

Base: Respondents who have used a commercial site and/or a library Web site.

■ Canada ▨ United States ■ Japan ■ France ▨ Germany ■ United Kingdom

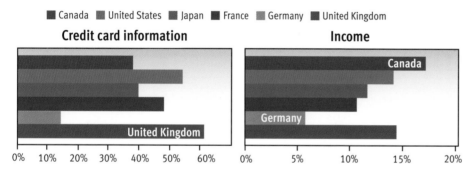

Credit card information

Income

Commercial site users in the U.K. (61%) were significantly more likely to have provided credit card information on a commercial site. (Total=46%)

Commercial site users in Canada (17%) were more likely to have provided their income on a commercial site, while users in Germany were least likely (6%). (Total=11%)

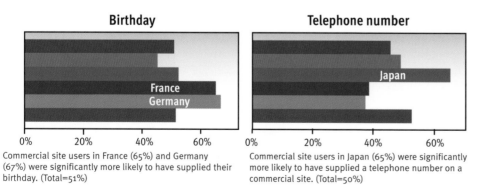

Birthday

Telephone number

Commercial site users in France (65%) and Germany (67%) were significantly more likely to have supplied their birthday. (Total=51%)

Commercial site users in Japan (65%) were significantly more likely to have supplied a telephone number on a commercial site. (Total=50%)

Source: *Sharing, Privacy and Trust in Our Networked World,* OCLC, 2007, question 765.

Users of commercial sites shared information to purchase goods and they were also likely to have shared information to keep current and receive alerts. Well over half of respondents (60%) have used commercial electronic notification services.

Over a quarter of commercial site users report they have created a "my favorites" list, which entails providing information about preferences and desires.

Electronic newsletters and e-mail alerts are the most popular notification services and use was particularly dominant among commercial site users in Canada, Germany, the U.S. and the U.K. Overall, the French commercial site users were the least likely to have used these electronic notification services; 52% say they have used none of these services.

60%
of commercial site users have used **commercial electronic notification services.**

Use of Commercial Electronic Notification Services
By Country

Which of the following activities have you done during the last 12 months while browsing for and/or purchasing music, movies, books and other retail items?

Base: Respondents who have used a commercial site and/or a library Web site.

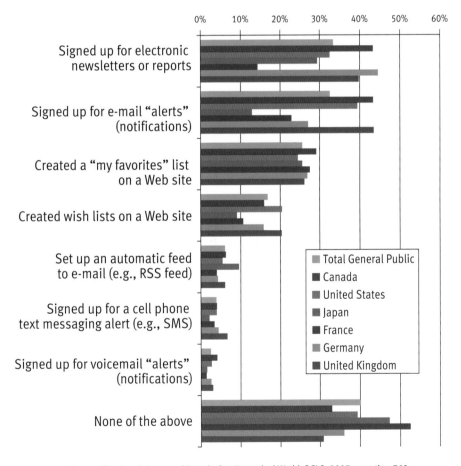

Source: *Sharing, Privacy and Trust in Our Networked World,* OCLC, 2007, question 760.

Information Shared on Social Networking Sites—Country Comparisons

Social networking users were likely to have shared a wide variety of personal information on their favorite sites. The majority of social networking users have shared their *birthday, marital status, subjects of interest* and *photos/videos*. More than a third of respondents have shared *personality attributes, books read, sexual preference, physical attributes* and *religious affiliations* on social networking sites.

Even with consistency in sites used (MySpace was the top social networking site in all countries except Japan), the personal information users have provided shows wide variation across geographies. Overall, Japanese social networking users reported the lowest rate of information sharing on social networking sites. While Japanese social networking users indicated that they have shared their *subjects of interest* and *books they have read* on a social networking site at a rate comparable to users from other countries surveyed, they were significantly less likely to have provided many other types of personal information. Overall, social networking users in Germany, the U.S., Canada and the U.K. were most likely to have provided personal information on social networking sites. Users in the U.S. and Canada were the most likely to have shared their *personality attributes, physical attributes* and *religious affiliations* on social networking sites. Users in Germany report the highest rates of having shared *association affiliations, political affiliations, books read* and *self-published information*. Social networking users in the U.K. (6%) and Japan (3%) were the least likely to have provided their *political affiliations*; users in Germany (22%) and the U.S. (21%) were the most likely.

Information Shared on Social Networking Sites
By Country

Which of the following types of information have you ever supplied about yourself on social networking Web site(s)?

Base: Respondents who have used a social networking site.

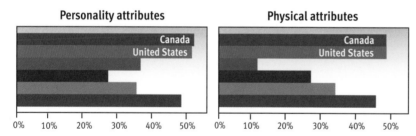

Personality attributes

Social networking users in Canada (51%) and the U.S. (50%) were more likely to have shared their personality attributes on a social networking site. (Total =46%)

Physical attributes

Social networking users in Canada (49%) and the U.S. (49%) were more likely to have shared their physical attributes on a social networking site. (Total=42%)

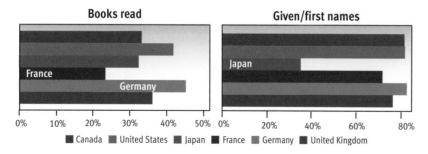

Books read

Social networking users in Germany (45%) were most likely to have shared books they have read; the French (23%) were least likely. (Total =39%)

Given/first names

Japanese users of social networking sites were significantly less likely to have shared their given/first names (36%). Total=73%)

■ Canada ■ United States ■ Japan ■ France ■ Germany ■ United Kingdom

Source: *Sharing, Privacy and Trust in Our Networked World*, OCLC, 2007, question 625.

Information Shared on Social Networking Sites
By Country

Which of the following types of information have you ever supplied about yourself on social networking Web sites?

Base: Respondents who have used a social networking site.

The types of *personal information* shared on social networking sites *varies* across countries surveyed.

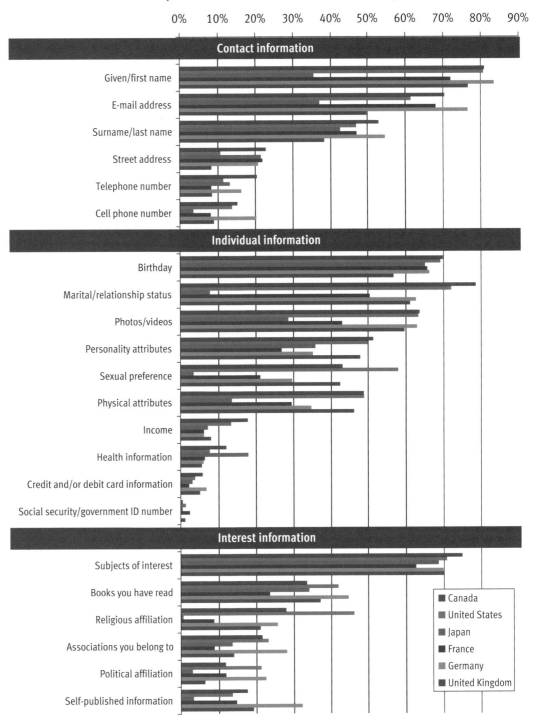

Source: *Sharing, Privacy and Trust in Our Networked World*, OCLC, 2007, question 625.

Information Shared on Social Media Sites—Country Comparison

Sharing personal information on social media sites showed sharing patterns more consistent with commercial site use than with social networking sites. Overall, users of social media sites were much less likely to have shared information on these sites than social networking site users have shared on social networking sites, including "content" information generally associated with social media sites.

More than half of total social networking users (57%) have shared *photos/videos* and 14% have shared *self-published information* on social networking sites, compared to 30% and 7%, respectively, of social media users on social media sites. Social media users in Germany, the U.S. and Canada were more likely to have provided information on social media sites than those in other countries surveyed. The Japanese social media users shared less on these sites, and often significantly less, than users in the others countries surveyed.

Significantly more French social media users were likely to have uploaded or linked to *videos* (60%) during the last 12 months on a social media site, almost twice the rate of users in any other country. More Canadian and French social media users uploaded or linked to *music* than any other respondents. The Canadian and American social media users were the most likely to have uploaded or linked to *pictures* on a social media site.

57% have shared photos/videos on a social networking site; 30% on a social media site.

Uploading or Linking on Social Media Sites
By Country

Which of the following have you uploaded or linked to a social media
Web site during the last 12 months?

Base: Respondents who have used a social media site.

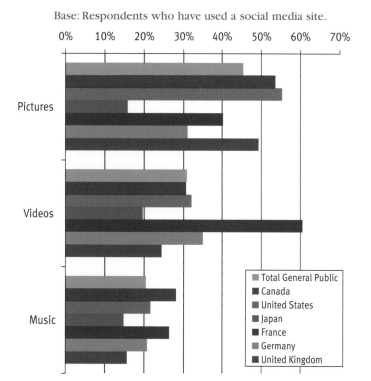

Source: *Sharing, Privacy and Trust in Our Networked World*, OCLC, 2007, question 705.

Leaving Social Sites

Over 80% of the total general public indicated that once started, they have not stopped using a social networking or social media site.

Just 16% of the total social networking users reported that they have stopped using a site within the last 24 months. And only 9% of social media users have stopped using a site.

The top two reasons for discontinuing the use of a particular social networking site were *the Web site was not as useful as I thought it would be* (40%) and *the Web site was not as much fun as I thought it would be* (33%). While the top reason for using a social networking site is because *my friends use the same site,* only 17% of those who stopped using a social networking site did so because their friends stopped using it.

The top reason for discontinuing use of a social network site is that the site was not as useful as anticipated. The 16% of users who stopped using a social networking site gave the following reasons:

- The Web site was not as useful as I thought it would be (40%)
- The Web site was not as much fun as I thought it would be (33%)
- I found other sites I liked better (26%) and other Web sites offer more options (17%)
- I did not have the time to devote to it (26%)
- My friends stopped using it (17%)
- I did not trust the people I met online (13%)
- My parents required me to stop using it (9%)
- My spouse/partner asked me to stop using it (6%)

The top reason for discontinuing use of a social media site is lack of time. The 9% of users who stopped using a social media site gave the following reasons:

- I did not have the time to devote to it (28%)
- The Web site was not as much fun as I thought it would be (21%)
- The Web site was not as useful as I thought it would be (20%)
- I found other sites I liked better (17%) and other Web sites offer more options (9%)
- Other Web sites are easier to use (14%)
- I did not trust the people I met online (8%)

Stopped Using a Social Networking Site?
By Country

Did you stop using a social networking Web site
within the past 24 months?

Base: Respondents who have used a social networking site.

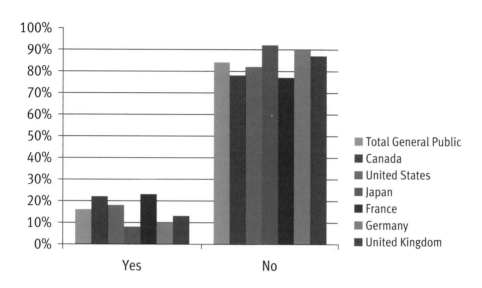

- Total General Public
- Canada
- United States
- Japan
- France
- Germany
- United Kingdom

Source: *Sharing, Privacy and Trust in Our Networked World*, OCLC, 2007, question 660.

*Without social
networking ...*
it would kill me,
*because I'd feel that all
of those connections
I spent this time making
would be lost.*

Source: *Sharing, Privacy and Trust in
Our Networked World*, OCLC, 2007,
discussion group.

Summary

More than a quarter of the online population surveyed (28%) are active users of social sites–sites defined especially to provide exchange and content sharing. At the time of the survey, a few social sites were the most preferred sites across all countries: MySpace and YouTube were clear favorites; Mixi dominated social networking use in Japan. Users are spending a large amount of time on these sites. Almost three-quarters of social networking users spend time on social networking sites each week and half of the social media site users visit social media sites weekly.

While online users across all groups surveyed are using social sites, frequency of use among the youth (ages 14/15–21) is the highest. Social site users appear to be quickly becoming comfortable in these new spaces; over half of social networking users report they are *extremely* or *very familiar with* these sites.

Social site users are sharing information about themselves on social sites that commercial sites users are far less likely to provide on commercial sites. Nearly half or more have provided *subjects of interest* and *books read* and just over 20% have provided *association affiliation* on social networking sites. And, once started, very few users of social networking sites report they have stopped using them. They are building the social Web.

Social Networking Thoughts and Opinions

In three social networking focus groups moderated by OCLC, participants discussed their thoughts on communication, privacy and security in social spaces. They also told us what social networking meant to them and how their lives would be different without these services.

PRIVACY

How important is this service or this product to me? They're asking this much information of me. Is it worth it?

Undergraduate student, McMaster University, Hamilton, Ontario, Canada

SECURITY

You don't know who's watching or what's being done with the information that you're using online. The conversation you're having is private between you and the person on the next computer but not really, because it's on the Internet ... You don't know who's watching and what they can get.

Undergraduate student, McMaster University, Hamilton, Ontario, Canada

WITHOUT SOCIAL NETWORKING

It would kill me, because I'd feel that all of those connections I spent this time making would be lost.

Hairstylist, Columbus, Ohio, U.S.

SECURITY

And it's [social networking's] good because it prompts you. If you click "I don't know this person," it will ask you "Well, then, why are you adding them?" It allows you to think a little bit more about who you're letting into your world.

Graduate student, McMaster University, Hamilton, Ontario, Canada

DESCRIBE SOCIAL NETWORKING

It's like a house. You put everything you like or want in the house and invite other people to the house.

Graduate student, McMaster University, Hamilton, Ontario, Canada

COMMUNICATION

I just use it to connect with friends.

Hairstylist, Columbus, Ohio, U.S.

WITHOUT SOCIAL NETWORKING

PRIVACY

I wouldn't say anything I didn't want the whole world to know about me, because the whole world is going to know.

Undergraduate student, McMaster University, Hamilton, Ontario, Canada

I have everyone's e-mail on there—like, 300 people that I stay in contact with. I don't know—if I lost all of those e-mails, it would be impossible to get them all back. And, I wouldn't want to do that work and I probably wouldn't, so that would just be the end of so many relationships in my life.

Undergraduate student, McMaster University, Hamilton, Ontario, Canada

2-40 Sharing, Privacy and Trust in Our Networked World

DESCRIBE SOCIAL NETWORKING

I describe Facebook as sort of a profile that you put out there—out there meaning the Internet—about yourself, and it has details like your name, your hobbies, that sort of thing. And you have this imaginary wall and people can write things on your wall and when they write on your wall you can go back to the other person's wall and write on theirs.

Graduate student, McMaster University, Hamilton, Ontario, Canada

WITHOUT SOCIAL NETWORKING

So many of my friends are like, "I have to get home and Facebook." So, if that was missing, they'd just be at home not knowing what to do with themselves, because it's such a way that they communicate with so many people.

Undergraduate student, McMaster University, Hamilton, Ontario, Canada

PRIVACY

At first, I was kind of naïve about it. Now, I know a little more about it—not to put super personal information on it about myself.

Hairstylist, Columbus, Ohio, U.S.

SECURITY

It seems there are a lot more passwords—pretty much every site you go into has a password. So, I think it's definitely more secure than it was several years ago.

Hairstylist, Columbus, Ohio, U.S.

COMMUNICATION

When you pick up the telephone to call, you're only talking to one person. But, when you go online, you can have multiple conversations in the same amount of time. So, I find that beneficial.

Graduate student, McMaster University, Hamilton, Ontario, Canada

PRIVACY

I only leave my true information [on social networking sites] when necessary.

Graduate student, McMaster University, Hamilton, Ontario, Canada

DESCRIBE SOCIAL NETWORKING

A student came in and she went through the whole salon [during a job interview]. Then we said we have a Web page, and she goes, "I already looked at it and I went to everybody's MySpace and looked at everybody that worked here," and she goes, "I want to work here."

Hair salon owner, Columbus, Ohio, U.S.

SECURITY

I won't post anywhere unless they have a security policy where you have to check off that you've read the whole thing. That makes me feel a little bit safer.

Hairstylist, Columbus, Ohio, U.S.

Privacy, Security and Trust

This is an opportunity to build a new kind of international understanding, not politician to politician, great man to great man, but citizen to citizen, person to person.

It's a chance for people to look at a computer screen and really, genuinely wonder who's out there looking back at them.

—From *Time,* "Time's Person of the Year: You," by Lev Grossman, Dec. 13, 2006

People engage in a growing variety and number of Web activities on today's social Internet, from buying on commercial sites, to blogging, to online dating, to social networking. Many of the activities require participants to share information about themselves with people and institutions they have no previous relationship with. As Web users create "friendship" with dozens, often hundreds, of other Internet users, new rules of communities begin to form.

We were interested to learn more about how respondents evaluate what they are willing to share, with whom and on what sites. Did their participation in an increasing number of Internet services change users' views about personal privacy or information privacy?

We asked respondents about their top privacy concerns in general, if any. We also evaluated how private they viewed their online activities, including their interactions with the library. We asked about privacy policies, remaining anonymous and building trust on the Internet.

And, finally, we asked respondents to help us better understand how they make decisions about when to share and what is expected in return.

Views on Privacy and Security

Approximately a quarter of the total general public surveyed feel their personal information is kept more private and kept more secure on the Internet than it was two years ago. An almost equal number feel their information is kept less private. And a roughly equal number are not sure.

Eleven percent (11%) have had their personal online information used without their consent.

Internet Privacy

Respondents were fairly evenly divided regarding changes in Internet privacy over the last two years. A quarter of the total general public surveyed feel their personal information on the Internet is *kept more private* (23%), is *kept less private* (27%), showed *no change* (29%) or are *not sure* (21%).

Internet Privacy
By Total General Public

Generally, do you think that your personal information on the Internet is kept more private than, less private than, or the same as it was two years ago?

Source: *Sharing, Privacy and Trust in Our Networked World,* OCLC, 2007, question 930.

Respondents had similar opinions on Internet privacy across all countries surveyed. While the Canadian, American, French, German and U.K. respondents were more likely than the Japanese respondents to feel their personal information is *kept more private* on the Internet, approximately half or more of the respondents from each country feel their personal information is kept as private or more private as it was two years ago.

52% *of the general public surveyed feel their personal information on the Internet is* **kept as private, or more private,** *as it was two years ago.*

Internet Privacy
By Country

Generally, do you think that your personal information on the Internet is kept
more private than, less private than, or the same as it was two years ago?

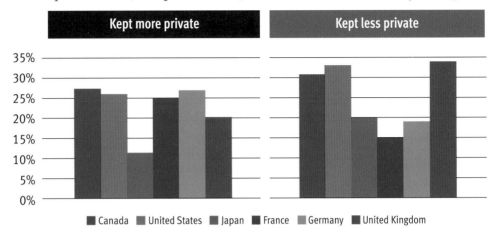

Source: *Sharing, Privacy and Trust in Our Networked World,* OCLC, 2007, question 930.

Respondents age

50+

*are more likely to
feel their personal
information is*

kept less private
on the Internet

*than two years ago
compared to the
younger age groups.*

We observed similar views on privacy among respondents ages 14/15–21 and ages
22–49. Roughly a quarter of each age group feel their personal information is *kept
more private* on the Internet than it was two years ago. Twenty percent (20%) of
respondents ages 14/15–21 and 26% of respondents ages 22–49 feel their personal
information is *kept less private.*

Compared to the younger age groups, respondents age 50+ are slightly less likely to
feel their personal information is *kept more private*, at 20%. Older respondents were
more likely to feel that privacy is weakening on the Internet; more than a third (35%)
feel their personal information is *kept less private.*

Internet Privacy
By Age

Generally, do you think that your personal information on the Internet is kept
more private than, less private than, or the same as it was two years ago?

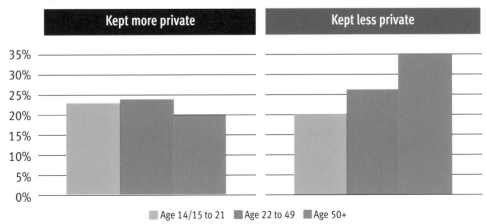

Source: *Sharing, Privacy and Trust in Our Networked World,* OCLC, 2007, question 930.

Internet Security

The public's opinion about security of their personal information on the Internet is similar to their views on privacy.

Just over a quarter of the total general public surveyed (26%) feel their personal information on the Internet is *kept more secure* than it was two years ago; an equal number, 25%, feel it is *kept less secure*. Nearly half of the general public feel there is *no change* (30%) or are *not sure* (19%).

Our research showed a relationship exists between the views on privacy and security on the Internet. Respondents who feel their personal information is *kept more private* on the Internet tend to feel it is *kept more secure* as well. In fact, 74% of those who feel their personal information is *kept more private* also feel it is *kept more secure*.

Internet Security
By Total General Public

Generally, do you think that your personal information on the Internet is kept more secure than, less secure than, or the same as it was two years ago?

Source: *Sharing, Privacy and Trust in Our Networked World*, OCLC, 2007, question 935.

56% *of the total general public surveyed feel their personal information is* **kept as secure, or more secure, on the Internet** *as it was two years ago.*

40%

of French respondents feel their personal information on the Internet is

kept more secure

than two years ago, the highest of any country surveyed.

More than a third of Japanese respondents (36%) feel their information on the Internet is *kept less secure*—significantly more than respondents in the other countries surveyed; only 6% feel their personal information is *kept more secure*. Forty percent (40%) of French respondents feel their personal information is *kept more secure* than it was two years ago—the highest of any country. Only 10% of French respondents feel it is *kept less secure*. Nearly a third or more of respondents in Canada, the U.S. and the U.K. feel their personal information on the Internet is *kept more secure* than it was two years ago.

Internet Security
By Country

Generally, do you think that your personal information on the Internet is kept more secure than, less secure than, or the same as it was two years ago?

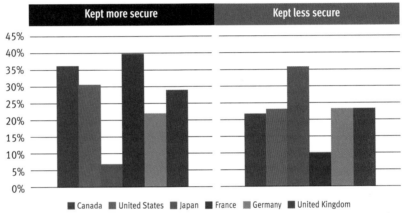

Source: *Sharing, Privacy and Trust in Our Networked World*, OCLC, 2007, question 935.

Security attitudes roughly matched privacy attitudes across total age groups. Approximately a quarter of the general public ages 14/15–21, 22–49 and 50+ feel their personal information is *kept more secure* on the Internet than it was two years ago. As with privacy, respondents age 50+ had the strongest belief that Internet security was declining, at 31%.

Internet Security
By Age

Generally, do you think that your personal information on the Internet is kept more secure than, less secure than, or the same as it was two years ago?

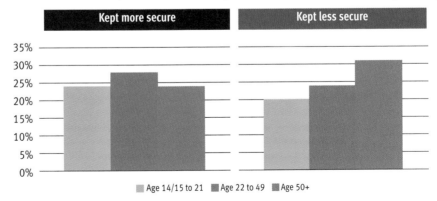

Source: *Sharing, Privacy and Trust in Our Networked World*, OCLC, 2007, question 935.

Improper Use of Information

While attitudes and perceptions about changes in Internet privacy and security are generally split, actual experiences with security breaches were fairly low. Eleven percent (11%) of the total general public surveyed have personally had their personal information used without their consent. And, 11% know someone who has had their information used without consent. The majority of respondents have not had their personal information misused online.

Improper Use of Personal Information Online
By Country

Have you or has anyone you know ever had personal information used online without consent? Please select all that apply.

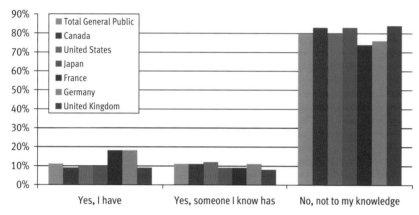

Source: *Sharing, Privacy and Trust in Our Networked World*, OCLC, 2007, question 1135.

Passwords

Respondents are generally comfortable using the same password on multiple sites. When registering on Web sites, 42% of the total general public revealed they *always* (16%) or *often* (26%) use the same password; just 13% *never* do so.

Use of the Same Password
By Total General Public

In general, when registering at any Web site, how often do you use the same password as you do with other sites?

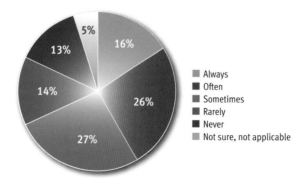

Source: *Sharing, Privacy and Trust in Our Networked World*, OCLC, 2007, question 836.

42%

of the total general public surveyed always or often

use the same password

when registering at a Web site.

Top Privacy Concerns among the General Public

Overall, what types of concerns do you have about keeping your personal information private?

Abuse **Ads/Spam** Confidentiality Credit/financial theft

Data security **Data sharing/leaks** E-mail/Web site security Financial security

Finding me/my address Fraud General concern Government abuse Government ID Hackers

Identity theft Library privacy Limit information provided **No concerns**

No guarantee No one's business No trust Privacy policy Privacy rights Profiling

Protect personal information Safety issues

Security issues Selling my information Spying Stalkers Telephone calls/number

Tracing me Trust particular companies/Web sites Use of information Who has access to my information?

Source: *Sharing, Privacy and Trust in Our Networked World*, OCLC, 2007, question 905.

Verbatim responses were categorized and are presented in this tag cloud. Tag clouds present the most frequently expressed opinions in larger font text and less frequently expressed opinions in smaller font text.

Over 10,000 comments regarding privacy concerns were summarized and are presented in the tag cloud.

The highest privacy concerns were of two types: *advertising/spam* and *identity theft/protecting personal information*. Roughly 14% of respondents have concerns about unwanted advertising or telephone calls. Several of the categories—*data sharing/leaks, protect personal information, fraud, abuse, hackers* and *credit/financial theft* reflect concerns about privacy related to possible criminal activity. Many comments exposed issues about personal information being protected from deliberate misuse. What we see in the responses from the general public are primarily concerns about losses of privacy that lead to security problems.

Very few respondents indicated concerns related to ideas of privacy from nonfraudulent sources. More than 10% had *no concerns* about privacy and just 3% of the general public listed concerns with *privacy rights*. Government abuse of privacy was expressed by 1.6%. Just 0.45% of the general public's concerns were related to library/reading privacy issues.

Privacy and Everyday Activities

Of 11 everyday activities ranging from banking to cable television to cell phones, only online banking was considered to be an extremely or very private activity by the majority of respondents. Just 11% felt that using the library Web site was extremely or very private.

Respondents exhibited a wide range of attitudes about the privacy of many everyday activities. These varying attitudes toward privacy extend to activities not only conducted online, but using offline services as well. Overall, respondents felt their activities while online at banking/investment sites, using their telephones and cell phones and e-mail at home are private. Most other activities were not rated as particularly private.

Respondents felt most private when conducting online banking/investing activities. Over 60% of total respondents rated activities on online banking/investment Web sites as *extremely* or *very private*, by far the most private of the activities surveyed. Nearly 60% or more of the respondents in all countries, except Japan (52%), feel their online banking/investing activity is *extremely* or *very private*.

Phone conversations, both landline and cellular, are also rated fairly high in privacy among the total general public surveyed, at 43% and 41%, respectively. German respondents were significantly more likely than those in the other countries surveyed to feel their activity while using landline phones is *extremely* or *very private*, at 55%. The German respondents also feel their cell phone use is private, as do the Japanese respondents.

E-mail at home is another activity that respondents felt was reasonably private. Nearly half or more of the general public in each country surveyed considered their activity while using e-mail at home to be *extremely* or *very private*.

Privacy ratings for activities on search engines, social networking sites, social media sites, cable TV, online bookstores, library Web sites and the library's print collections were significantly lower than the other activities evaluated. Just 15% of respondents felt that their use of search engines and social networking sites were *extremely* or *very private*. Using the library's Web site and print collection were considered the least private activities, at 11% and 9%, respectively.

63%

of the total general public surveyed feel *online banking is extremely or very private.*

11%

feel activity on a *library Web site is extremely or very private.*

Privacy and Everyday Activities
By Country

For each of the following, please rate how private, if at all,
your activity is while using:

Note: The chart shows the *extremely private* and *very private* responses.

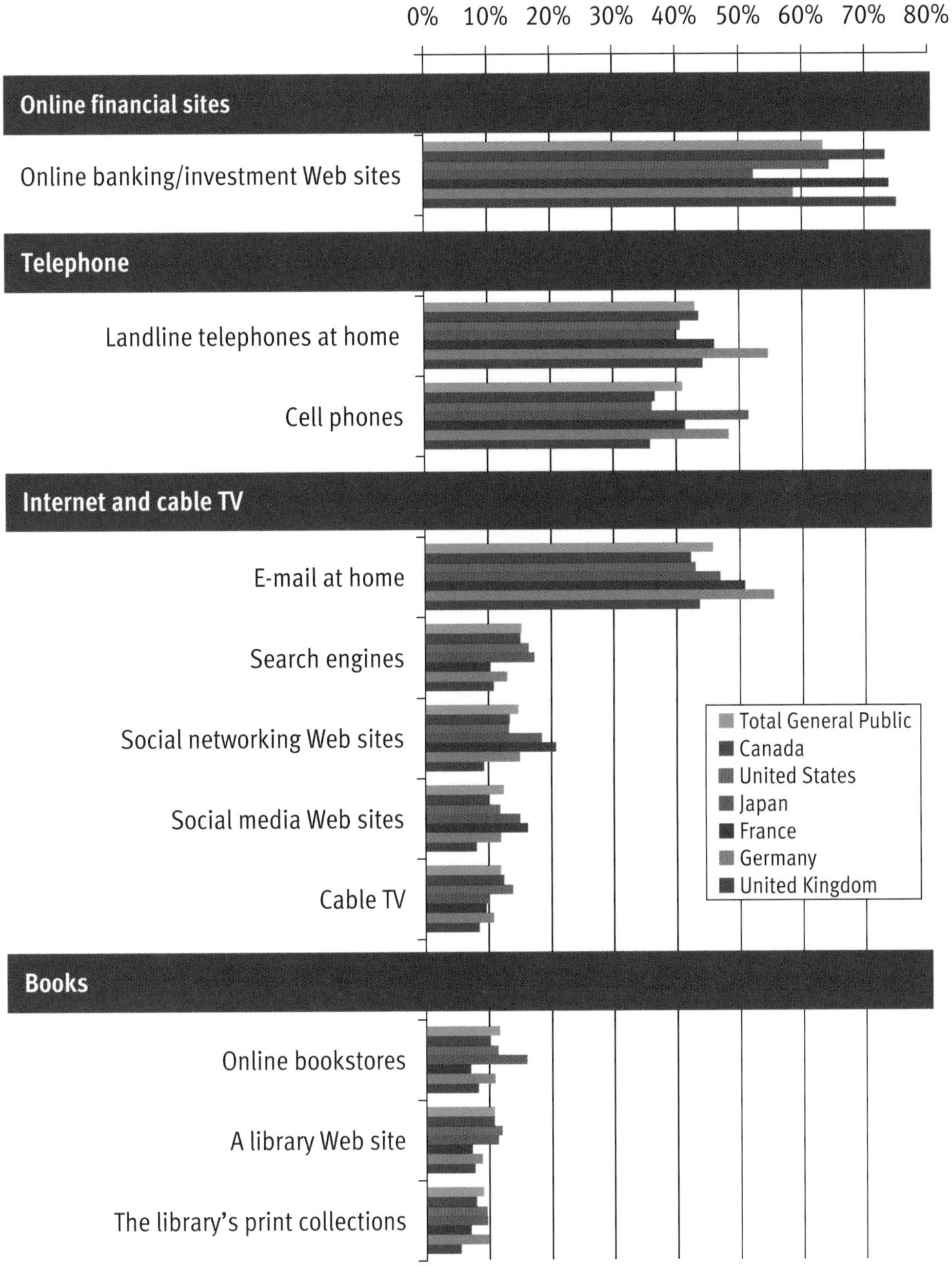

*Very few everyday
activities are considered
extremely or
very private.*

Categories shown in chart:

Online financial sites
- Online banking/investment Web sites

Telephone
- Landline telephones at home
- Cell phones

Internet and cable TV
- E-mail at home
- Search engines
- Social networking Web sites
- Social media Web sites
- Cable TV

Books
- Online bookstores
- A library Web site
- The library's print collections

Legend:
- Total General Public
- Canada
- United States
- Japan
- France
- Germany
- United Kingdom

*I feel [the Internet] is
more connected
to my home,
and therefore
my safety.*

22-year-old from Canada

Source: *Sharing, Privacy and Trust in Our
Networked World*, OCLC, 2007, question
915, "Why do you feel that the subjects
that you have searched on the Internet
are private?"

Source: *Sharing, Privacy and Trust in Our Networked World*, OCLC, 2007, question 926.

Overall, the youth, ages 14/15–21, were less likely than the older age groups surveyed to feel that many of the everyday activities are private.

Privacy and Everyday Activities

By Age

For each of the following, please rate how private, if at all, your activity is while using:

Note: The chart shows the *extremely private* and *very private* responses.

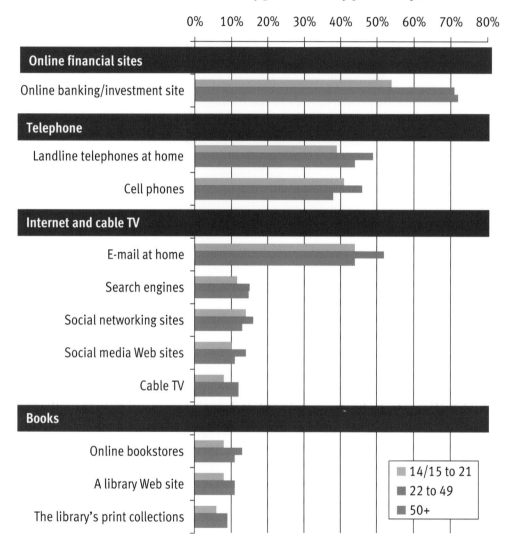

Youth are less likely to feel that online activities are extremely or very private.

Source: *Sharing, Privacy and Trust in Our Networked World*, OCLC, 2007, question 926.

Sharing Personalities Online

Over half of online users surveyed are at least somewhat more comfortable sharing their true personalities in person than online. A third or more of users prefer to remain anonymous on commercial, social and library Web sites, but often share their real name, e-mail address and age when registering on Web sites.

Despite significant online activity, most respondents are still more comfortable sharing their true personalities in person than online. Half or more of the general public in each country surveyed are *somewhat more comfortable* (*much more comfortable* or *somewhat more comfortable*) sharing their true personalities in person than online. The exception is among the French respondents; a third are more comfortable in person, but 40% are equally comfortable in person and online.

Less than one fifth of the total general public (16%) are *somewhat more comfortable* online than in person. Again, French respondents are the exception, indicating the most comfort expressing their true personalities online, at 26%.

Almost a third of online users surveyed are just as comfortable sharing their true personalities online as in person.

Sharing Your True Personality
By Country

Please indicate where you are more comfortable sharing your true personality (e.g., feelings, attitudes, interests, etc.).

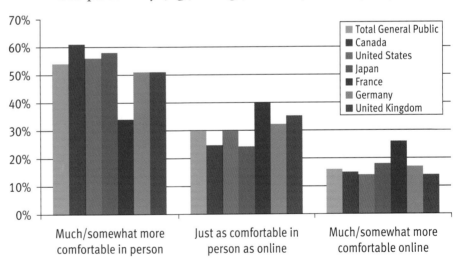

Source: *Sharing, Privacy and Trust in Our Networked World*, OCLC, 2007, question 940.

Age differences were uncovered regarding comfort levels in sharing true personalities. Well over half of the total general public age 50+ surveyed (62%) are *somewhat more comfortable* sharing their true personalities in person than online. Nearly a quarter of the 14/15–21-year-olds are at least *somewhat more comfortable* sharing their true personalities online.

Sharing Your True Personality
By Age

Please indicate where you are more comfortable sharing your true personality (e.g., feelings, attitudes, interests, etc.).

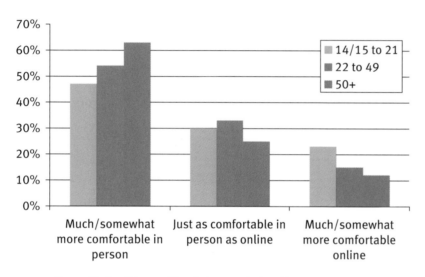

Source: *Sharing, Privacy and Trust in Our Networked World*, OCLC, 2007, question 940.

Our Online Personality

Respondents feel they have the same personalities online and offline. More than half of the total general public in each country surveyed *agree (strongly agree* or *somewhat agree)* they have the same personalities online as they do in person while using social networking (61%), social media (52%), commercial (61%) and library Web sites (54%).

The Japanese respondents are significantly less likely to *agree* they have the same personalities online as they do in person when using social networking and social media sites; they are also significantly less likely, along with respondents in Germany, to *agree* they have the same personalities online when using commercial and library Web sites as they do in person.

Personality Online vs. in Person
By Country

Thinking about the [social networking, social media, commercial and/or library Web sites you use], how strongly do you agree or disagree that you have the same personality online as you do in person?

Base: Respondents who have used a social networking, social media, commercial and/or library Web site.

Note: The chart shows the *strongly agree* and *somewhat agree* responses.

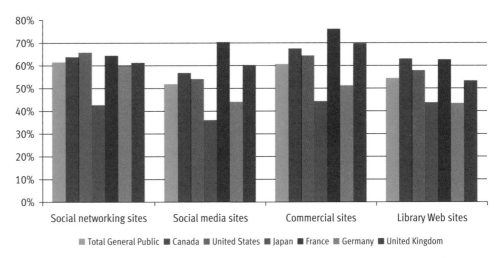

Source: *Sharing, Privacy and Trust in Our Networked World,* OCLC, 2007, questions 971, 1011, 1046 and 1086.

Remaining Anonymous

Approximately half or more of respondents *agree* (*strongly agree* or *somewhat agree*) they have the same personalities while using social, commercial and library Web sites as they do in person and most do not feel the need to remain anonymous on these sites. The desire to remain anonymous varied by type of site. More than a third of respondents *agree* that they prefer to remain anonymous on social networking sites (35%). More respondents prefer to remain anonymous on social media sites (45%) and commercial sites (44%); fewer respondents, 34%, wish to remain anonymous at the library (in person or online).

Japanese respondents are more likely than respondents in the other countries surveyed to *agree* (*strongly agree* or *somewhat agree*) they prefer to remain anonymous on social networking and social media sites. The Japanese respondents are significantly less likely to *agree* they prefer to remain anonymous with respect to using the library (in person or online), at just 20%.

Anonymity
By Country

Thinking about the [social networking site, social media site, commercial site and/or the library you use], how strongly do you agree or disagree that you prefer to remain anonymous?

Base: Respondents who have used a social networking, social media, commercial site and/or the library.

Note: The chart shows *strongly agree* and *somewhat agree* responses.

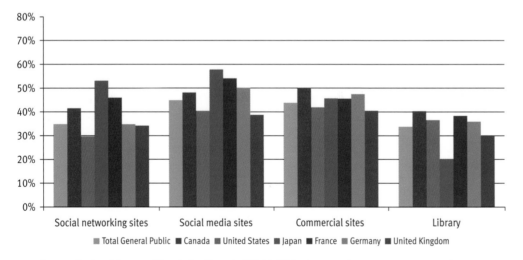

■ Total General Public ■ Canada ■ United States ■ Japan ■ France ■ Germany ■ United Kingdom

Source: *Sharing, Privacy and Trust in Our Networked World*, OCLC, 2007, questions 971, 1011, 1046 and 1086.

35%
of respondents prefer to
remain anonymous on social networking sites;

34%
prefer to
at the library (in person or online).

Information Provided While Registering

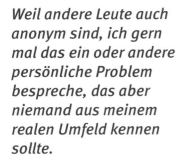

Weil andere Leute auch anonym sind, ich gern mal das ein oder andere persönliche Problem bespreche, das aber niemand aus meinem realen Umfeld kennen sollte.

Because others are also anonymous, I occasionally like to discuss a personal problem that no one from the real world should know.

48-year-old from Germany

Source: *Sharing, Privacy and Trust in Our Networked World*, OCLC, 2007, question 1015, "Why do you prefer to remain anonymous on social media Web sites?"

Most respondents are willing to provide their true identities when registering on a Web site. Nearly two-thirds or more of the total general public *always* or *often* use their real names (65%), real e-mail addresses (80%) and real ages (81%) when registering at any Web site. Just over half provide their real telephone numbers.

Information Provided While Registering
By Country

In general, when registering at any Web site, how often do you … ?

Note: The chart shows the *always* and *often* responses.

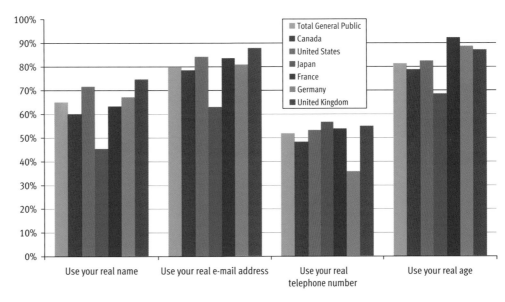

Source: *Sharing, Privacy and Trust in Our Networked World*, OCLC, 2007, question 836.

Respondents are engaging in more activities online that involve more personal aspects and as a result, require some level of trust, both with the people they are interacting with and the sites themselves. This comfort level very well could be due to the controls Web sites have in place to protect personal information, such as privacy policies.

Privacy Rules

The majority of respondents feel that it is important to have controls over their personal information on the Internet, such as the ability to remain anonymous, specifying who can use and view it, and knowing there are privacy policies in place. Respondents frequently do not take advantage of privacy controls that are available.

Respondents place a high importance on the ability to protect their identities and personal information on the Internet. Well over half of the total general public (62%) feel it is *extremely* or *very important* to have the ability to remain anonymous on the Internet. This view was very consistent among respondents across all countries. Canadian respondents had the highest concern for anonymity, at 70%. Significantly fewer Japanese respondents feel this way, at 48%.

Importance of Remaining Anonymous on the Internet
By Country

How important is each of the following with respect to providing your personal information on the Internet?

Ability to remain anonymous

Note: The chart shows the *extremely important* and *very important* responses.

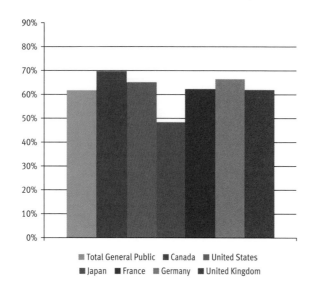

■ Total General Public   ■ Canada   ■ United States
■ Japan   ■ France   ■ Germany   ■ United Kingdom

Source: *Sharing, Privacy and Trust in Our Networked World*, OCLC, 2007, question 1131.

Respondents want the ability to remain anonymous and they want to be informed about how their information will be used on the Internet. Over two-thirds of the total general public surveyed (69%) also feel it is *extremely* or *very important* to know how their personal information will be used on the Internet. Nearly two-thirds or more of respondents in each country expressed the importance of remaining informed. Significantly fewer Japanese respondents are likely to feel it is *extremely* or *very important* to remain informed on how their personal information will be used on the Internet, at 53%.

Importance of Remaining Informed on the Internet
By Total General Public

How important is each of the following with respect to providing your personal information on the Internet?

Ability to remain informed on how it will be used

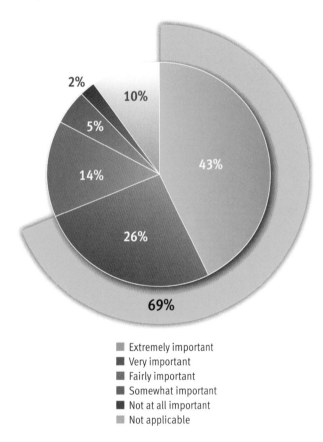

- Extremely important
- Very important
- Fairly important
- Somewhat important
- Not at all important
- Not applicable

Source: *Sharing, Privacy and Trust in Our Networked World*, OCLC, 2007, question 1131.

Respondents want to control their identities online; they want to remain informed on how their information will be used and they want to be able to set parameters around who can view and who can use their personal information.

Nearly three-fourths of the total general public surveyed feel it is *extremely* or *very important* to be able to specify who can use and view their personal information on the Internet. Canadian respondents expressed the highest desire for controls; Japanese respondents expressed the lowest.

Importance of Controlling Personal Information on the Internet
By Country

How important is each of the following with respect to providing your personal information on the Internet?

The ability to specify who is able to **use** it

The ability to specify who is able to **view** it

Note: The chart shows *extremely important* and *very important* responses.

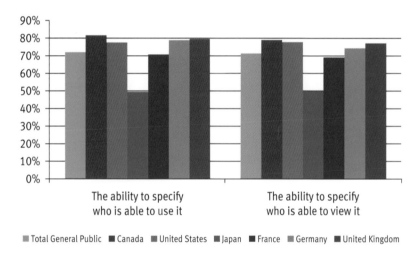

■ Total General Public   ■ Canada   ■ United States   ■ Japan   ■ France   ■ Germany   ■ United Kingdom

Source: *Sharing, Privacy and Trust in Our Networked World*, OCLC, 2007, question 1131.

I want to control who knows what about me.

62-year-old from the United States

Source: *Sharing, Privacy and Trust in Our Networked World*, OCLC, 2007, question 1015, "Why do you prefer to remain anonymous on social media Web sites?"

Although 71% of the total general public place a high importance on controlling who can view their personal information on the Internet, they are much less likely to specify who can view their personal information. Forty-five percent (45%) of social networking users *always* or *often* specify who can view their information. These percentages are even lower for users of social media sites (36%) and the library (24%).

The Japanese respondents are the least likely to place a high importance on setting controls regarding who can view their personal information on the Internet. They are also the least likely to actually *always* or *often* do so when using social networking sites, social media sites and the library (in person or online). German respondents are more likely to *always* or *often* specify who can view their personal information on social media sites. Significantly more German respondents do so while using a library in person or online, at 35%.

Specifying Who Can View Personal Information
By Country

In general, when using [social networking sites, social media sites and/or the library (in person or online)], how frequently do you specify who is able to view your personal information?

Base: Respondents who have used a social networking site, social media site, and/or the library (in person or online).

Note: The chart shows the *always* and *often* responses.

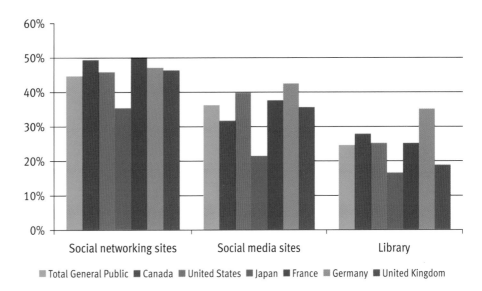

Source: *Sharing, Privacy and Trust in Our Networked World,* OCLC, 2007, questions 966, 1006 and 1081.

Policies and Icons

Privacy policies inform Internet users how a particular Web site will use their personal information. They are often the primary tool users have to determine if they are comfortable supplying information on a site.

As we have reported, the majority of respondents place a high importance on the ability to have controls on who can view and use their personal information, but fewer actually take steps to specify who can view and use their information while using social networking sites, social media sites and at the library (in person or online). Even fewer *always* or *often* review the privacy policies before registering on a site. Less than 40% of total respondents review privacy policies on social networking, social media, commercial and library sites before registering. The Japanese general public is less likely to do so, while the German general public are most likely to review privacy policies on all four types of sites.

For those who review privacy policies on commercial sites, many are either satisfied with what they read or are unconcerned with the policy stated. Forty percent (40%) *rarely* or *never* decide not to make a purchase after reviewing the policy. A third of respondents *sometimes* decide not to purchase an item online after reviewing a site's privacy policy; just 12% *often* or *always* decline to make a purchase.

Frequency of Reviewing Privacy Policies
By Country

In general, when using [social networking sites, social media sites, commercial sites and/or the library (in person or online)], how frequently do you review the Web site's privacy policy before registering?

Base: Respondents who have used a social networking site, social media site, commercial sites, and/or the library (in person or online).

Note: The chart shows the *always* and *often* responses.

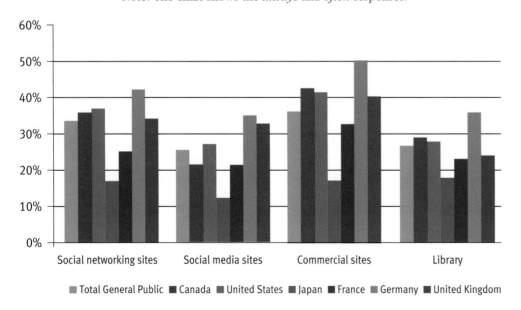

■ Total General Public ■ Canada ■ United States ■ Japan ■ France ■ Germany ■ United Kingdom

Source: *Sharing, Privacy and Trust in Our Networked World*, OCLC, 2007, questions 966, 1006, 1051 and 1081.

40% of respondents *rarely or never decide not to purchase* an item online after reviewing *privacy policies.*

While approximately a third or more of respondents usually review Web sites' privacy policies when registering, many more will look for security icons while browsing or purchasing.

Security icons are visual symbols that Internet users can often use to quickly gauge the security of their personal information while using Web sites, especially commercial sites. Over half of the total general public (54%) *always* or *often* look for security icons when browsing or shopping on Web sites.

Respondents in Japan and Germany are least likely to *always* or *often* look for security icons while using commercial sites, at 18% and 38%, respectively. Respondents in Canada, the U.S., France and the U.K. were very similar in their responses, with over 40% indicating they *always* look for security icons.

54%

of respondents always
or often look for
security icons
while browsing and/or
purchasing on
commercial sites.

Frequency of Looking for Security Icons
By Country

In general, when you browse/purchase on Web sites, how often do you look for security icons on the Web site (e.g., VeriSign)?

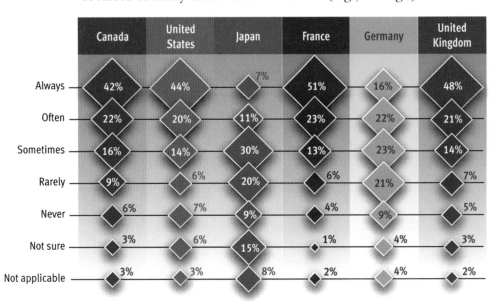

	Canada	United States	Japan	France	Germany	United Kingdom
Always	42%	44%	7%	51%	16%	48%
Often	22%	20%	11%	23%	22%	21%
Sometimes	16%	14%	30%	13%	23%	14%
Rarely	9%	6%	20%	6%	21%	7%
Never	6%	7%	9%	4%	9%	5%
Not sure	3%	6%	15%	1%	4%	3%
Not applicable	3%	3%	8%	2%	4%	2%

Source: *Sharing, Privacy and Trust in Our Networked World*, OCLC, 2007, question 1051.

lese immer die
sicherheitsvorkehrungender
Seite

[I] always read the safety notice on the site.

24-year-old from Germany

Source: *Sharing, Privacy and Trust in Our Networked World*, OCLC, 2007, question 1140,"Please describe the situation [you or anyone you know having had personal information used online without consent] and the impact it had on your and/or their Internet use."

Trust

Many respondents agree that online trust increases with use. Currently, about half of users trust commercial sites, 34% trust social networking sites and 32% trust social media sites. Most users (65%) feel commercial sites keep their personal information secure; about half think library Web sites keep their information secure.

Understanding how respondents establish and evaluate trust is important to examining online relationships on the social Web. Respondents shared their attitudes about trust of the people they communicate with and meet online and trust about the Web sites themselves.

Survey respondents who have used social networking sites and/or social media sites have established some trust with the people they communicate with. Approximately a third of social networking site users *always* or *often* trust the people they communicate with on these sites and 70% at least *sometimes* trust who they communicate with on social networking sites. Fewer social media site users (15%) *always* or *often* trust those they communicate with on social media sites but nearly half of the respondents at least *sometimes* trust who they communicate with on social media sites.

Less than a quarter (23%) *rarely* or *never* trust the people they communicate with on social networking sites; 32% *rarely* or *never* they trust the people they communicate with on social media sites.

60%
of library users agree they
trust the library.

Trust the People with Whom I Communicate
By Total General Public

In general, when using [social networking sites and/or social media sites], how frequently do you trust the people you communicate with?

Base: Respondents who have used a social networking site and/or social media site.

Note: The chart shows the *always*, *often* and *sometimes* responses.

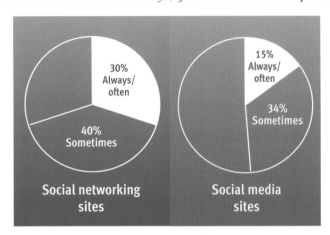

Source: *Sharing, Privacy and Trust in Our Networked World,* OCLC, 2007, questions 966 and 1006.

A quarter or more of respondents across all countries who use social networking sites *always* or *often* trust who they communicate with on these sites; fewer social media users trust who they communicate with on social media sites. Overall, French social site users are more likely to trust the people they communicate with when using either social networking or social media sites than the respondents in the other countries surveyed.

While the Japanese respondents who use social networking sites trust the people they communicate with on these sites at similar rates to the general public in the other countries surveyed, at 25% (*always* or *often*), they are significantly less likely to *always* or *often* trust those they communicate with while using social media sites, at approximately 5%.

Trust the People with Whom I Communicate
By Country

In general, when using [social networking sites and/or social media sites], how frequently do you trust the people you communicate with?

Base: Respondents who have used a social networking site and/or social media site.

Note: The chart shows the *always* and *often* responses.

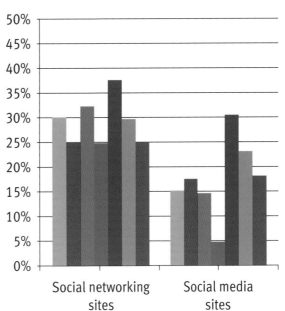

■ Total General Public ■ Canada ■ United States ■ Japan ■ France ■ Germany ■ United Kingdom

Source: *Sharing, Privacy and Trust in Our Networked World,* OCLC, 2007, questions 966 and 1006.

Respondents are largely uncertain about the people they meet online. Respondents have some level of trust with whom they meet on both social and library Web sites but at least a third are neutral in their agreement they trust who they meet online.

Less than a quarter of the total general public *agree (strongly agree* or *somewhat agree)* they trust the people they meet on social networking (21%), social media (15%) and library Web sites (18%). Nearly a third of the general public are *neutral* in their agreement to trusting who they meet on social and library Web sites and well over a third do not trust who they meet on social networking and media sites.

Trusting Whom We Meet Online
By Total General Public

Thinking about the [social networking, social media and/or library Web sites you use], how strongly do you agree or disagree that you trust the people you meet on these sites?

Base: Respondents who have used a social networking, social media and/or library Web site.

Note: The chart does not show the *not sure* and *not applicable* responses.

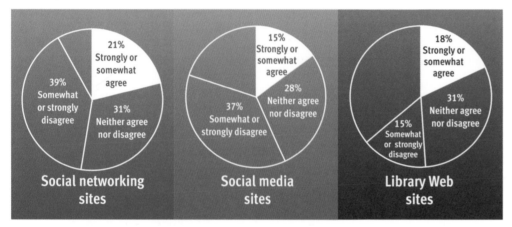

Source: *Sharing, Privacy and Trust in Our Networked World,* OCLC, 2007, questions 971, 1011 and 1086.

With two exceptions, there is little variation among respondents surveyed across all countries regarding their agreement on trusting the people they meet on social networking, social media and library Web sites. The French respondents are significantly more likely to *agree* they trust those they meet through the online library, at 30%; and more German respondents *agree* they trust the people they meet on social media sites, at 26%.

Trusting Whom We Meet Online
By Country

Thinking about the [social networking, social media and/or library Web sites you use], how strongly do you agree or disagree that you trust the people you meet on these sites?

Base: Respondents who have used a social networking, social media and/or library Web site.

Note: The chart shows the *strongly agree* and *somewhat agree* responses.

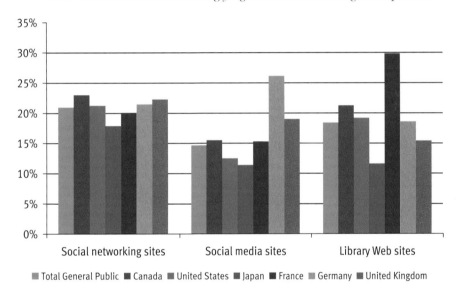

Source: *Sharing, Privacy and Trust in Our Networked World*, OCLC, 2007, questions 971, 1011 and 1086.

There are steps in establishing friendships.
On-line a sense of trust is important first. The social controls that apply in face-to-face relationships are not present in on-line relationships. Certainly not initially.

61-year-old from Canada

Source: *Sharing, Privacy and Trust in Our Networked World*, OCLC, 2007, question 975, "Why do you prefer to remain anonymous on social networking Web sites?"

Youth are more likely than older respondents to trust who they meet on social sites but slightly less trusting of people they meet through a library Web site. The 14/15–21- and 22–49-year-old respondents are more likely to *agree* they trust those they meet on social networking sites than those age 50+. As age increases, so does the agreement they trust the people they meet on library Web sites.

Trusting Whom We Meet Online
By Age

Thinking about the [social networking, social media and/or the library Web sites you use], how strongly do you agree or disagree that you trust the people you meet on these sites?

Base: Respondents who have used a social networking, social media and/or library Web site.

Note: The chart shows the *strongly agree* and *somewhat agree* responses.

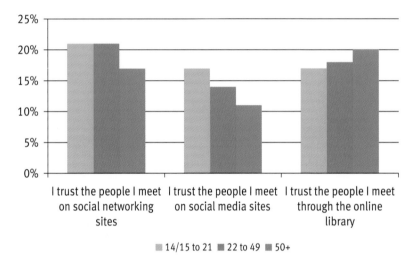

■ 14/15 to 21   ■ 22 to 49   ■ 50+

Source: *Sharing, Privacy and Trust in Our Networked World*, OCLC, 2007, questions 971, 1011 and 1086.

More users of social and library Web sites *disagree than agree they trust those they meet online;* about a third are neutral.

Trust of Web sites is at a modest level; many respondents remain neutral. Trust is strongest among those who use commercial sites; nearly half of commercial site users (48%) *agree* (*strongly agree* or *somewhat agree*) they trust these sites; 29% are *neutral* and 15% *disagree* (*strongly disagree* or *somewhat disagree*). A third of the social networking users *agree* they trust these sites (34%), 38% are *neutral* and 21% *disagree*. Ratings are similar among social media sites users; 32% of those who use these sites *agree* that they trust them, 32% are *neutral* and 23% *disagree*.

Trusting Online Sites
By Total General Public

Thinking about the [social networking, social media and commercial sites you use], how strongly do you agree or disagree that you trust the Web sites?

Base: Respondents who have used a social networking, social media and/or commercial site.

Note: The chart shows the *strongly agree* and *somewhat agree* responses.

More users trust than distrust social and commercial sites; about a third are neutral.

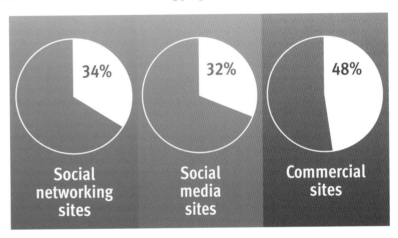

Source: *Sharing, Privacy and Trust in Our Networked World,* OCLC, 2007, questions 971, 1011 and 1046.

Overall, more French social and commercial site users *agree* that they trust social networking, social media and commercial sites than respondents in the other countries—they are significantly more likely to *agree* they trust commercial sites, at 65%. The Japanese respondents are less likely than those in the other countries surveyed to *agree* they trust social networking, social media or commercial sites.

Trusting Online Sites
By Country

Thinking about the [social networking, social media and commercial sites you use], how strongly do you agree or disagree that you trust the Web sites?

Base: Respondents who have used a social networking, social media and/or commercial site.

Note: The chart shows the *strongly agree* and *somewhat agree* responses.

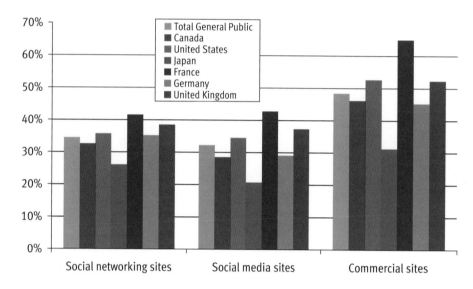

Source: *Sharing, Privacy and Trust in Our Networked World*, OCLC, 2007, questions 971, 1011 and 1046.

For many respondents, Web site trust increases with use. Most commercial site users (50%) *agree* (*strongly agree* or *somewhat agree*) the more they use commercial sites, the more they trust them.

Forty-one percent (41%) *agree* the longer they use social networking sites, the more they trust them, while a third or more feel this way about library Web sites (32%) and social media sites (37%). Nearly a third or more of respondents are *neutral* in their agreement that the longer they use social, commercial and library Web sites, the more they trust them.

Web Site Trust Increases with Use
By Total General Public

Thinking about the [social networking, social media, commercial and/or library Web sites you use], how strongly do you agree or disagree that the longer you use the Web sites, the more you trust them?

Base: Respondents who have used a social networking, social media, commercial and/or library Web site.

Note: The chart shows the *strongly agree* and *somewhat agree* responses.

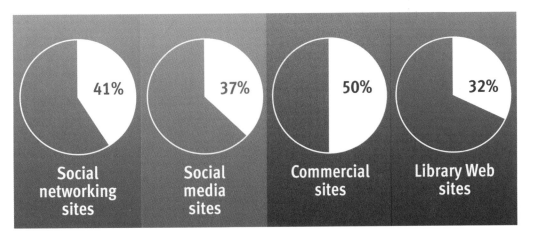

Source: *Sharing, Privacy and Trust in Our Networked World*, OCLC, 2007, questions 971, 1011, 1046 and 1086.

German and U.K. social site users are the most likely to *agree* that the more they use social networking and social media sites, the more they trust them; the French are among the least likely to *agree*.

Nearly half or more of respondents in each country *agree* the longer they use commercial sites, the more they trust them, except for the Japanese respondents; they are the least likely. The French respondents are most likely to *agree* the longer they use commercial sites, the more they trust them, at 60%.

Canadian respondents are more likely to *agree* the more they use library Web sites, the more they trust them. Agreement ratings for the American, French and German respondents are similar for the longer they use library Web sites, the more they trust them; Japanese and U.K. respondents are the least likely to *agree*.

Web Site Trust Increases with Use
By Country

Thinking about the [social networking, social media, commercial and library Web sites you use], how strongly do you agree or disagree that the longer you use the Web sites, the more you trust them?

Base: Respondents who have used a social networking, social media, commercial and/or library Web site.

Note: The chart shows the *strongly agree* and *somewhat agree* responses.

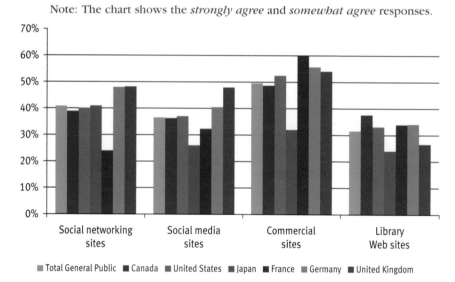

Source: *Sharing, Privacy and Trust in Our Networked World*, OCLC, 2007, questions 971, 1011, 1046 and 1086.

Keeping My Personal Information Secure

Most respondents feel that commercial sites keep their personal information secure; fewer feel this way about social and library Web sites. Sixty-five percent (65%) of commercial sites users *agree* (*strongly agree* or *somewhat agree*) that these sites keep their information secure. Just over half of library Web sites users *agree* that library Web sites keep their information secure, and 47% of social networking users *agree* social networking sites keep their personal information secure. Respondents are least likely to *agree* social media sites keep their personal information secure; just a third of social media users *agree*. Approximately a quarter of respondents are *neutral* in their agreement that social networking sites (24%) and social media sites (23%) keep their personal information secure; 12% and 26% are *not sure*, respectively.

Thirteen percent (13%) of commercial site users are *not sure* if commercial sites keep their information secure; 20% of library Web site users are *not sure*.

65%

of users agree
commercial
sites keep their
personal
information
secure.

Agree Sites Keep My Personal Information Secure
By Total General Public

Considering the [social networking, social media, commercial and/or library Web site you use], please rate the degree to which you agree or disagree that it keeps your personal information secure.

Base: Respondents who have used a social networking, social media, commercial and/or library Web site.

Note: The chart shows the *strongly agree* and *somewhat agree* responses.

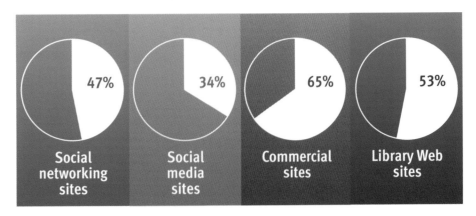

Source: *Sharing, Privacy and Trust in Our Networked World,* OCLC, 2007, questions 956, 1001, 1041 and 1066.

20%

of library users are
not sure
if the
library Web site
keeps their
personal
information
secure.

Unsure if Sites Keep My Personal Information Secure
By Total General Public

Note: The chart shows the *not sure* responses.

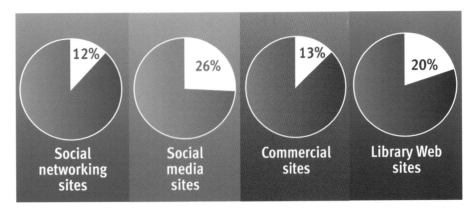

Source: *Sharing, Privacy and Trust in Our Networked World,* OCLC, 2007, questions 956, 1001, 1041 and 1066.

Well over half of commercial sites users across all countries surveyed agree commercial sites keep their personal information secure. Half or more of library Web site users agree library Web sites keep their personal information secure, with the Canadian and the U.K. users showing the highest agreement rates.

Agree Sites Keeps My Personal Information Secure
By Country

Considering the [social networking, social media, commercial and/or library Web sites you use], please rate the degree to which you agree or disagree that it keeps your personal information secure.

Base: Respondents who have used a social networking, social media, commercial and/or library Web site.

Note: The chart shows the *strongly agree* and *somewhat agree* responses.

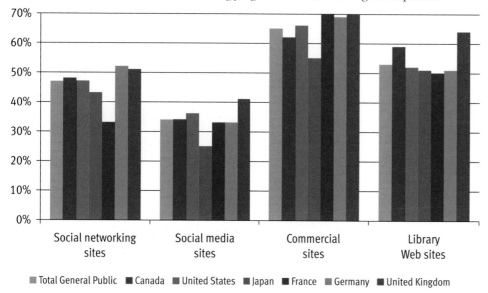

■ Total General Public ■ Canada ■ United States ■ Japan ■ France ■ Germany ■ United Kingdom

Source: *Sharing, Privacy and Trust in Our Networked World*, OCLC, 2007, questions 956, 1001, 1041 and 1066.

64%

of U.K. library Web site users agree the sites **keep their personal information secure,** *the highest rate among all library Web site users across all the countries surveyed.*

Rules on How My Personal Information Will Be Used

Commercial site users are more likely to *agree* that commercial sites keep their information secure, and they are also more likely to *agree* that commercial sites have rules on how this information will be used. Seventy percent (70%) *agree* commercial sites have rules on the use of personal information.

About half of library Web site users *agree* their personal information is kept secure on a library Web site and an equal number also *agree* the Web site has rules on use of personal information. About a quarter of library Web site users are unsure if the library has rules on the use of personal information.

Agree that Sites Have Rules on How
My Personal Information Will Be Used
By Total General Public

Considering the [social networking, social media, commercial and/or library Web sites you use], please rate the degree to which you agree or disagree that it has rules on how your personal information will be used.

Base: Respondents who have used a social networking, social media, commercial and/or library Web site.

Note: The chart shows the *strongly agree* and *somewhat agree* responses.

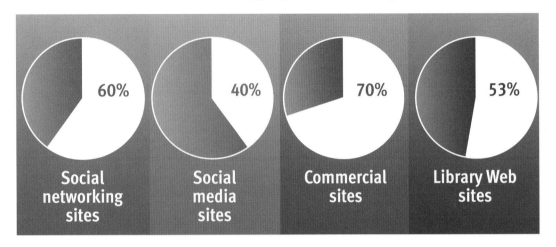

Source: *Sharing, Privacy and Trust in Our Networked World,* OCLC, 2007, questions 956, 1001, 1041 and 1066.

24%

of library Web site users are

unsure if the site has rules

on how their personal information will be used.

Unsure if Sites Have Rules on How
My Personal Information Will Be Used
By Total General Public

Note: The chart shows the *not sure* responses.

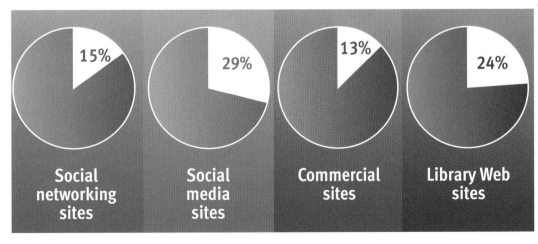

Source: *Sharing, Privacy and Trust in Our Networked World,* OCLC, 2007, questions 956, 1001, 1041 and 1066.

Information Privacy

Less than a third of the total general public surveyed consider most information searching, browsing or buying activities as extremely or very private.

While most do not feel information-seeking activities are extremely or very private to them, half or more feel it is extremely or very important that the library keep many of these same activities private.

Earlier, we reviewed privacy attitudes of everyday activities such as using search engines, online banking, social networking or library Web sites, cell phones and watching cable TV. Of these activities, respondents considered only a few of these activities to be *extremely* or *very private*.

We were equally interested in learning more about privacy attitudes surrounding information and online information-seeking activities. We asked respondents to rate the relative privacy of 11 activities ranging from subjects searched on the Internet to items purchased at a bookstore to books they had read.

Only one of these activities—subjects searched on the Internet—was considered *extremely* or *very private* by more than 25% of respondents. Most other activities were even less private, with just 16% of respondents rating the books they had read as *extremely* or *very private* information.

Slightly more of the total general public surveyed feel that items they have purchased from a bookstore (in person or online) are *extremely* or *very private* compared to items they have checked out from the library (in person or online).

Attitudes about information privacy varied by country. The Japanese and German respondents are substantially more likely to consider their subjects of interest and books they have read to be *extremely* or *very private* when compared to the respondents from the other countries surveyed. The Japanese respondents are significantly more likely to feel that the items they purchased from the bookstore (in person or online) are *extremely* or *very private*.

Privacy of Searching/Browsing Information
By Country

Please rate how private, if at all, the following information is to you.

Note: The chart shows the *extremely private* and *very private* responses.

Respondents feel that subjects searched on
the Internet are more private
to them than subjects searched on a library Web site.

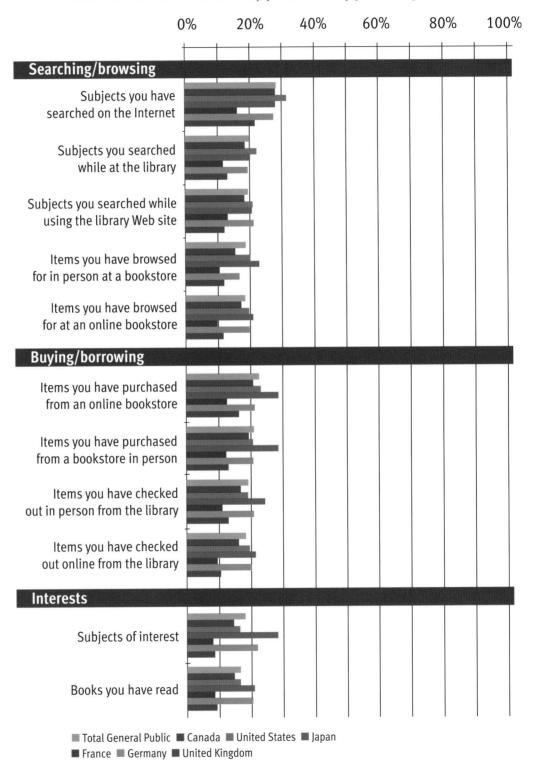

Source: *Sharing, Privacy and Trust in Our Networked World,* OCLC, 2007, question 911.

Although activities conducted at the library are considered *extremely* or *very private* by just 20% of respondents, approximately half the respondents feel it is *extremely* or *very important* for the library to keep this information private.

Approximately half or more of the total general public feel it is *extremely* or *very important* for their library to keep their personal information and activities conducted at the library or library Web site private.

While respondents were most concerned about the privacy of their personal information, about half expressed a desire to keep all library activities private.

More than 60% of respondents also feel it is *extremely* or *very important* their library keeps a policy on privacy. Yet as reported earlier, half as many indicated they review the library privacy policy before registering on the site.

Importance of Keeping Library Information Private
By Country

In thinking about privacy, how important, if at all, is it to you that the library you primarily use would keep ... [private]?

Base: Respondents who have used the library (in person or online).

Note: The chart shows the *extremely important* and *very important* responses.

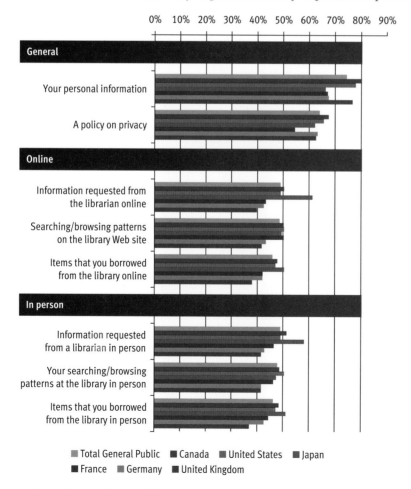

Source: *Sharing, Privacy and Trust in Our Networked World*, OCLC, 2007, question 1076.

Sixty-four percent (64%) of the total general public surveyed feel that it is *extremely* or *very important* for the library to keep a privacy policy, yet only 26% actually *always* or *often* review the library's Web site privacy policy before using the library Web site.

Frequency of Reviewing Library's Web Site Privacy Policy
By Total General Public

In general when using the library in person or online, how frequently do you review the Web site's privacy policy before registering?

Base: Respondents who have used the library (in person or online).

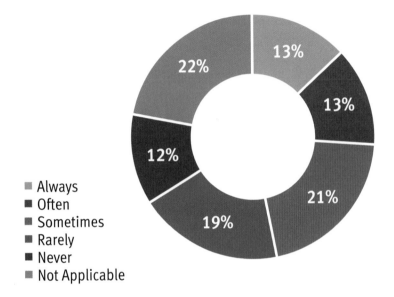

- Always
- Often
- Sometimes
- Rarely
- Never
- Not Applicable

Source: *Sharing, Privacy and Trust in Our Networked World*, OCLC, 2007, question 1081.

Privacy Trade-offs

Respondents see a higher value in providing their contact information on social networking sites than on social media, commercial or library Web sites.

Social networking users indicated that they are more likely to share their contact information provided on social networking sites in exchange for other services when compared to users of social media sites, commercial sites or the library. About a quarter or more of users would be willing to share their contact information provided on social networking sites *to connect with others with similar interests*, *to set up personalized services* or *to receive free or discounted goods or services*.

16%

of library users are
willing to share
their personal contact information supplied at the library in exchange for setting up personalized services.

Contact Information Trade-Off
By Total General Public

For each of the following types of information you may have provided on [social networking sites, social media sites, commercial sites and/or library (in person or online)], please indicate if you would be willing to share your contact information.

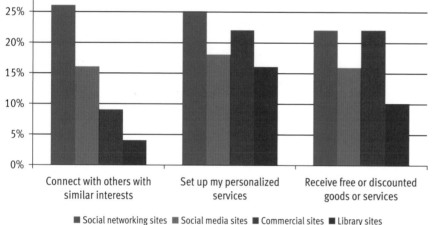

Base: Respondents who have used a social networking site, social media site, commercial site and/or the library (in person or online).

■ Social networking sites ■ Social media sites ■ Commercial sites ■ Library sites

Source: *Sharing, Privacy and Trust in Our Networked World*, OCLC, 2007, questions 991, 1031, 1056 and 1091.

Some interesting differences surfaced when we analyzed the willingness of the different age groups to provide contact information provided on social networking, social media and commercial sites, and at the library in exchange for different services. Respondents age 50+ would be substantially more likely to provide contact information provided on social networking sites *to connect with others with similar interests* than any other age group.

The respondents ages 22–49 would be generally more willing than those ages 14/15–21 and 50+ to share their contact information provided on social networking, social media and commercial sites, and at the library *to receive free or discounted goods or services*. And, respondents ages 14/15–21 would be least likely to share their contact information provided on social networking, social media and library sites *to set up personalized services*. Overall, all groups saw more value in exchanging contact information provided on social networking sites in exchange for other services than any other type of site.

Contact Information Trade-Off
By Age

For each of the following types of information you may have provided on [social networking sites, social media sites, commercial sites and/or library sites], please indicate if you would be willing to share your contact information.

Base: Respondents who used a social networking site, social media site, commercial site and/or the library (in person or online).

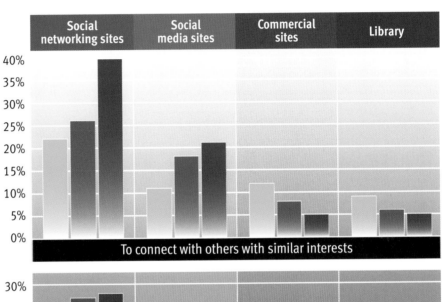

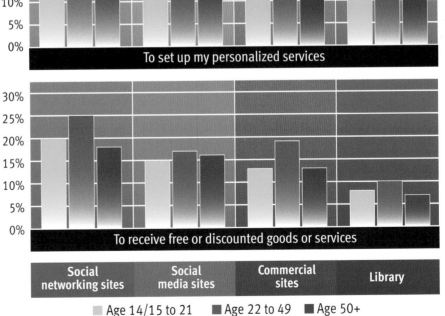

Source: *Sharing, Privacy and Trust in Our Networked World*, OCLC, 2007, questions 991, 1031, 1056 and 1091.

Users are more **willing to share** *personal information provided on* **social networking sites** *than on social media, commercial and library sites, in* **exchange for services**.

Summary

Overall, respondents are split on their feelings on how private and secure their personal information has been kept on the Internet in the last two years. Roughly a quarter each feel their personal information is *kept more private*, *kept less private*, there has been *no change* or they are *not sure*. Views among respondents across the countries surveyed revealed half or more feel their personal information has been kept as private or more private than it was two years ago. While overall ratings for how secure their personal information has been kept on the Internet were similar to Internet privacy among total respondents, there were some noteworthy differences among respondents across the countries regarding Internet security. Respondents in France were more likely to feel their personal information is *kept more secure* on the Internet; significantly more Japanese respondents are likely to feel their personal information is *kept less secure*.

Eleven percent (11%) of the total general public surveyed have had their personal information used online without their consent, while the vast majority have not.

Identity theft was among the top privacy concerns among respondents. *Ads/spam* and *protecting personal information* were also top concerns. While many expressed overall concerns, over 10% of respondents had *no concerns*.

The majority of respondents feel online banking is very private. Less than half of respondents felt landline phones, cell phones and e-mail at home are very private. Other activities such as search engines, social sites, online bookstores and library Web sites are considered very private by 15% or less of respondents. These attitudes were consistent among respondents across the countries surveyed.

While many respondents do not feel many browsing/searching activities—such as books read, subjects searched on the Internet and checking out items from the library—are very private, approximately half feel it is very important for the library to keep this information private.

Having controls and rules on how personal information will be used and viewed on the Internet is important to respondents. The ability to remain anonymous, to specify who can view and use their information, privacy policies and security icons are all important to respondents, but respondents do not frequently use these controls on social sites and often share their real identities when registering on Web sites.

There is some level of trust with the people respondents communicate with and meet among users of social networking and media sites, but overall, more respondents trust the site itself and agree the longer they use the site, the more they trust the site. Nearly half or more of respondents agree that social networking, commercial and library Web sites keep their personal information secure and also that the sites have rules on how it will be used.

U.S. Library Directors

The study ... reveals that other agencies of mass communication reach far larger groups and reach them more frequently and regularly, with a wealth of words and images designed to inform, to persuade, and to entertain. The public library cannot match this quantitative distribution without a drastic revolution in its operations.

The direct question raised by the data is whether the public library can profitably enter into any such competition, or whether it might better develop its own unique strength ...

—From the Foreword to *The Library's Public*, by Bernard Berelson, 1949, based on data from a 27-month Social Science Research Council (SRC) report to the American Library Association, funded by the Carnegie Corporation

Understanding how users interact with library services and librarians provides important information for guiding services and creating value for constituents and the community. But, as the quote above from the 1949 ALA study points out, it is equally important to understand the changing information environment in which libraries operate and compete. That task is hardly a new one.

We are not, however, anthropologists studying an Internet culture foreign to us in an attempt to contrast it to our own. Libraries exist within the same dynamic digital environment as their users, and librarians use many, if not most, of the same Web tools and services as users.

Library directors have been on the Internet longer than the U.S. general public and are using all of the same online resources. How they use these resources, their privacy views and what personal information they are willing to share online differ, sometimes widely, from the actions and preferences of the members of their online communities.

The views of 382 U.S. library directors are presented on the following pages. The views of the U.S. general public respondents are often presented alongside those of the U.S. library directors for comparison.

Library Directors' Life on the Internet

While the data indicate that library directors do in fact read more than the U.S. general public, they also are intense Internet users. The digital pioneers of the Internet Age may well be librarians. More than half of the librarians surveyed have been using the Internet for over a decade, nearly two times longer than any U.S. general public age group. Librarians are engaged in the same online activities as the U.S. general public, often outpacing their level of participation.

Librarians read substantially more than the U.S. general public. More than a third of the U.S. general public spend five to ten hours a week reading (including books, magazines, online Web pages, blogs, etc.), and almost another third spend 11 or more hours a week reading. Comparatively, nearly 75% of library directors read 11 or more hours per week, while just 31% of the U.S. general public read at this level.

Books Read Annually

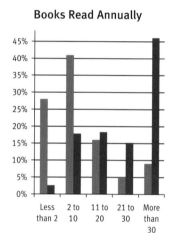

Total U.S. Respondents ■ Total U.S. Library Directors

Source: *Sharing, Privacy and Trust in Our Networked World*, OCLC, 2007, question 510.

Time Spent Reading Per Week

Overall, how much time do you estimate you spend reading on a weekly basis (including books, magazines, online Web sites, blogs, etc.)?

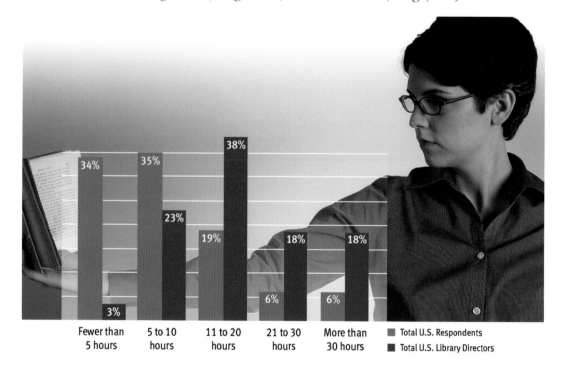

	Fewer than 5 hours	5 to 10 hours	11 to 20 hours	21 to 30 hours	More than 30 hours
Total U.S. Respondents	34%	35%	19%	6%	6%
Total U.S. Library Directors	3%	23%	38%	18%	18%

■ Total U.S. Respondents
■ Total U.S. Library Directors

Source: *Sharing, Privacy and Trust in Our Networked World*, OCLC, 2007, question 515.

Librarians may well be the digital pioneers of the Internet Age. The Internet has been used longer by librarians than any population or age group surveyed. Ninety percent (90%) of librarians have been online seven years or more, compared to 64% of the U.S. general public. Over half of librarians have used the Internet for more than a decade.

Length of Time Using the Internet

Thinking of your overall usage of the Internet, how many years would you estimate you have been using the Internet?

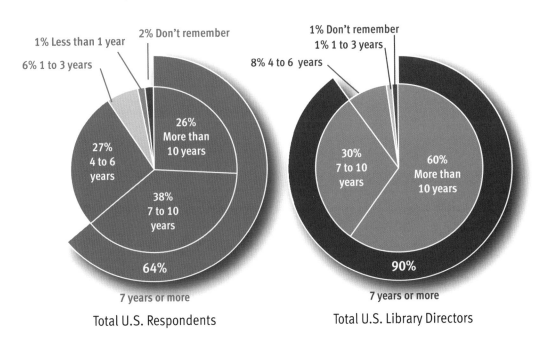

Total U.S. Respondents   Total U.S. Library Directors

Source: *Sharing, Privacy and Trust in Our Networked World*, OCLC, 2007, question 525.

60%

of U.S. library directors have

used the Internet for over a decade,

compared to

26%

of the U.S. general public.

Librarians have participated in a wide range of online activities. On average, library directors are more likely to have participated in many of these activities than the users they serve. Many of these online activities could be categorized as "content-centric" and are similar in nature to the daily professional services and programs that many librarians perform and direct.

Library directors are more likely than the U.S. general public to have:

- Borrowed items or searched for specific items at a library Web site: +67%
- Browsed for or purchased books online: +42%
- Read someone's blog: +24%
- Created a Web page: +19%
- Browsed for information using a search engine: +11%

Library directors are less likely than the U.S. general public to have:

- Sent or received instant messages: −21%
- Used a social networking site: −15%

Online Activities

What type of online activities have you done or participated in during the last 12 months? Please select all that apply.

	Total U.S. Respondents	Total U.S. Library Directors
Browsing/purchasing activities		
Used search engines	86%	97%
Browsed for or purchased items online	76%	92%
Used an online banking or investment Web site	58%	63%
Browsed for or purchased books online	52%	94%
Used an online question service	45%	50%
Read someone's blog	44%	68%
Searched for or borrowed items from the library Web site	23%	90%
Read online (electronic) books	17%	32%
Interacting activities		
Sent or received e-mails	96%	99%
Sent or received instant messages	59%	38%
Used a social networking site	37%	22%
Used chat rooms	18%	11%
Used online dating sites	9%	7%
Accessed business-related social networking sites	6%	7%
Creating activities		
Used a social media site	32%	36%
Blogged or wrote an online diary/journal	19%	19%
Created a Web page	18%	37%
Contributed information to others' Web pages	18%	27%

Source: *Sharing, Privacy and Trust in Our Networked World*, OCLC, 2007, question 530.

97% of library directors and **86%** of the U.S. general public *have used search engines.*

22% of library directors and **37%** of the U.S. general public *have used social networking sites.*

There are noteworthy differences in the adoption of certain Internet activities when we compare librarians ages 22–49 and 50+ to the respective U.S. general public age groups. We find librarians have a much broader adoption of many Internet activities, especially among those Internet activities categorized as "creating" or "browsing" (e.g., creating Web pages, using search engines, reading blogs, etc).

Online Activities

What type of online activities have you done or participated in during the last 12 months? Please select all that apply.

57%
of library directors ages 22–49
have created Web pages
compared to
20%
of the U.S. general public ages 22–49.

	Age 22–49 U.S. Library Directors compared to U.S. Respondents	Age 50+ U.S. Library Directors compared to U.S. Respondents
Browsing/purchasing activities		
Used search engines	+ 10%	+ 9%
Browsed for or purchased items online	+ 17%	+ 11%
Used an online banking or investment Web site	+ 10%	- 9%
Browsed for or purchased books online	+ 36%	+ 45%
Used an online question service	+ 1%	+ 7%
Read someone's blog	+ 31%	+ 33%
Searched for or borrowed items from the library Web site	+ 67%	+ 72%
Read online (electronic) books	+ 25%	+ 17%
Interacting activities		
Sent or received e-mails	+ 2%	+ 3%
Sent or received instant messages	- 5%	- 16%
Used a social networking site	+ 0%	+ 0%
Used chat rooms	- 6%	- 2%
Used online dating sites	+ 1%	- 3%
Accessed business-related social networking sites	+ 2%	+ 1%
Creating activities		
Used a social media site	+ 23%	+ 13%
Blogged or wrote an online diary/journal	+ 18%	+ 7%
Created a Web page	+ 37%	+ 18%
Contributed information to others' Web pages	+ 20%	+ 8%

Source: *Sharing, Privacy and Trust in Our Networked World*, OCLC, 2007, question 530.

Library directors are more likely than the U.S. general public to have multiple online addresses. Most library directors (74%) have two to four e-mail addresses. Over half of library directors also have at least one instant messaging account. Library directors ages 22–49 also are more likely than both their age 50+ colleagues and the U.S. general public to have multiple e-mail addresses and instant messaging accounts.

More library directors ages 22–49 and 50+ have created an alias, avatar or pseudonym than the U.S. general public.

Online Addresses and Avatars

How many e-mail addresses and IM (instant messaging) accounts do you have?
How many aliases, avatars or pseudonyms have you created for the Web?

Base: Respondents who have sent or received an e-mail and/or instant message.

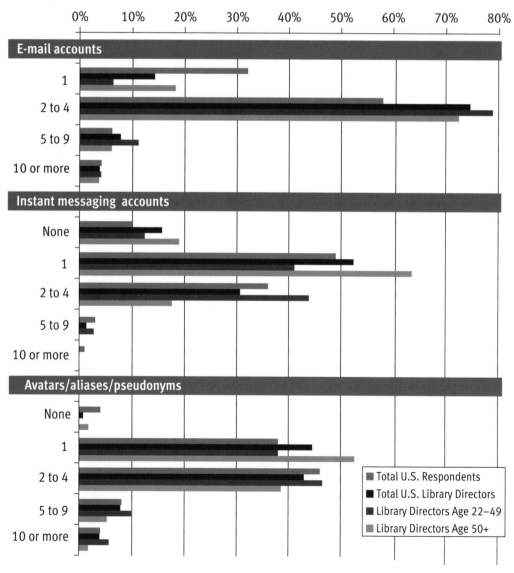

*Library directors are more likely to have **created an alias** than the U.S. general public.*

Source: *Sharing, Privacy and Trust in Our Networked World*, OCLC, 2007, questions 535, 540 and 830.

Favorites Sites

Library directors show a higher usage of commercial sites compared to the U.S. general public but lag behind in the use of social networking sites. Amazon is their top choice of commercial sites. MySpace is the most used social networking site among U.S. library directors. YouTube tops the list of social media sites.

Commercial Sites

Library directors report strong use of commercial Internet sites. Overall, library directors are also more likely than the U.S. general public to have used commercial banking/investment (+5%) and retail shopping sites (+16%).

Library directors browse and shop for books. While Amazon is the most popular commercial site for both library directors and the U.S. general public, a remarkable 92% of librarians report having shopped at Amazon in the past year, a rate nearly double that of the U.S. general public. More than half of library directors have browsed for or purchased items at Barnesandnoble.com, compared to 25% of the U.S. general public.

Among commercial site users, only 13% of the U.S. general public used a library Web site in the last 12 months to browse for books compared to 77% of library directors

92%

of library directors have **used Amazon,**

56%

of the U.S. general public have.

**Frequency of
Library Web Site Use**

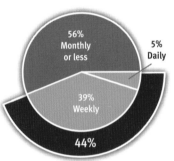

Total U.S. Respondents

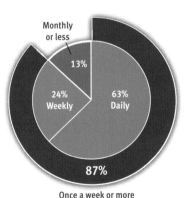

Once a week or more

Total U.S. Library Directors

Frequency of Amazon Use

Typically, how frequently do you log in to (your preferred commercial site)?

Base: Respondents who have used a commercial and/or library Web site.

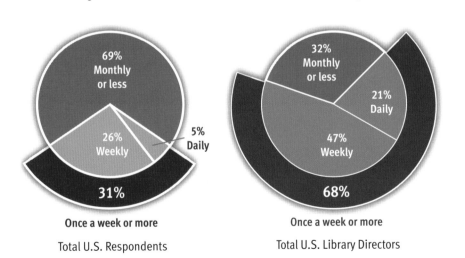

Once a week or more

Total U.S. Respondents

Once a week or more

Total U.S. Library Directors

Source: *Sharing, Privacy and Trust in Our Networked World*, OCLC, 2007, question 790.

Favorite Commercial Sites

Below is a list of Web sites commonly used to browse for and/or purchase music, movies, books and other retail items (e.g., clothing, electronics, etc.). Please select all the Web sites you have used in the past 12 months.

Base: Respondents who have used a commercial and/or library Web site.

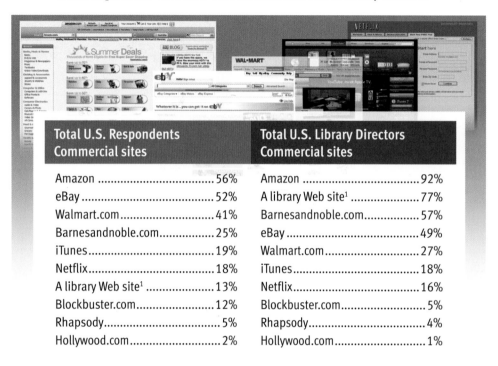

Total U.S. Respondents Commercial sites		Total U.S. Library Directors Commercial sites	
Amazon	56%	Amazon	92%
eBay	52%	A library Web site[1]	77%
Walmart.com	41%	Barnesandnoble.com	57%
Barnesandnoble.com	25%	eBay	49%
iTunes	19%	Walmart.com	27%
Netflix	18%	iTunes	18%
A library Web site[1]	13%	Netflix	16%
Blockbuster.com	12%	Blockbuster.com	5%
Rhapsody	5%	Rhapsody	4%
Hollywood.com	2%	Hollywood.com	1%

Note: The chart shows the top 10 sites.

[1]Library Web site was grouped with commercial sites to provide a view of relative usage across respondent groups.

Source: *Sharing, Privacy and Trust in Our Networked World,* OCLC, 2007, question 770.

Social Networking Sites

The U.S. general public's use of social networking sites (37%) is higher than all other regions surveyed; the use of social networking sites among all library directors is notably less than the U.S. general public, at 22%.

Usage across the two librarian age groups varied. While only 13% of library directors age 50+ have used a social networking site, use by library directors ages 22–49 is significantly higher, at 38%. This usage rate is on par with the overall usage rate of the U.S. general public.

Librarians generally use the same social networking sites, but their usage rates indicate some interesting differences. MySpace, Facebook and Classmates.com are among the most used social networking sites for both librarians and the U.S. general public; MySpace is the most used site for both groups.

Classmates.com is the second most used social networking site for both librarians and the U.S. general public. It was equally used by the public and academic library directors.

Not surprisingly, Facebook, which began as a social networking site for college students, was used significantly more by academic library directors (58%) than by public library directors (10%).

Significantly more academic library directors used del.icio.us than their public library colleagues, 45% compared to 20%. While 30% of total library directors have used del.icio.us in the last year, only 3% of the U.S. general public have used the site. This usage difference may be due to the nature of the del.icio.us service. While the social features of del.icio.us are unmistakably important to its purpose, the general function of the service is to provide reference/search recommendations based on user categorizations, a domain of particular importance and expertise in the library community.

MySpace is the *most used social networking site* among librarians and the U.S. general public.

Favorite Social Networking Sites

Below is a list of social networking Web sites. Please select all the Web sites you have used in the past 12 months.

Base: Respondents who have used a social networking site.

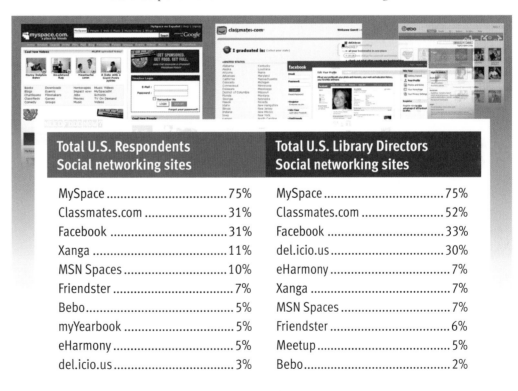

Total U.S. Respondents Social networking sites		Total U.S. Library Directors Social networking sites	
MySpace	75%	MySpace	75%
Classmates.com	31%	Classmates.com	52%
Facebook	31%	Facebook	33%
Xanga	11%	del.icio.us	30%
MSN Spaces	10%	eHarmony	7%
Friendster	7%	Xanga	7%
Bebo	5%	MSN Spaces	7%
myYearbook	5%	Friendster	6%
eHarmony	5%	Meetup	5%
del.icio.us	3%	Bebo	2%

Note: The chart shows the top 10 sites.
Source: *Sharing, Privacy and Trust in Our Networked World*, OCLC, 2007, question 605.

Frequency of MySpace Use

Typically, how frequently do you log in to
(your preferred social networking site)?

Base: Respondents who have used a social networking site.

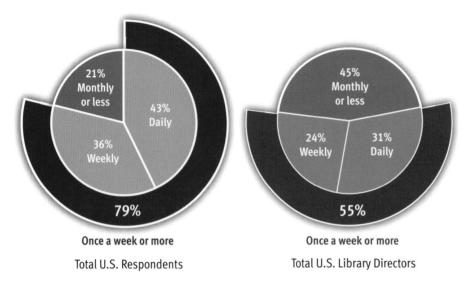

| Total U.S. Respondents | Total U.S. Library Directors |

Source: *Sharing, Privacy and Trust in Our Networked World*, OCLC, 2007, question 635.

Social Media Sites

YouTube is the dominant social media service of choice for both library directors and the U.S. general public. It is also the social media service of choice across all geographies surveyed.

Flickr is the second most popular social media site for librarians; almost half of the librarians (49%) have used the service in the last year. Flickr is a feature-rich photo-sharing service, offering the ability to post pictures for direct sharing, storage and use on the site itself, as well as providing its application programming interface (API) for program enhancements by users. This service is similar to the content collection and distribution model used by many U.S. libraries. In contrast, much of the use of Photobucket and Yahoo! Photos is connected to collaboration and communication functions and tied to services of other social networking and portal sites. Photobucket and Yahoo! Photos were used by more U.S. respondents than librarians. [NOTE: After the survey was conducted, Yahoo! closed Yahoo! Photos in September 2007.]

The same social media sites were generally used by academic and public library directors.

Favorite Social Media Sites

Below is a list of social media Web sites. Please select all the
Web sites you have used in the past 12 months.

Base: Respondents who have used a social media site.

18%
*of library
directors and*

19%

*of the U.S.
general public*
*have used
iTunes.*

Total U.S. Respondents Social media sites		Total U.S. Library Directors Social media sites	
YouTube	73%	YouTube	72%
Photobucket	28%	Flickr	49%
Yahoo! Photos	22%	Snapfish	33%
MySpace Videos	22%	Kodak Gallery	25%
Snapfish	22%	Yahoo! Photos	22%
Kodak Gallery	14%	Shutterfly	19%
Shutterfly	13%	Webshots	10%
Flickr	11%	Photobucket	9%
Webshots	9%	MySpace Videos	5%
Imageshack	7%	iFilm	3%

Note: The chart shows the top 10 sites.
Source: *Sharing, Privacy and Trust in Our Networked World*, OCLC, 2007, question 710.

Frequency of YouTube Use

Typically, how frequently do you log in to (your preferred social media site)?

Base: Respondents who have used a social media site.

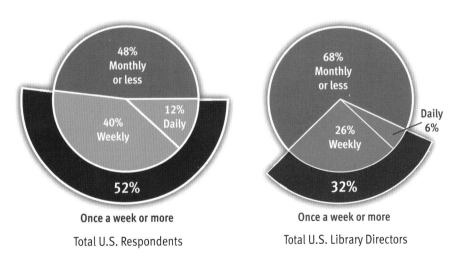

Total U.S. Respondents: 48% Monthly or less, 40% Weekly, 12% Daily — 52% Once a week or more

Total U.S. Library Directors: 68% Monthly or less, 26% Weekly, Daily 6% — 32% Once a week or more

Source: *Sharing, Privacy and Trust in Our Networked World*, OCLC, 2007, question 740.

When looking at the three types of Internet sites surveyed—social networking, social media and commercial sites—our results indicate library directors are using social media and commercial sites at roughly the same rate or more than the U.S. general public. Overall, librarians age 50+ lag in their use of social networking sites, but librarians ages 22–49 are using them at a rate equal with U.S. general public. Together, U.S. library directors and the U.S. general public ages 22–49 lead the use of social networking sites across the six countries surveyed, at 38%.

Library directors are using the same sites as the U.S. general public, but are they using the sites for the same reasons?

Why Library Directors Use Social Sites

The survey results highlight that library directors and the U.S. general public are using many of the same social Internet sites, but their primary motivations for using these services vary. Library directors are more likely to utilize social sites for browsing services or content creation, rather than for social exchange. A quarter are motivated to use social networks as a part of their business.

Motivations for Using Social Networking Sites

Library directors and the U.S. general public use social networking sites for a variety of reasons. While *my friends use the same site* is the most common reason why both the library directors and the U.S. general public use social networking sites, the degree to which this is the top motivator greatly varies. Seventy percent (70%) of the U.S. general public cite *my friends use the same site* as their main reason for using a social networking site, compared to 37% among library directors.

Library directors reported a balanced set of reasons for using social networking sites, with almost equal emphasis given to *my friends use the same site*, *being part of a group or community*, *the Web site is useful*, *to network or to meet new people* and *I use as part of my business*. In sharp contrast to the U.S. general public at 42%, only 17% of library directors use a social networking site because *the Web site is fun*. Over a quarter of librarians (27%) say that they use the social networking sites *as part of their business* compared to only 4% of the U.S. general public. Nearly half (49%) of the U.S. general public age 50+ cite being *part of a group or community* as the primary motivator for using a social networking site, compared to only 21% of library directors age 50+.

27%
of library directors and

4%
of the U.S. general public **use social networking sites for business.**

Why Library Directors Use Social Networking Sites

Which of the following describe why you use your preferred social networking Web site(s)? Please select all that apply.

Base: Respondents who have used a social networking site.
Note: The chart represents responses of 25% or more.

Total U.S. Respondents	
My friends use the same site	70%
The Web site is fun	42%
To network or to meet new people	38%
To be a part of a group or community	30%
The Web site is useful	28%
Total U.S. Library Directors	
My friends use the same site	37%
To be a part of a group or community	31%
The Web site is useful	30%
To network or to meet new people	27%
I use it as a part of my business	27%

Source: *Sharing, Privacy and Trust in Our Networked World*, OCLC, 2007, question 626.

Motivations for Using Social Media Sites

The top motivation for library directors to use a social media site is *the Web site is useful* (35%). While a third of the U.S. general public also report using Web sites for utility, this motivation ranked first for librarians, but third for the U.S. general public. Twenty-three percent (23%) of library directors use a social media site because *it is part of my business*, compared to just 3% of the U.S. general public. As with social networking sites, library directors are less likely to say that they use social media sites because *the Web site is fun* (26%) than the U.S. general public (43%); the community-building components of social media sites are also less utilized by library directors.

23% *of library directors and* **3%** *of the U.S. general public* use social media sites for business.

Why Library Directors Use Social Media Sites

Which of the following describe why you use your preferred social media Web site(s)? Please select all that apply.

Base: Respondents who have used a social media site.
Note: The chart represents responses of 15% or more.

Total U.S. Respondents	
The Web site is fun	43%
My friends use the same site	34%
The Web site is useful	33%
To document and share personal experiences	16%
Total U.S. Library Directors	
The Web site is useful	35%
The Web site is fun	26%
I use it as part of my business	23%
My friends use the same site	19%

Source: *Sharing, Privacy and Trust in Our Networked World*, OCLC, 2007, question 730.

Sharing Personal Information Online

Library directors and the U.S. general public use many of the same social networking, social media and commercial sites. While the usage rates are similar, the survey results identified several notable differences in the amount of personal information that library directors and the U.S. general public are willing to share.

Librarians are more likely than the general public to provide information on commercial sites and to sign up for alert notifications, but less likely to provide personal information on social sites.

Survey respondents who used social networking, social media and commercial sites were asked to indicate the types of personal information they have supplied on each type of site. The survey respondents were presented with 22 different information types and were asked which they have supplied on these sites in the past 12 months.

The information types were grouped into three general categories: **contact information**, including information such as name, address, e-mail and phone; **individual information**, including marital status, personality attributes, sexual preference, physical attributes and birthday; and **interest information** such as subjects of interest, books read and association affiliations.

Library directors were less likely than the U.S. general public to have supplied **contact**, **individual** and **interest information** on either social networking or social media sites. The directors were more likely to have supplied **contact information** on commercial sites.

The higher the level of **social interaction or community** *on a site, the more personal information both the library directors and the U.S. general public are willing to provide.*

Information Shared on Commercial Sites

Over half of library directors have supplied general **contact information**, including *e-mail address*, *phone number* and *credit card information* on commercial sites. Library directors are more likely than the U.S. general public to have supplied general **contact information** and *credit card information* on a commercial site, but less likely to have provided *subjects of interest, income* or other individual and interest information.

Information Shared on Commercial Sites

Which of the following types of information have you ever supplied about yourself when you were browsing for and/or purchasing music, movies, books and other retails items? Please select all that apply.

Base: Respondents who have used a commercial site.

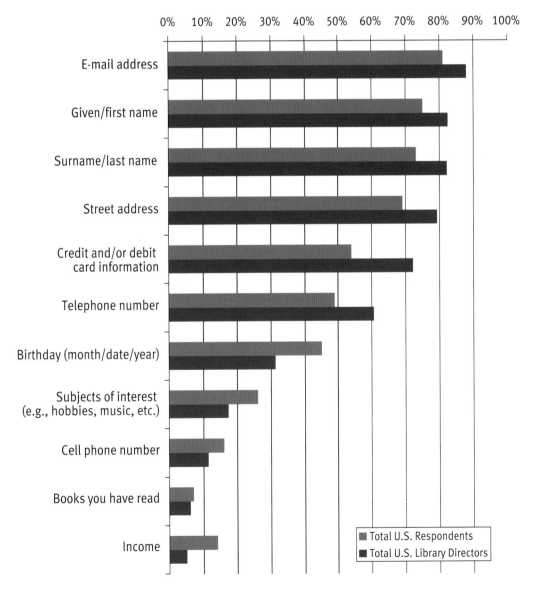

Source: *Sharing, Privacy and Trust in Our Networked World,* OCLC, 2007, question 765.

Notification services, often used as a way to stay abreast of news and information from a company or service, were used by more library directors than the U.S. respondents.

Almost half of the library directors (46%) have registered to receive e-mail alerts compared to 39% of the U.S. general public.

Library directors were also more likely than the U.S. general public to have signed up for electronic newsletters, created wish lists or "favorites" or to have set up RSS feeds on commercial sites.

A larger percentage of library directors have used

notification and alert services
on commercial sites compared to the U.S. general public.

Use of Commercial Electronic Notification Services

Which of the following types of activities have you done during the last 12 months while browsing for and/or purchasing music, movies, books and other retails items? Please select all that apply.

Base: Respondents who have used a commercial site.

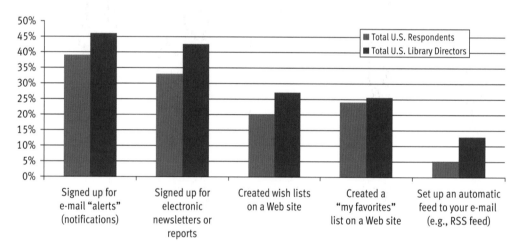

Source: *Sharing, Privacy and Trust in Our Networked World,* OCLC, 2007, question 760.

Information Shared on Social Networking Sites

Library directors were less likely to have shared personal information on social networking sites than the U.S. general public, with some differences including *marital status, birthday, physical attributes* and *sexual preference.*

In only three instances did library directors provide information in proportion to the U.S. general public: *books they had read, associations they belong to* and s*elf-published information.* In all instances, librarians ages 22–49 were more likely than their age 50+ colleagues to have shared personal information on social networking sites. Approximately 30% of library directors age 50+ indicated they have not shared any of the information evaluated, making it likely that they are using social networking sites only as readers and not as active participants.

50%
of U.S. respondents and

28%
of U.S. library directors have shared **personality attributes** *on social networking sites.*

Information Shared on Social Networking Sites

Which of the following types of information have you ever supplied about yourself on social networking Web sites? Please select all that apply.

Base: Respondents who have used a social networking site.
Note: No library directors age 50+ have supplied information related to sexual preference.

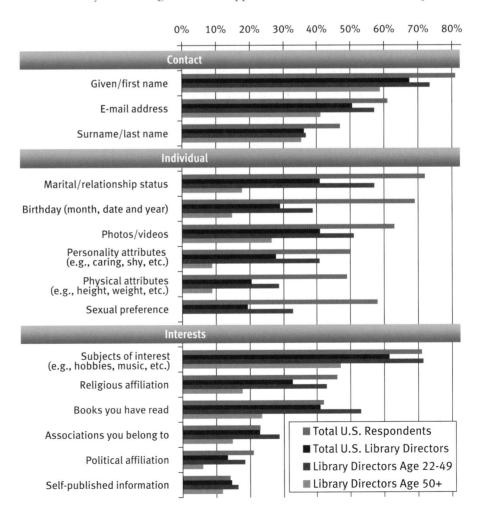

Source: *Sharing, Privacy and Trust in Our Networked World,* OCLC, 2007, question 625.

Information Shared on Social Media Sites

Library directors are less likely to have shared personal information on social media sites than the U.S. general public. Over 50% of library directors indicated that they have not provided any personal information on social media sites.

The data indicate similar information-sharing behavior on both social media and social networking sites. As with social networking sites, library directors are less likely to have provided information on social media sites than the U.S. general public. Again, library directors ages 22–49 were more likely to have shared information than their age 50+ colleagues.

Information Shared on Social Media Sites

Which of the following types of information have you ever supplied about yourself on social media Web sites? Please select all that apply.

Base: Respondents who have used a social media site.

Note: No library directors age 50+ indicated they have shared the following attributes: personality and physical attributes, sexual preference, associations and self-published information.

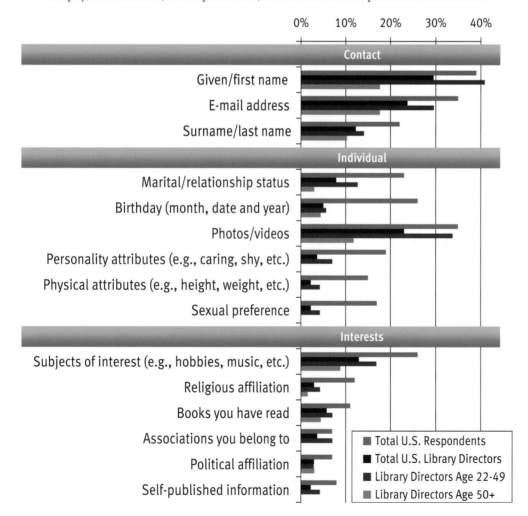

Source: *Sharing, Privacy and Trust in Our Networked World,* OCLC, 2007, question 725.

Sharing *pictures* is the top social media activity for both library directors and the U.S. general public. At rates equal to the U.S. general public, over half of the library directors have uploaded or linked to *photos* on social media sites.

Library directors are less likely to have uploaded or linked to *videos* or *music* on a social media site.

Uploading or Linking on Social Media Sites

Which of the following have you uploaded or linked to on a social media Web site(s) during the last 12 months? Please select all that apply.

Base: Respondents who have used a social media site.

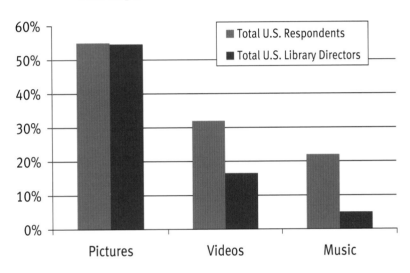

Source: *Sharing, Privacy and Trust in Our Networked World*, OCLC, 2007, question 705.

Views on Privacy and Security

Overall, library directors see a trend toward less Internet privacy and less Internet security, while the U.S. general public feels privacy and security on the Internet is stable.

It can be difficult to separate the concepts of privacy and security on the Internet. In the physical environment, people can interact with a person or organization with relatively little thought to personal privacy or information security. But on the Internet, where most communication is remote and requires the transmission of personal information to interact at any level with an organization or individual, new issues around privacy and security begin to shape relationships.

To understand how the perceptions of privacy and security among librarians compare to the U.S. general public, we asked a series of questions about both general and specific attitudes concerning Internet privacy and security over the past two years.

Internet Privacy

About a quarter of the U.S. general public and library directors feel there was *no change* in the privacy of their personal information online over the last two years, at 22% and 23%, respectively. Slightly more of the U.S. general public feel their personal information on the Internet is *kept less private* (33%) today than feel it is *more private* (26%) when compared to two years ago. Comparatively, 42% of the library directors feel that their personal information is *kept less private* today than it was two years ago, while only 15% feel it is *kept more private*.

Library directors were also asked to predict how the public feels their personal information has been kept on the Internet. Their estimations are labeled as "Total U.S. Library Directors: Estimation of Users' Views" when presented in the charts.

Library directors' estimate of the public's view of Internet privacy were close to their own views. Fifty-one percent (51%) of library directors estimated the public feels their personal information is *kept less private* on the Internet than it was two years ago; 33% of the U.S. general public actually reported feeling this way, whereas 42% of the library directors feel their own personal information is *kept less private* on the Internet.

Ten percent (10%) of library directors estimated that the public feels their personal information on the Internet is *kept more private*. Twenty-six percent (26%) of the U.S. general public hold this view. Again, directors estimated that users' views closely reflected their own privacy views; 15% of library directors feel their own personal information is *kept more private* on the Internet.

Internet Privacy

Generally, do you think that your personal information on the Internet is kept more private than, less private than, or the same as it was two years ago?

Generally, do you believe the public feels their personal information on the Internet is kept more private than, less private than, or the same as it was two years ago?

I have no concerns

46-year-old from Germany

Source: *Sharing, Privacy and Trust in Our Networked World*, OCLC, 2007, question 905, "Overall, what types of concerns do you have about keeping your personal information private?"

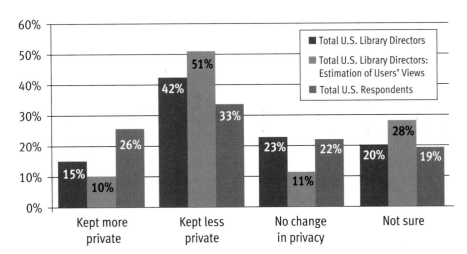

Source: *Sharing, Privacy and Trust in Our Networked World*, OCLC, 2007, questions 930 and 1195.

I worry that maybe my bank information will be stolen, but I've used online banking for more than 6 years at 2 different banks and never had a problem, so i feel fairly safe.

30-year-old librarian from the United States

Source: *Sharing, Privacy and Trust in Our Networked World*, OCLC, 2007, question 905, "Overall , what types of concerns do you have about keeping your personal information private?"

Top Privacy Concerns

Overall, what types of concerns do you have about keeping your personal information private?

U.S. Library Directors

Ads/spam   **Credit/financial theft**
Data sharing/leaks   Finding me   Fraud   Government abuse   Government ID
Hackers **Identity theft**   Library privacy   Limit information provided
No concerns   No guarantee   No trust   Privacy policy   **Privacy rights**   Safety issues
Security issues   Selling my information   Spying   Stalkers   Tracing me
Trust particular companies/Web sites   Use of information   Who has access to my information?

U.S. General Public

Abuse   Ads/spam   Confidentiality   Credit/financial theft   Data security   Data sharing/leaks
E-mail/Web site security   Financial security   Finding me/my address   Fraud   General concern
Government ID Government abuse Hackers **Identity theft**   Library privacy
Limit information provided   No concerns   No guarantee   No one's business   No trust
Privacy policy   Privacy rights   Profiling   Protect personal information
Safety issues   Security issues   Selling my information   Spying   Stalkers   Telephone calls/number
Tracking of Information   Trust particular companies/Web sites   Use of information   Who has access to my information?

Source: *Sharing, Privacy and Trust in Our Networked World*, OCLC, 2007, question 905.

Over 700 comments by U.S. library directors and nearly 3,000 comments from the U.S. general public about their privacy concerns have been categorized and presented as the tag clouds above.

The most pressing privacy concern for both U.S. library directors and the U.S. general public is *identity theft*. Librarians were slightly more concerned about *ads/spam* than were respondents from the U.S. general public, but unwanted solicitations were a top concern for both.

Librarians were more concerned about *privacy rights* in general than the U.S. general public. Library privacy was mentioned as a top concern by less than 1% of each group.

Internet Security

In general, library directors hold similar views of Internet security trends as they do of Internet privacy. More library directors feel the Internet is less secure than it was two years ago.

Twenty-one percent (21%) of library directors feel their personal information on the Internet is *kept more secure* (slightly more than those who indicated the Internet was *kept more private* at 15%) compared to over 30% of the U.S. general public.

Library directors estimated the public would have more negative views on Internet security than what they estimated with Internet privacy. Nearly half of the library directors (46%) estimated the public would feel their personal information has been *kept less secure* than it was two years ago, which is double the rate of what the U.S. general public actually reported (23%). Eleven percent (11%) of library directors predicted the public feels their personal information has been *kept more secure* in the last two years compared to 31% of the U.S. general public who actually rated the Internet as *more secure*.

Internet Security

Generally, do you think that your personal information on the Internet is kept more secure than, less secure than, or the same as it was two years ago?

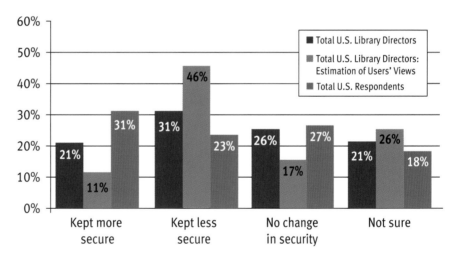

Source: *Sharing, Privacy and Trust in Our Networked World*, OCLC, 2007, questions 935 and 1200.

While library directors are more likely than the U.S. general public to feel their personal information is *kept less secure* on the Internet, their experiences with unauthorized use of personal information on the Internet is very similar to the U.S. general public's experiences. Twelve percent (12%) of library directors and 10% of the U.S. general public have experienced improper use of personal information.

Improper Use of Personal Information Online

Have you or has anyone you know ever had personal information used online without consent? Please select all that apply.

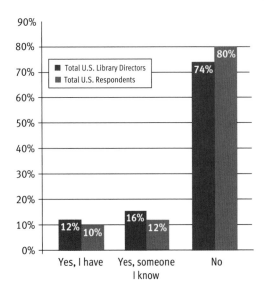

Source: *Sharing, Privacy and Trust in Our Networked World,* OCLC, 2007, question 1135.

Library directors feel the Internet is less secure than it was two years ago, and they are less likely than the U.S. general public to use the same password at multiple sites as a security measure. A third of library directors *always* or *often* use the same password when registering at Web sites compared to 41% of the U.S. general public.

Use of the Same Password

In general, when registering at any Web site, how often do you use the same password as you do with other sites?

Total U.S. Respondents

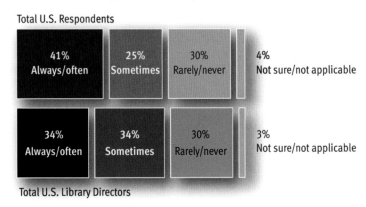

Total U.S. Library Directors

Source: *Sharing, Privacy and Trust in Our Networked World,* OCLC, 2007, question 836.

Privacy and Everyday Activities

Overall, the U.S. general public feel that many of their everyday activities are more private than do library directors. The only areas in which library directors ranked the privacy of activities as more private than the U.S. general public are the library's print collection, and a library Web site.

The majority of library directors feel their online banking/investment service activity is *extremely* or *very private* (60%). This activity is considered to be substantially more private than any other activity evaluated by both librarians and the U.S. general public. E-mail at home is seen as the second most private activity by the U.S. general public, at 43%; library directors rate e-mail third at 25%.

Both librarians and the U.S. general public rated social networking and social media activities similar to search engines, online bookstores and cable television. A third or more of library directors and the U.S. general public feel their activity while using landline phones at home is *extremely* or *very private*, at 33% and 41%, respectively. Over a third (36%) of the U.S. general public feel their use of cell phones is *extremely* or *very private*, nearly two times more than library directors, at 20%.

43%

of the U.S. general public feel

e-mail at home is extremely or very private,

compared to

25%

of library directors.

Privacy and Everyday Activities

For each of the following, please rate how private, if at all, your activity is while using it.

Note: The chart shows the *extremely private* and *very private* responses.

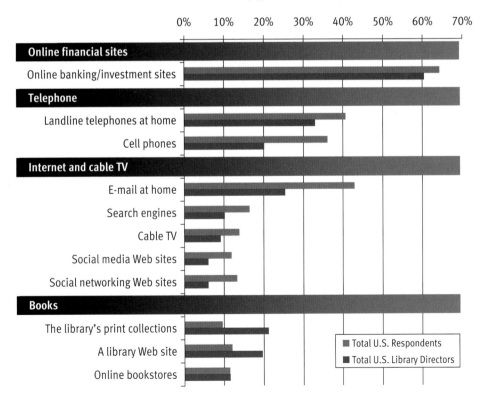

Source: *Sharing, Privacy and Trust in Our Networked World*, OCLC, 2007, question 926.

Sharing Personalities Online

Most respondents, both library directors and the U.S. general public, indicated they were more comfortable sharing their true personalities in person than online. While most comfortable in person, both groups indicated that they have the same personalities online as they do in person. Library directors are more likely than the U.S. general public to prefer to remain anonymous on social and commercial sites.

Library directors are more comfortable sharing their true personality in person than online. More than two-thirds of librarians (69%) indicated they are at least *somewhat more comfortable* sharing their true personalities in person than online compared to 56% of the U.S. general public.

Nearly a third of the U.S. general public are equally comfortable sharing their personalities online as in person, compared with just over 20% of library directors. Only a very small percentage of both the U.S. general public and library directors are more comfortable sharing their true personalities online than in person.

Sharing Your True Personality

Please indicate where you are more comfortable sharing your true personality (e.g., feelings, attitudes, interests, etc.).

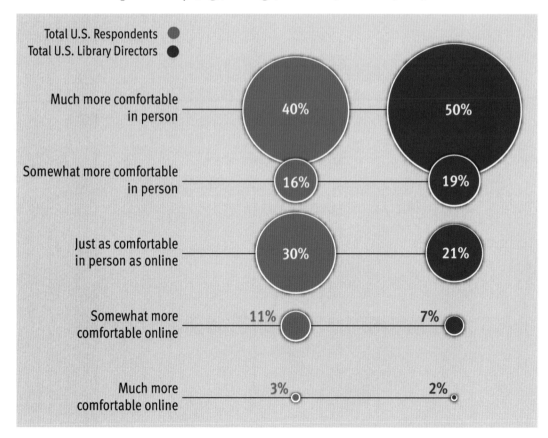

Source: *Sharing, Privacy and Trust in Our Networked World,* OCLC, 2007, question 940.

While most respondents are at least *somewhat more comfortable* sharing their true personalities in person, the majority of both librarians and U.S. respondents (over 60%) *agree* (*strongly agree* or *somewhat agree*) that they have the same personality while using social networking and commercial sites as they do in person; approximately half of both groups *agree* they have the same personality while using social media sites. Seventy percent (70%) of librarians *agree* to having the same personalities on commercial sites as they do in person.

Half of library directors *agree* they prefer to remain anonymous when using commercial and social media sites. Just over 40% also prefer anonymity on social networking sites.

Personality and Anonymity Online

Thinking about the [social networking, social media, and/or commercial Web sites you use], how strongly do you agree or disagree with each of the following statements?

Base: Respondents who have used a social networking, social media and/or commercial site.

Note: The chart shows the *strongly agree* and *somewhat agree* responses.

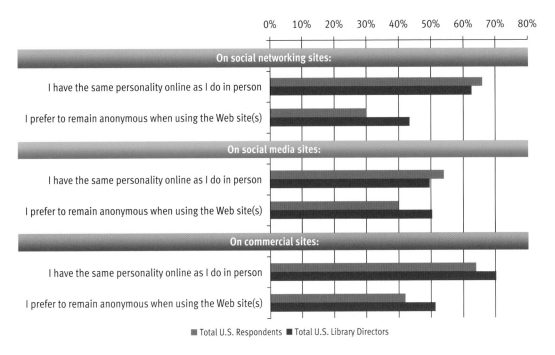

Source: *Sharing, Privacy and Trust in Our Networked World*, OCLC, 2007, questions 971, 1011 and 1046.

While many librarians indicate they prefer to remain anonymous when using social networking, social media and commercial sites, over 70% are willing to *always* or *often* use their real names when registering on a Web site and the majority (80%) *always* or *often* use their real e-mail addresses. More than half of both librarians and the U.S. general public *always* or *often* use their real phone numbers and real ages.

Information Provided While Registering

In general, when registering at any Web site, how often do you ...?

Note: The chart shows the *always* and *often* responses.

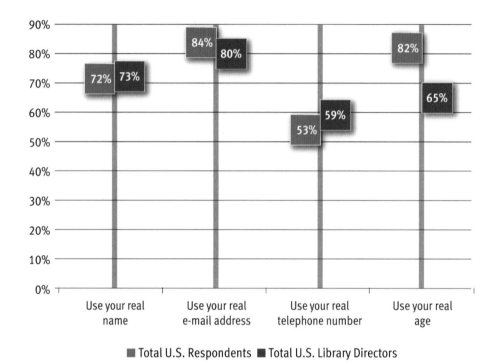

■ Total U.S. Respondents ■ Total U.S. Library Directors

Source: *Sharing, Privacy and Trust in Our Networked World*, OCLC, 2007, question 836.

Frequency of Completing the Entire Web Registration Form

Note: The chart shows the *always* and *often* responses.

Total U.S. Respondents

Total U.S. Library Directors

Source: *Sharing, Privacy and Trust in Our Networked World*, OCLC, 2007, question 836, "In general, when registering at Web sites, how often do you fill out the complete form, not just the required information?"

Privacy Rules

Most librarians and U.S. respondents look for symbols of privacy and security. Most do not review privacy policies, and less than 10% use privacy policies as a determination on whether or not to make a purchase on a commercial site.

Both librarians and U.S. respondents share similar attitudes on the importance of setting controls and remaining informed on how their personal information will be used on the Internet. Three-quarters of librarians and U.S. respondents say that establishing guidelines on how their personal information will be used or viewed is *extremely* or *very important* to them. The ability to have controls on their personal information is more important than the ability to remain anonymous on the Web for both librarians and U.S. respondents.

Importance of Controlling Personal Information on the Internet

How important is each of the following with respect to providing your personal information on the Internet?

Ability to specify who can view it
Ability to specify who can use it
Ability to remain informed about how it will be used

Note: The chart shows the *extremely important* and *very important* responses.

Controlling the use of personal information is more important than remaining anonymous on the Web for both library directors and the U.S. general public.

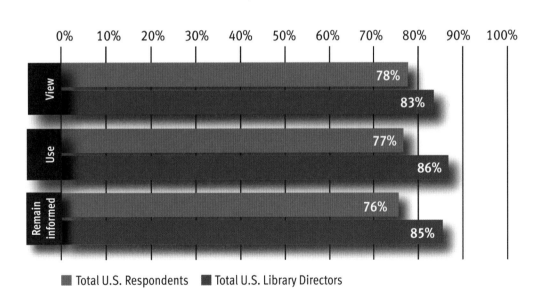

■ Total U.S. Respondents ■ Total U.S. Library Directors

Source: *Sharing, Privacy and Trust in Our Networked World*, OCLC, 2007, question 1131.

Importance of Remaining Anonymous on the Internet

How important is each of the following with respect to providing
your personal information on the Internet?

Ability to remain anonymous

Note: The chart shows the *extremely important* and *very important* responses.

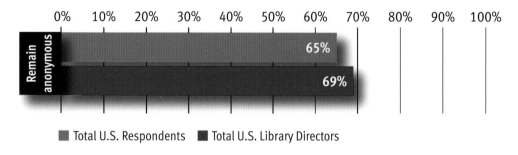

Total U.S. Respondents   Total U.S. Library Directors

Source: *Sharing, Privacy and Trust in Our Networked World*, OCLC, 2007, question 1131.

Attitudes and behavior are not always congruent. While over 70% of librarians and
U.S. respondents indicated it is important to be able to specify who may view their
personal information, a smaller percentage actually specify who could view their
personal information on social networking and social media sites. Half or less of
librarians and the U.S. general public who use social networking and social media
sites *always* or *often* specify who is able to view their personal information on these
sites.

Specifying Who Can View Personal Information

In general when using [social networking and/or social media sites], how frequently
do you specify who is able to view your personal information?

Base: Respondents who have used a social networking and/or a social media site.

Note: The chart shows the *always* or *often* responses.

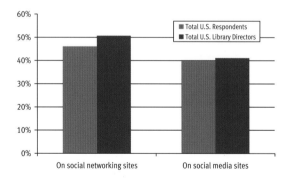

Source: *Sharing, Privacy and Trust in Our Networked World*, OCLC, 2007, questions 966 and 1006.

While 70% of librarians and U.S. respondents rated the ability to establish controls on how personal information is viewed as *extremely* or *very important*, a relatively smaller number of respondents indicated that they *always* or *often* reviewed a Web site's privacy policy before registering.

Forty-one percent (41%) of library directors review privacy policies on social networking sites before registering. Library directors are only slightly more likely to *always* or *often* review privacy policies on social networking, social media and commercial sites than the U.S. general public.

Few librarians and U.S. respondents have *always* or *often* decided not to purchase an item online after reviewing a company's privacy policy, 9% and 14% respectively.

Frequency of Reviewing Privacy Policies

In general when using [social networking, social media and/or commercial sites], how frequently do you review the Web sites' privacy policies before registering?

Base: Respondents who have used a social networking, social media and/or commercial site.

Note: The chart shows the *always* and *often* responses.

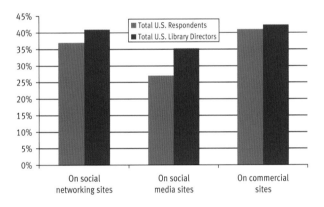

Source: *Sharing, Privacy and Trust in Our Networked World*, OCLC, 2007, questions 966, 1006 and 1051.

More librarians and U.S. respondents report they look for security icons than review privacy policies on commercial sites. Two-thirds of librarians and the U.S. general public *always* or *often* look for security icons on commercial Web sites (69% and 64%, respectively). Librarians ages 22–49 are even more likely than their age 50+ colleagues to look for security icons; 74% compared to 66%.

Frequency of Looking for Security Icons

In general, when you browse/purchase on Web sites, how often do you look for security icons on the Web site (e.g., VeriSign)?

Base: Respondents who have used a commercial site.

Note: The chart shows the *always* and *often* responses.

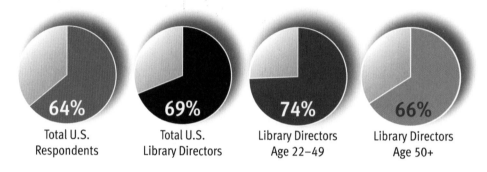

Total U.S. Respondents	Total U.S. Library Directors	Library Directors Age 22–49	Library Directors Age 50+
64%	69%	74%	66%

Source: *Sharing, Privacy and Trust in Our Networked World*, OCLC, 2007, question 1051.

Trust

Library directors are slightly more likely to trust commercial sites than U.S. respondents. U.S. respondents trust social sites more.

Both librarians and the U.S. respondents place a high level of importance on the ability to control how their personal information will be used online and to some extent take steps to use controls on Web sites. Having the ability to control how their personal information will be used, knowing there are privacy policies in place and identifying known security icons on Web sites can contribute to establishing trust.

Use and familiarity also can contribute to a sense of trust. Librarians and the U.S. general public both trust commercial sites notably more than they trust social networking or social media sites. The U.S. general public are more likely than librarians to trust social networking and social media sites, but librarians were slightly more likely to trust commercial Web sites. While over half of library directors feel that the longer they use commercial sites, the more they trust the sites, they did not feel as strongly that use translated into greater trust for social networking and media sites.

36%
of U.S. respondents
trust social
networking
sites,
compared to

25%
of library directors.

Trusting Online Sites

Thinking about the [social networking, social media and commercial sites you use], how strongly do you agree or disagree with each of the following statements?

Base: Respondents who have used a social networking, social media and/or commercial site.
Note: The chart shows the *strongly agree* and *somewhat agree* responses.

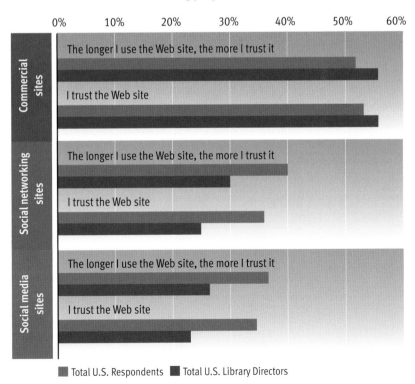

Source: *Sharing, Privacy and Trust in Our Networked World*, OCLC, 2007, questions 971, 1011 and 1046.

Just 21% of the U.S. general public and 18% of librarians *agree* (*strongly agree* or *somewhat agree*) they trust the people they meet on social networking sites.

Trust Whom We Meet Online

In general, when using [social networking, social media and/or library Web sites], how frequently do you trust the people you meet?

Base: Respondents who have used a social networking site, social media site and/or the library Web site.

Note: The chart shows the *strongly agree* and *somewhat agree* responses. Librarians were not asked about library sites for this question.

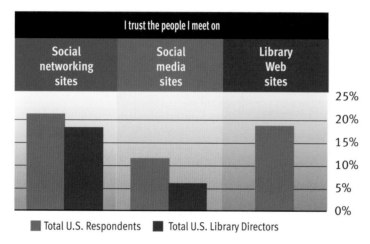

Source: *Sharing, Privacy and Trust in Our Networked World*, OCLC, 2007, questions 971, 1011 and 1086.

Both librarians and the U.S. general public *agree* that commercial sites keep their information secure. Two-thirds or more of both librarians (74%) and the U.S. general public (66%) *agree* (*strongly agree* or *somewhat agree*) that commercial sites keep their personal information secure. More than half of the U.S. general public (52%) also *agree* that library Web sites keep their personal information secure.

The U.S. general public are more likely than librarians to *agree* that social networking and social media sites keep their personal information secure. Librarians are more likely to indicate they are *not sure* if these sites keep their personal information secure.

Agree Sites Keep My Personal Information Secure

In general, when using [social networking, social media, commercial and library Web sites], how strongly do you agree that it keeps your personal information secure?

Base: Respondents who have used a social networking, social media, commercial and/or a library Web site.

Note: The chart shows the *strongly agree* and *somewhat agree* responses. Librarians were not asked about library sites for this question.

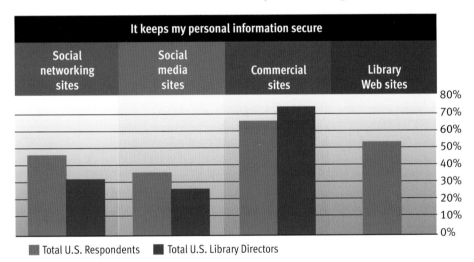

Source: *Sharing, Privacy and Trust in Our Networked World*, OCLC, 2007, questions 956, 1001, 1041 and 1066.

Information Privacy

Library directors rate the privacy of library services high and the survey results indicate that directors feel that their users also share similarly high views of privacy regarding library information and library access.

Library directors overestimated the privacy views of their users.

Not only did we ask the U.S. general public and the library directors questions about how private they felt specific searching/browsing information is to them, such as books they have read, subjects they have searched on the Internet, or items checked out from the library, we also asked the library directors to predict how private this information is to their users. Their estimations are labeled as "Total U.S Library Directors: Estimation of Users' Views" when presented in the charts.

Library directors overestimated the privacy views of their users regarding searching/browsing activities ranging from books read to subjects searched on the Internet to items checked out online from the library. In no instance did library directors underestimate their users' views on the importance of privacy.

The largest spread between actual and perceived user views of online privacy related to library activities. For example, over 50% of library directors estimated their users would view items checked out online from the library to be *extremely* or *very private;* just 19% of U.S. respondents actually rated this information as *extremely* or *very private.* Nearly half of the library directors (48%) felt their users would rate books read as *extremely* or *very private*; actual response among U.S. respondents was 16%.

It is interesting to note that library directors rated their own privacy levels of these activities lower than the levels they predicted their users would report on every activity.

Librarians overestimated privacy views of their users in every instance.

Privacy of Searching/Browsing Information

Please rate how private, if at all, the following information is to you.
Please rate how private, if at all, you feel the following information is to your users.

Note: The chart shows the *extremely private* and *very private* responses.

54%
of library directors estimate that
users view items checked out from the library as extremely or very private;

19%
of the U.S. general public agrees.

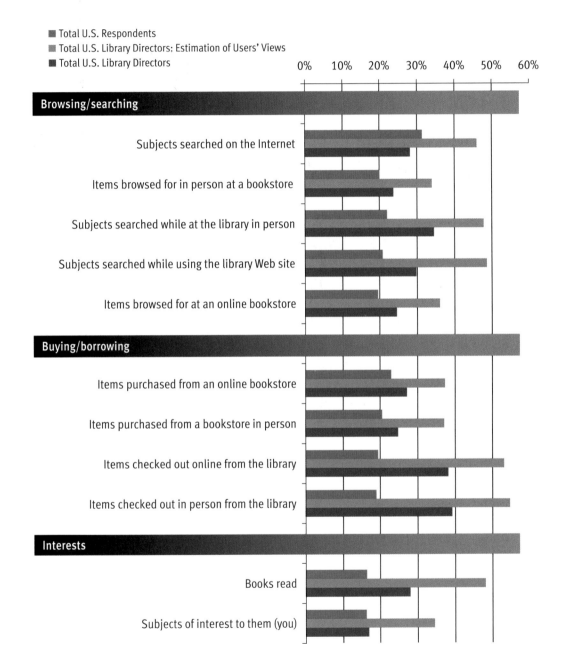

Source: *Sharing, Privacy and Trust in Our Networked World*, OCLC, 2007, questions 911 and 1161.

Library directors more closely estimated their users' views on the importance of keeping library information private, but still overestimated these views.

Over three-quarters (78%) of the U.S. respondents indicated that it was *extremely* or *very important* for the library to keep personal information private, while 87% of librarians perceived their users would feel this way.

Approximately half of the U.S. respondents feel it is *extremely* or *very important* that all other library activities are kept private, compared with approximately 70% of library directors' perceptions.

Importance of Keeping Library Information Private

In thinking about privacy, how important, if at all, is it to you that the library you primarily use would keep ... [private]?
In thinking about privacy, how important, if at all, is it to your users that your library keeps ... [private]?

Base: For the U.S. respondents, those who have used a library in person or online.

Note: The chart shows the *extremely important* and *very important* responses.

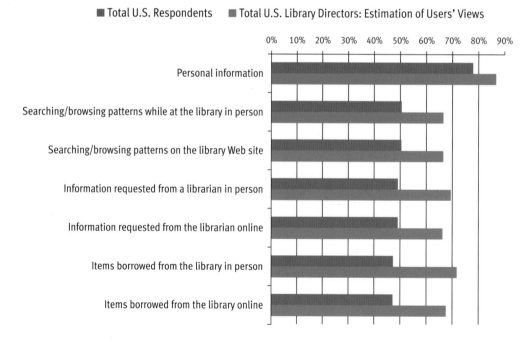

Source: *Sharing, Privacy and Trust in Our Networked World*, OCLC, 2007, questions 1076 and 1166.

66%
of the U.S. general public feel that **a policy on privacy on a library Web site is extremely or very important.**

Many libraries do not have a specific privacy policy posted on their Web sites.

Librarians' Responsibility to Keep Users' Information Private

As a librarian, what is your responsibility, if any,
for keeping users' library usage information private?

Important   Law   Library technology—safeguard information   Library/ALA policy   None

Not sure   Privacy Act   **Professional responsibility**

Release information for safety reasons only   State law   Usage information—internal use

Usage information—not retained   User confidentiality   User trust   Users don't care   Users' rights

Source: *Sharing, Privacy and Trust in Our Networked World*, OCLC, 2007, question 1175.

Over 400 comments from librarians were categorized and are presented in the tag cloud above.

Most librarians indicated that their reason for keeping library usage information private was one of *professional responsibility*. Responses related to library policy and law were also important to respondents.

Professional responsibility, as a term, often refers to specific codes written into the by-laws or ethical canons of professional groups. The American Library Association (ALA) Code of Ethics provides important guidelines to members. Article 3 of the ALA Code of Ethics relates to privacy as a professional value:

> *We protect each library user's right to privacy and confidentiality with respect to information sought or received and resources consulted, borrowed, acquired or transmitted.*

A small number of library directors (0.5%) specifically noted users' rights. A few librarians indicated that they were not sure about their responsibility for keeping users' library information private (0.5%).

All states in the U.S. have statutes or opinions concerning the confidentiality of library information.

All interactions in the library are expected to be confidential.

55-year-old librarian from
the United States

Source: *Sharing, Privacy and Trust in Our Networked World*, OCLC, 2007, question 1162,
"Why do you think that subjects your patrons have searched on the Internet are (private, very private or extremely private)?"

Two-thirds (66%) of U.S. respondents feel that having a privacy policy on a library Web site is *extremely* or *very important*. Yet, when U.S. respondents register on social networking, social media, commercial and/or library Web sites, approximately 40% or less *always* or *often* review these policies; just 28% check the privacy policy on library Web sites.

Frequency of Reviewing Privacy Policies

In general, when using [social networking, social media, commercial and/or library Web sites], how frequently do you review the Web site's privacy policy before registering?

Base: Respondents who have used a social networking, social media, commercial and/or library Web site.

Note: The chart shows the *always* and *often* responses. Librarians were not asked about library sites for this question.

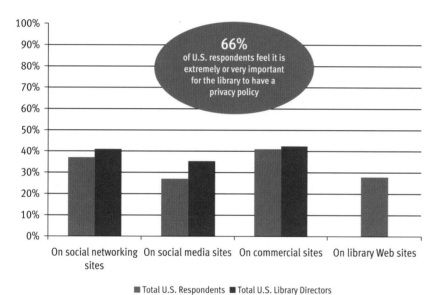

■ Total U.S. Respondents ■ Total U.S. Library Directors

Source: *Sharing, Privacy and Trust in Our Networked World,* OCLC, 2007, questions 966, 1006, 1051 and 1081.

28%
of U.S. respondents always or often **review privacy policies** *before registering on a library's Web site.*

Privacy Trade-Offs

While the majority of library users do not rate the privacy of their library activities as *extremely* or *very important*, when asked directly about sharing library information, their views were more strict.

Less than 20% of U.S. respondents indicate that they would be willing to share their library activities of searching/browsing patterns, questions asked of a librarian online, or the items they borrowed from the library. Library directors fairly closely estimated user views on sharing their library activities.

Library Information Trade-Off

For each of the following types of information you may have provided at the library, please indicate if you would be willing to share your contact information.

For each of the following types of information that can be provided at the library, please indicate which of the following you think your users would be willing to share for their contact information.

Activities: Searching/browsing activities from the library Web site or resources, questions asked of a librarian online, and items borrowed from the library.

Base: For the U.S. respondents, those who have used a library in person or online.

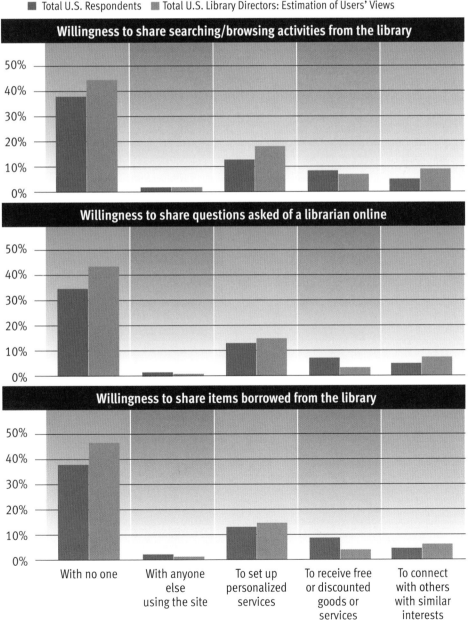

Source: *Sharing, Privacy and Trust in Our Networked World*, OCLC, 2007, questions 1091 and 1171.

Summary

In many ways, the online activities and preferences of U.S. library directors parallel those of the users they serve. Library directors are using most Internet services at levels equal to or greater than their users. U.S. library directors are more tenured and, in many areas such as Web searching and e-commerce, are more active than their users. They are as much a part of the Web culture as the users they serve.

Yet, several distinctions are worth noting. Overall, librarians have notably greater concerns about Internet privacy and Internet security. They feel that the Web is less safe, less private and less trustworthy than the general public. And library directors are more likely to use online social spaces for work than for relationship building or fun.

While users want libraries to keep their information private, the majority do not rate most library services as very private. About a quarter of U.S. respondents are unsure if libraries have rules about how their personal information will be used. The majority do not read library privacy policies. Library directors have a strong sense of professional responsibility to keep their users' information private.

These attitudinal differences may explain the hesitancy of many librarians to enter into social networking when compared to other Internet activities that they embraced and often pioneered. As a group, librarians are using social spaces measurably less than their communities.

Libraries and Social Networking

"To continue to be vital to society, libraries must adopt new objectives. In particular, they must strive to participate with individuals in their cultural activities; passive, depersonalized service is no longer enough."

—Frederick Kilgour, "Evolving, Computerizing, Personalizing," in *American Libraries*, February 1972

6%

of the total general public would be extremely or very likely **to describe their collection on a library social site.**

5%

would share photos/videos *on a library social site.*

The general public respondents surveyed do not currently see a role for libraries in their new social networked world.

The general public respondents do not see a role for libraries in constructing social sites, and most would not be very likely to contribute content, self-publish or join discussion groups if a library were to offer these services. Interest in participating in activities on a library-hosted social networking site was low among respondents. Most activities evaluated garnered the interest of less than 10% of the total general public who indicated they would be either *extremely* or *very likely* to participate.

This general level of disinterest held very constant across countries surveyed. French respondents would be the most likely to use library social networking services, although the likelihood level was still quite low.

Of most interest to respondents was the ability to be notified of new items of interest. Again, French respondents would be the most likely to use this service, at roughly a quarter of respondents.

In large part, this lack of interest or excitement may be a result of relatively few examples of library "social" services. For respondents who saw a social networking role for libraries, "book clubs" was their top recommendation.

Like the general public, U.S. library directors do not see a role for social networking in libraries. Just 14% see it as the library's role to build social networking sites for their communities. A few pioneers see some potential. And a few libraries are beginning to participate in social networking in a variety of ways and for different purposes. This chapter concludes with a few examples.

Participating in Library-Hosted Social Networking Activities
by Country

How likely would you be to participate in each of the following activities on a social networking/community site if built by your library?

Base: Respondents who have used a library in person or online.

Note: The chart shows the *extremely likely* and *very likely* responses.

■ Total General Public ■ Canada ■ United States ■ Japan ■ France ■ Germany ■ United Kingdom

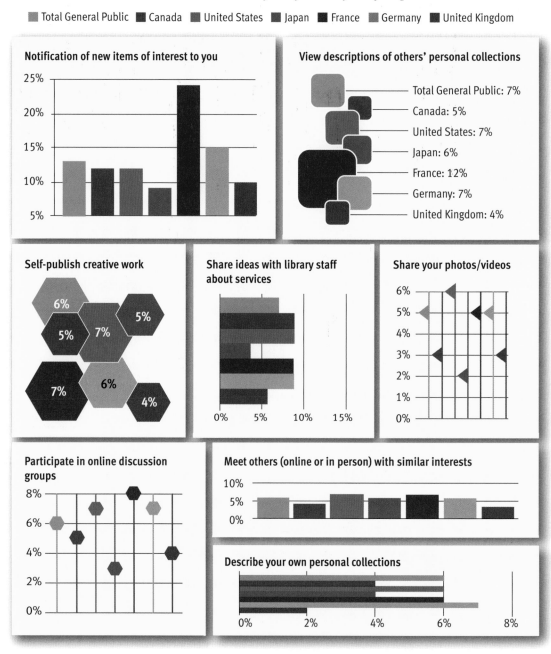

Library directors were also asked to predict how likely the public would be to participate in library-hosted social networking activities. Their estimations are labeled as "Total U.S. Library Directors: Estimation of Users' Views" when presented in the chart.

Although at relatively low levels, library directors felt the public would be very likely to participate in most activities at a higher rate than the U.S. general public actually reported. About twice as many library directors felt the public would be *extremely* or *very likely* to get notification of new items that are of interest and to share ideas with the library staff about services. Both of these notification activities are offered by most traditional Internet services and are closely related to customer service.

While library directors overestimated the public's interest in notification services, they fairly accurately estimated the public's low appetite for sharing and publication services—services offered by social networking and social media sites.

Participating in Library-Hosted Social Networking Activities
By U.S. General Public and Library Directors' Estimation of Users' Views

How likely would you be to participate in each of the following activities on a social networking/community site if built by your library?

How likely do you feel the public would be to participate in each of the following activities on a social networking/community site if built by your library?

Base: Respondents who have used a library in person or online.

Note: The chart shows the *extremely likely* and *very likely* responses.

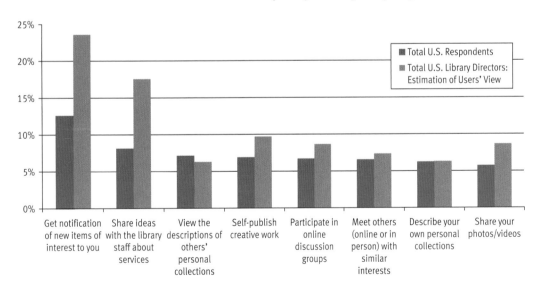

Source: *Sharing, Privacy and Trust in Our Networked World*, OCLC, 2007, questions 1096 and 1206.

When the general public respondents were asked if they thought it was the role of the library to build social networking sites for their community, responses were split between "no" and "not sure."

Just 13% of total general public respondents indicated "yes," it should be the role of the library to build a social networking site for its community.

Although the use of social networking is highest among respondents in the U.S. across all countries surveyed (37% vs. 28% of total general public), they were least likely (9%) to say "yes" that building these spaces is the library's role, and most likely (57%) to say "no."

German respondents were most likely, at 22%, to see a role for libraries and social networking. The majority of respondents in Japan were unsure about the role of libraries and social networking.

At

22%,

German respondents were most likely to say

libraries should build social networking sites

for their communities.

Role of the Library to Build a Social Site
By Country

Do you think it should be the library's role to build
social networking sites for your community?

Base: Respondents who have used a library in person or online.

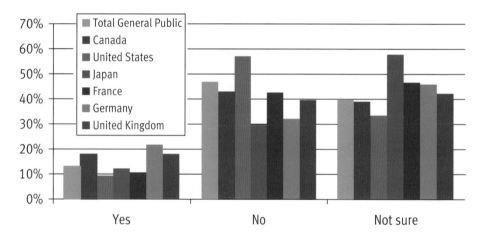

Source: *Sharing, Privacy and Trust in Our Networked World*, OCLC, 2007, question 1100.

The library is there to be
a place where you can borrow books
and sometimes use computers, not for people's social lives.

**15-year-old from the
United Kingdom**

Source: *Sharing, Privacy and Trust in Our Networked World*, OCLC, 2007, question 1113, "Why do you think that it should not be the library's role to build social networking sites in your community?"

Views across U.S. age groups were consistent with survey totals. The majority of U.S. respondents of all ages do not see a role for social networking sites in libraries.

Although slightly more positive than the U.S. general public, less than 20% of U.S. library directors see a role for social networks in libraries. Younger library directors are only slightly more likely than their age 50+ colleagues to suggest that it is the library's role.

Role of the Library to Build a Social Site
By U.S. Library Directors and U.S. General Public

Do you think it should be the library's role to build
social networking sites for your community?

Base: For U.S. respondents, those who have used a library in person or online.

There should definately **be chatrooms where you can discuss anything, roleplay, or simply have a random conversation,** *not just for discussing books or specific topics.*

14-year-old from Canada

Source: *Sharing, Privacy and Trust in Our Networked World*, OCLC, 2007, question 1112, "Please describe the top two most interesting activities that could be included in a library's social networking/community site."

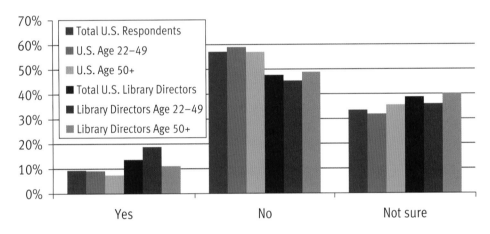

Source: *Sharing, Privacy and Trust in Our Networked World*, OCLC, 2007, questions 1100 and 1210.

Why social networking is *not* the library's role

The total general public and U.S. library directors surveyed do not currently see a role for libraries in building social networking spaces. Both groups believe that the library is for learning/information and do not see the connection with social networking and libraries. The general public saw social networks as personal/individual spaces and noted concerns about the library not knowing its community and issues of the library potentially exercising too much control. Librarians feel there are enough social networking sites existing already. Not unexpectedly, librarians also voice concerns about funding and resources.

The total general public

Why don't you think it should be the library's role to build social networking sites for your community?
Base: Respondents who do not think it should be the role of the library to build a social networking site.

Abuse of information   Could be too controlled   Don't care/no opinion   Enough social networking sites exist already
Interaction should happen in person   Libraries do enough already   Library does not have the equipment/skills   Library does not know its community
Library is a physical place   **Library is for learning/information**
Library is not for socializing   Library not used   Limited/no funding   n/a
No connection between libraries and social networking   No need/interest   No time/resources
Not the role of the library   Other organizations should build, but library could offer   Other organizations should do it
Other priorities for tax dollars   Personal/individual matter   Potential legal issues   Privacy concerns
Security issues   Should be city hall/community obligation   Valid for public but not academic libraries
Would add more burden to the library   Would be nice but not the library's role

Source: *Sharing, Privacy and Trust in Our Networked World*, OCLC, 2007, question 1113.

- Library is for learning/information (25%)
- Not the role of the library/librarian (16%)
- Personal/individual matter (7%)
- Library is not for socializing (7%)
- Don't care/no opinion (7%)

U.S. Library Directors

Why don't you think it should be the library's role to build social networking sites for your community?
Base: Library directors who do not think it should be the role of the library to build a social networking site.

Abuse of information   Against library's policies   **Enough social networking sites exist already**
Library is for learning/information   Library provides means to access existing sites
Library sponsors book clubs   Limited/no funding   No need/interest   No time/resources
Not the role of the library   Other organizations should do this
Other priorities for tax dollars   Personal/individual matter   Potential legal issues   Privacy concerns
Tried and didn't work   Valid for public but not academic libraries   Valid for public or larger academic libraries

Source: *Sharing, Privacy and Trust in Our Networked World*, OCLC, 2007, question 1212.

- Not the role of the library/librarian (30%)
- Enough social networking sites exist already (16%)
- Library is for learning/information (14%)
- No time/resources (9%)

Top social networking services a library could provide

Book clubs were the social services that the majority of the total general public surveyed would like to see their libraries adopt. Activities around books were cited in 17% of suggestions. As of September 2007, MySpace has over 195 groups with "book club" in the name.

U.S. librarians view potential opportunities for using social networking very similarly to the general public and view book clubs as the service with the highest potential.

The total general public

Please describe the top two most interesting activities that could be included
in a library's social networking/community site.
Base: Respondents who think it should be the role of the library to build a social networking site.

Book clubs Book reviews/recommendations Book swap/sale Book/article lists
Circulation **Community events** **Discussion groups**
Education services Hobbies Homework help Internet sites Library collection Library information
Library services Local information Meeting people Physical library suggestions Research Searching
Sharing interests Sharing music/videos/photos Support groups Topic information Writing Youth activities

Source: *Sharing, Privacy and Trust in Our Networked World*, OCLC, 2007, question 1112.

- Book clubs (17%)
- Discussion groups (13%)

U.S. Library Directors

Please describe the top two most interesting activities that could be included
in a library's social networking/community site.
Base: Library directors who think it should be the role of the library to build a social networking site.

Blog/wiki **Book clubs** Book recommendations **Book reviews**
Community events Discussion groups Education services
Hobbies **Library services** Local information Reading lists/tags Research
Sharing interests **Support groups** **Writing** Youth activities

Source: *Sharing, Privacy and Trust in Our Networked World*, OCLC, 2007, question 1211.

- Book clubs (15%)
- Community events (15%)

How a Few Pioneering Libraries are Using Social Networking

While nearly half (48%) of U.S. library directors feel it is not the libraries' role to create social networking sites and while most are not optimistic about users' likelihood to participate in social networking activities, a few libraries are experimenting with and piloting social networking and social media projects. Several of these early projects are content-focused, utilizing social media tools. Librarians are using del.icio.us tags to provide more intuitive links into their online catalogs. Some libraries are posting instructional and "day-in-the-life" videos to YouTube. And, as we identified earlier in the report, librarians are blogging. As of September 2007, Technorati, a catalog of Web site blogs, listed 10,004 blogs about "library" or "librarian."

Several libraries are also experimenting with MySpace, Facebook and other social networking sites. Social networking tools are providing libraries and museums with new opportunities to engage users and establish interactive Web communities. These library social networks are starting ongoing, online conversations—often an online forum for community building. Discussions among these Web audiences involve sharing materials, programs and exhibits and provide users with opportunities to learn about the library's online and physical building programs. A few examples follow:

There are **10,004** *blogs about libraries or librarians.*

Technorati, September 2007

The Social Catalog: Ann Arbor District Library—SOPAC

Using open-source code from Drupal, the Ann Arbor District Library (Ann Arbor, Michigan, U.S.) has added personal tagging, ratings and reviews to its online public access catalog. The library revamped its Web site to create a highly personalized space where users can make comments, post blog entries and sign up for RSS feeds, including feeds for holds and checkouts.

www.flickr.com/photos/jblyberg/sets/72157594489472951/
www.aadl.org/catalog

My Exhibits: Brooklyn Museum—Building an online community with social networking tools

Using BlipTV, podcasts, Flickr and MySpace, the Brooklyn Museum (Brooklyn, New York, U.S.) provided interactive exhibit experiences online to extend its reach and advance its mission. In one project, the online community established the first archive of local street artists by uploading digital images to the museum. In another, the museum created an online gallery of drawings using a virtual spray can, marker, pencil and pen. The museum discovered that social software furthers the goals of both the exhibition and institution and are as valuable as any wall label or text panel, as noted in a paper by Nicole J. Caruth and Shelley Bernstein at Museums and the Web 2007.

www.flickr.com/groups/brooklynmuseum/discuss/72157594192198447/
www.flickr.com/groups/visualstory/discuss/72157594356288683

Open Library: University of Kentucky— Reaching users with MySpace

The University of Kentucky Libraries (Lexington, Kentucky, U.S.) work hard to reach students in a variety of ways: open houses, flyers, campus or community events. Today that effort includes a profile on MySpace, and the library is seeing a steady growth in the number of students who become "friends" of the library online. The library's online profile includes contact information, tips for using the library and other items of interest, such as advice for new students. The library also has included sketches of the future Information Commons, a collection of banners on display in the library and a fun photo album of librarians on vacation. The library says that as students increasingly use these social networks—some log on and remain there all day—having a library presence makes sense. It is a high visibility arena and participation is cheap and easy, according to an article in the *Kentucky Librarian,* Fall 2006 issue.

http://www.myspace.com/uklibraries

Teen Space: Denver Public Library—Helping teens overcome library anxiety

The library is not always seen as the "cool" place to be for teenagers. But the Denver Public Library (DPL) (Denver, Colorado, U.S.) is giving this demographic a new idea of what the library is by using social networking tools that resonate with teens. When a library survey showed that teens' favorite Web site was MySpace, DPL established a hip profile and began promoting not only library services but fun activities for teens. These activities include a YouTube video contest on "How I Have Fun at the Library" (the winner gets an MP3 player); user-contributed reviews (submissions earn chances to win an iPod Shuffle); a bookmark design contest for the summer reading program; and a Flickr account for teen photos. Traffic to the library's teen Web site has increased 41% since the launch of its MySpace account.

www.myspace.com/denver_evolver

Social Day: St. Joseph County Public Library— "Day-in-the-life" video

Library staffers Dale Kerkman, Bob Lewandowski, Michael Stephens and Adam Tarwacki created a "day-in-the-life" video set to the tune of Madonna's "Ray of Light" for the library's staff in-service day at the St. Joseph County Public Library (South Bend, Indiana, U.S.). The video details a day in the life of a thriving public library system. As of September 2007, the video had garnered more than 34,600 views on YouTube and more than 77 links to the video on other blogs, according to a search on Technorati.

www.youtube.com/watch?v=vrtYdFV_Eak

Social PA System: Vancouver and Niagara-On-The-Lake Libraries—Promoting to friends

The Vancouver (British Columbia, Canada) and Niagara-On-The-Lake (Ontario, Canada) public libraries are using MySpace to promote events, provide links into their catalogs and other systems, and connect with users through announcements, contact information and public messages.

www.myspace.com/vancouverpubliclibrary
www.myspace.com/notlpl

Virtual Tour: British Library's YouTube video

The British Library (London, U.K.) hired Tim Campbell, winner of the BBC's *The Apprentice,* to host an Internet video explaining what is offered to visitors and information seekers. The video, *From Bones to Bytes,* goes through the specialized materials available at the library and on its Web site, including special collections, business resources and user classes. The library posted the video to YouTube and hosts it on its own site.

www.youtube.com/watch?v=7O_oyuAY2tE

SecondLibrary: Info Island

The Alliance Library System (East Peoria, Illinois, U.S.) and OPAL (Online Programming for All Libraries, www.opal-online.org/) have teamed up to create a library-specific space in the virtual world of Second Life. Their mission is to extend current programs into the online virtual world. Info Island is the name of the area in Second Life they have devoted to their projects, which include a genealogy research center, a library gallery, a performance center, "Mystery Manor," a science center and a science fiction/fantasy center.

Blog: http://infoisland.org
SLURL: secondlife://Info%20Island/89/122/33

2.0-It-Your-Self: Library 2.0 Ning Space

Ning (www.ning.com) is a service that provides features and tools that allow users to create their own social networks. Libraries are among the many organizations using these new social software tools. For example, the Library 2.0 Ning page, created by Bill Drew, librarian at Tompkins-Cortland Community College Library (Dryden, New York, U.S.) allows librarians interested in discussing "2.0" trends in library and information services to share group blog posts, photos, videos and forum discussions. The site also provides space to introduce oneself as a new member, and post resources, announcements and conference information. Previous discussions can be found via full-text search or through tags. As of September 2007, the Library 2.0 Ning space supports 2,282 members and 13 groups of 20 or more people, and was the third Google listing for the search term "library 2.0."

http://library20.ning.com

Beyond the Numbers

"... I followed about 50 student blogs for a year and set up alerts on terms such as 'assignment,' 'paper,' 'library' and 'class.'... Throughout the day I would check in and see if any of the students posted something matching my criteria.... Students would frequently post, 'I have to read this book or article,' 'I need to get going on this assignment or paper' and essentially chronicle their lives.... I saw this as a natural extension of library outreach and an open invitation for interaction.

"The benefit that I saw was in the opportunity to help students before they hit a point of frustration.... The objective was to be able to initiate contact early on, instead of waiting for them to approach the reference desk the day before an assignment was due. This is a chance to be preemptive."

—Brian Mathews, Information Services Librarian,
Georgia Institute of Technology, 2007

In the early adopter stages of technology and media, it is difficult to envision long-term possibilities from current statistics. It was not easy for most to forecast, for example, that computer-based instant messaging (IM) would become a communication method used by over half the population when the first "tiny little messages" began moving back-and-forth between a handful of users. Even after the invention of wikis, very few would have predicted the phenomenon that is now Wikipedia.

In this section, we explore the perspectives of thought leaders and industry experts, the early forecasters of what the future might hold for social networking and the implications for privacy and library policies and practice. These experts represent a wide variety of experiences and backgrounds. Some have used networked communities for many years, and a few are new to social spaces. Many of their observations and opinions support the findings from the survey results and provide perspective to the numbers.

We spoke with 14 professionals in the information technology landscape. The goal was to delve more deeply into the personalities, realities and possibilities of these social spaces. What follows are excerpts from these in-depth individual interviews.

Libraries in the Culture—Early Involvement

We asked the interviewees about their personal involvement with social networking tools and with new media. In most cases, their reasons for getting into social networking were largely personal. Most of the early experiences involved instant messaging and gaming, and a few experts started personal blogs in their spare time before getting involved professionally.

Houghton-Jan: In terms of what I have experience with in social networking, I've been using IM since 1995, so that's probably my biggest area of personal knowledge. I've been focusing on social networking as something to use in libraries for about the last two years and working with the big names in the field to get the word out about what these tools are, that they're free for the most part, and how libraries can use them to reach out to patrons in an online environment. Usually these patrons are those that we will not see in the brick and mortar library, so getting to them online is usually the only way to get to them.

Morin: In many ways, these online social networks have always been there for me, starting with e-mails and listservs, but they grow with the tools. And as the tools have grown a lot lately, the importance of these social networks has been growing fast, too. I think it is part of the appeal of these social networks that they do not represent a revolution but mesh with people's habits. It certainly was part of the appeal for me: I didn't feel I was stepping into something radically new; I felt, rather, like I was using a new cool tool, adding it to the range of stuff I was using already, and then another, and another.

Mathews: For me, the social Web started back in 1995 with America Online. Not only did AOL provide Internet access, but also chat rooms, message board forums, games, events, classes and instant messaging. In this sense, the Web has always been social and interactive for me. However, in the more contemporary 2.0 mindset, it began with LiveJournal in 2001. Many of my friends from college had taken jobs all across the country. Using LiveJournal, a personal blogging Web site, we could all stay connected. It was a way to know what was going on in people's lives and an outlet for self-expression.

Henry Bankhead is currently a principal librarian with the Los Gatos Public Library in California where he is developing a library blog and IM reference services. He recently left Santa Clara County Library Administration where he helped use the library blog to market library programs and electronic resources. There he was part of a committee developing a Learning 2.0 initiative for Santa Clara County Library. He was also responsible for developing, maintaining and troubleshooting the library's electronic resources. Bankhead has an MLS from San Jose State University, an MFA from San Francisco Art Institute and a BA from Stanford.

66 Our users know that we are good at doing books. But I think that they would be surprised to know about the other various electronic resources that we have available.... My conjecture would be that we would only improve by raising awareness of what we can do for people by making ourselves more visible on the Web, in general. 99

46%
2007

16%
2005

blog growth in the last 18 months

Source: Compares data from the U.S., Canada and the U.K. from the OCLC 2005 report, *Perceptions of Libraries and Information Resources* and the 2007 report, *Sharing, Privacy and Trust in Our Networked World.*

Krajewski: Let's say I've been using the online environment for about two years, but the question is tricky.

Wikipedia is quite old now. Web 2.0 tools were created during the 1990s, so that some cynical people can claim that there is no novelty left in it.

As for social networking tools, strictly speaking, I would say I've used it for the past six months, because I don't really like those tools where you lose a lot of time.

In libraries, I've participated in social networking via blogs, and through the community created on "ning.com." I've also joined forums on Second Life's Info Island.

Kelly: If e-mail is a social networking tool, then I've been using e-mail for about 25 years. I've been using social networking tools such as Facebook for about two years. I've participated in Facebook, Flickr, Ning, MySpace, etc., during the last year.

Hoffman Gola: Personally I do use quite of bit of social tools; I am actually a younger librarian. I have only had my MLS for about two years now. So I was well-involved with MySpace and IM chat tools with my own friends personally for the last five years. College was all about using IM, instant messaging. My friends and I don't e-mail each other as much as I do with work. I like the statement: "E-mail is for old people."

Other than using the IM, using text messaging, being a social Internet browser, responding to other people's blogs online, I love using social tools like Flickr and del.icio.us. I love looking at what other people are tagging.

Bankhead: I think one of the foundations of social networking is kind of the IM piece, so I've been familiar with that and using instant messaging probably since 1999. But as far as the more diverse Web services that are available, like Flickr and del.icio.us and other innovative tools, I have been only using them for the past couple of years.

Keith Enright, Esq., CIPP/G is Senior Attorney and Director of Enterprise Information Policy, Limited Brands, Inc. (LBI). He oversees legal and policy compliance of customer data usage for LBI's Fortune 500 family of fashion and personal care brands. A frequent speaker at leading industry events, Enright has often been quoted in the media regarding privacy and security issues. He has authored and contributed to a number of publications dealing with business and legal aspects of privacy and information management and was recently named to the charter Advisory Board of the *Privacy Advisor,* the leading periodical for privacy professionals, published by the International Association of Privacy Professionals. Enright holds the Certified Information Privacy Professional/Government (CIPP/G) certification. He has previously served as the Chair of the Privacy Working Group of Computer Professionals for Social Responsibility and has served on a number of American Bar Association committees relating to privacy and related legal issues. Disclaimer: None of the comments made by Keith Enright constitute legal advice, nor do they reflect the opinions of Limited Brands.

❝... it could be that libraries provide the only mechanism whereby large populations of people would even have the opportunity to interact with social networks—which would otherwise be entirely closed to them.❞

Fox: I dabbled a bit in the early days of MOOs [MOO = MUD Object Oriented; MUD = Multi-User Dungeon], when it was primarily text-based online worlds. My friends and I really saw them as an extension of our video games. But generally you were playing or interacting just with the computer, not other individuals. It's been the more recent Web-based applications that I've used more because of the advantages of connecting with other people and benefiting from their knowledge, advice and resources.

I must confess my last two close friends who got married met their significant others on Match.com—an early rendition of social networking—and my college-aged brothers don't send e-mail to the family much any more but do update their Facebook and MySpace profiles, so I have to go there if I want to know what they are up to. But besides the pure networking sites, I also got into other social software tools such as del.icio.us for shared bookmarks, Connotea for more academic bookmarking and Flickr for photos.

del.icio.us started purely as a personal need—I was working two jobs, at each of which I had my desktop computer and worked on a Reference Desk computer, plus teaching courses and library instruction across campus, plus using my computer at home. Finding a way to store my bookmarks remotely and access them from anywhere was a huge timesaver. And then I began to notice what other people had bookmarked, and see the possibilities for sharing lists, and it took off from there.

Enright: I've been involved with MySpace ... probably since its inception, out of intellectual curiosity. I've interacted with MySpace in two capacities: One, just out of curiosity to see who, in my age range [uses it]. I'm 32 years old and I think I'm on the outside edge of early adopters. They're [MySpace users are] typically much younger. So I was curious how many people that I went to high school with would actually be there and there were a handful of them. Periodically I log into that account, once a month or once every two months to see if anything interesting has happened there.

Wittmann: I have had access to the Internet since 1994. A few years prior to that, since around 1992, I used Deutsche Telekom's online service, interactive videotext (BTX), and at that time I was already participating in discussion forums as well. The

10% of the general public have used online dating sites.

Source: *Sharing, Privacy and Trust in Our Networked World*, OCLC, 2007, question 530.

Meredith Farkas is the Distance Learning Librarian at Norwich University in Vermont. In this position, she frequently has the opportunity to develop social software applications to connect with her library's users. She is the author of the monthly "Technology in Practice" column in *American Libraries* and of the blog *Information Wants To Be Free*. She is the creator and administrator of *Library Success: A Best Practices Wiki*. In March 2006, Farkas was named a Mover and Shaker by *Library Journal* for her innovative use of social software to serve the profession. In 2007, her book, *Social Software in Libraries: Building Collaboration, Communication and Community Online,* was published by Information Today.

   ❝ *I also see us having an important role in going where our patrons are; providing services inside of the tools that our patrons are already using like instant messaging, MySpace and Facebook.* ❞

reason for starting with BTX was online banking, but very quickly I began using it for other purposes, and even used it for discussion forums, too. As soon as I had access to the Internet, I used it amongst others for Usenet news, an early form of social networking.

I have played around with social networking in the newer sense (blogs, wikis, etc.) in more recent years, at least since 2002.

Powell: I'm defining social networking tools as including wikis, blogs, Flickr, Slideshare, community tools such as Facebook, and 3-D virtual worlds such as Second Life. I'm excluding e-mail mailing lists and Google groups.

I've used the online environment since about 1984 (such as it was then). More importantly, I've used it since the start of the Web. This includes significant use of e-mail mailing lists.

I've used social networking tools (wikis, blogs, Flickr, Slideshare, community tools such as Facebook, and 3-D virtual worlds such as Second Life) for about two years (possibly a little longer).

Vaidhyanathan: My expertise is in copyright and the ways that it affects digital communication and the way that digital communication affects copyright. So, about 15 years ago, I got very interested in the potential for electronic distribution, and copyright was an intimate part of that. So I started engaging in quite a few conversations and monitoring a lot of what was going on in terms of the almost idealistic perceptions of what might emerge from digital communication. And I've been fairly involved with all of the permutations since.

I have used social networking sites—primarily Facebook. I have used peer-to-peer file sharing. I have used e-mail. I have used the Web. I blog. I have contributed to Wikipedia. I have contributed to other wikis. I'm fostering a wiki in a class I'm teaching in the spring. I use Skype—online telephony and voice-over Internet protocol—I use instant messaging. I use online repository as a scholarship. I've done just about everything you can think of. I've posted videos on YouTube. I've watched thousands of videos on YouTube and on Google Video.

Megan Fox is the Web & Electronic Resources Librarian for the Simmons College Library. She manages the Library's Web site, negotiates contracts and subscriptions for online research databases, and assists the Public Services department with instruction, faculty outreach and marketing library services. Fox completed a BA in History and Literature from Trinity College in 1992. She received her MA in Literature from Boston College in 1994 and her MLS in Library and Information Science from Simmons in 1998. At Simmons, Fox also teaches graduate and continuing education courses for the Graduate School of Library & Information Science. Her specialties include online resources, business information and mobile technologies.

“ ... our average patron doesn't care that much about how libraries technically might be able to push privacy boundaries, such as tracking circulation records. They are willing to let the library keep a list of all the books they ever checked out, because the trade-off of letting go of a bit of privacy is worth it to be able to look back at a comprehensive list.... ”

Personal to Professional ...
the Lines Begin to Blur

After spending time in social networking spaces out of personal interest and need, most of our interviewees began to identify how these social technologies might overlap with their professional lives. Several of the experts have expanded their personal experience with social networking and created applications to collaborate and reach students and library users.

Mathews: While I was using LiveJournal to talk with my friends, I noticed several group blogs dedicated to colleges and universities. Current students and alumni used these forums to discuss sports, classes, homework, social events and other school-related topics. As I dug a little deeper, I found conversations about libraries. It was fascinating to read the problems, frustrations and misunderstandings they encountered not only with libraries, but the college experience in general.

This was an awakening because it allowed me to see beyond traditional assessment tools, such as focus groups and surveys, with their built-in limitations. Social networking Web sites allowed to me enter unobtrusively into the patron consciousness—to discover how they felt about the library, what services they actually used and their unfilled needs. Social networks also opened the door for a less formal method of interaction. At first I created a second account, designed to be my "professional" librarian identity, which I would use to communicate directly with students. However, I found that students responded better to my personal account because it was more authentic. They preferred a genuine member of the community, rather than a fabricated manifestation—rather than someone trying to fit in. The lesson learned was "be yourself" instead that who you think patrons want you to be.

Houghton-Jan: Using something like Skype to provide reference via voice online would be one example of a technology from my personal life that also has applications in my professional life. There are a couple of academic libraries—I think they're in Australia—who are doing that. Also providing services like text messaging, (SMS) and there are about a dozen libraries that are doing that right now in the U.S.

Christina Hoffman Gola is currently the Coordinator for Undergraduate Instruction and Outreach at Texas A&M University in College Station. She received her MSLS from the University of North Texas, School of Library and Information Sciences in December 2004. She provides outreach, instruction and specialized reference services to undergraduates across campus using a variety of social tools including an undergraduate blog, chat services and a Facebook account, and is currently working on additional virtual spaces to interact with students. Hoffman Gola is also interested in studying technology in the classroom and effectively teaching information literacy through the use of technology.

❝ I think, as librarians, we have a choice to make; we can ... continue to exist as we do today or we can choose to play a major role in social software and really learn a lot more about our users than [we've] ever been able to figure out before. ❞

Instant Messaging

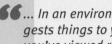

Source: *Sharing, Privacy and Trust in Our Networked World,* OCLC, 2007, question 530.

and elsewhere. The user sends a text message and it turns into an e-mail. The librarian answers via e-mail and it turns back into a text message. That's pretty exciting.

A few libraries have used blogs to present information that isn't like the traditional blog that you would think of. Libraries have used blogs to create book lists, to create recommended DVD lists and to create local history databases that are searchable.

Bankhead: I have been lobbying our administration to go to a more localized IM service, kind of based on the example of Marin County's Free Library.

I was using the Meebo Me widget, which allows you to put up a page with an IM box where the user doesn't even have to have an account; they just type into the box and say, "Hello, I have a question."

I am also really excited about del.icio.us as a way for libraries to organize their Web links. We spend a lot of time collecting free Web sites and putting them up on static home pages. It's pretty simple to use del.icio.us as an online Web service tool to add and subtract links instantly. San Mateo Library organizes their library-approved Web links on del.icio.us, and they organize them by Dewey right now. So if you go to del.icio.us/sanmateolibrary, you'll see tag bundles where they identify Web sites that are useful, like a tax Web site for IRS, and then tag it as "Taxes" and put it in the right Dewey classification.

Our library is also doing a MySpace. [Our] librarians are kind of excited about creating MySpace profiles for each library. [And] ... we are looking at mashups. One project we wanted to do is to try to build—using Google maps—[a mashup] to allow people to enter their ZIP code or street address to find the closest bookmobile stop.

Hoffman Gola: About nine months ago, we started using a blog in order to interact more with the students. We basically have an undergraduate blog where we make announcements and have helpful resources for them and when they're working on their assignments. It is a completely open commenting blog that students can comment back anonymously without having [to] log in to accounts or anything. The

Sarah Houghton-Jan has worked in libraries for a decade. She is currently the Information and Web Services Manager for the San Mateo County Library in Northern California. She also works as a consultant technology instructor for the Infopeople Project and serves on LITA's Top Technology Trends Committee. Houghton-Jan is the author of the blog *LibrarianInBlack.net,* the book *Technology Competencies and Training for Libraries* and a number of articles in library and technology publications. She also presents in-person and virtually at library conferences, workshops and events locally, nationally and internationally on libraries and technology topics.

“*... In an environment where Amazon tracks everything you buy and suggests things to you based on that, or even just based on the items that you've viewed recently, I think that people are more willing to give up a certain level of privacy if it means that they will get some kind of service in return.*”

other thing we have done is a couple of librarians [are] on Facebook. We are now [considering] ... whether we want to open a MySpace account for social software.

Powell: I have contributed [to wikis] on a fairly regular basis, particularly to the UKOLN wiki, the DCMI wiki, the Second Life Education wiki, Wikipedia (minimal contribution). I have contributed regularly to the eFoundations and ArtsPlace SL (Second Life) blogs. I have also read and commented on blogs in the area of Second Life, Identity Management, Libraries, the Semantic Web and Web 2.0.... I have been an active member [of Second Life] for about seven months, for personal and professional purposes. I have used it to host one national conference (for approximately 200 participants) and some smaller meetings (30 people), as well as for nonwork use.

We started using a blog ... to interact more with students.

Fox: The Reference staff at Simmons really saw the possibilities for how del.icio.us could be a great tool to allow the librarians and graduate assistants to work collaboratively and share our resources. We were all bookmarking sites for different areas, and this tool allowed us to put them all together and make our work much more effective. And then from there we started showing it in classes and coaching the students to use a del.icio.us folder to share their information for each of their projects—collaboratively identifying the best sources/best resources.

... Two years ago I was presenting at a conference where the planners came up with tags for the conference that we could use in del.icio.us, on a wiki, in Flickr. It was a great way to capture and share the collective wisdom and reaction of conference presenters and participants, again showing a strong professional application of social networking tools.

Usage of Social Media Sites

11% of the U.S. General Public use flickr, compared to 49% of Library Directors

Source: *Sharing, Privacy and Trust in Our Networked World,* OCLC, 2007, question 710. Base: Respondents who have used a social media site.

Brian Kelly is a national Web advisor to the U.K. higher and further education communities, and to the cultural heritage sector in England. Kelly works at UKOLN, a national centre of expertise in digital information management, located at the University of Bath. As a national advisor and Policy and Advice Team Leader, Kelly has an extensive list of publications and presentations (see www.ukoln.ac.uk/ukoln/staff/b.kelly/). He also maintains a blog at UK Web Focus (http://ukwebfocus.wordpress.com/).

66 *We will all have acceptable use policies [in the future] which address issues such as privacy, acceptable language and behaviour, etc. We will do this in order to clarify our policies and manage risks.* 99

Enright: I interact almost several times a week with things like LinkedIn and with several other blogs and other kinds of interactive communities that I think in the broadest sense are also social networks, but probably not what's typically captured in marketing statistics and research statistics, since we're talking about social networking, blog-like spaces.

Morin: I wrote an article for a peer-reviewed journal with a co-author using a wiki; I also used a wiki to design a Web site project with a group of people I didn't personally know. I tried out a few things like Ning and Facebook. I blogged and commented on other people's blogs. I got involved with a group of people I didn't know before: Americans living in France who blog. I put my personal library up on librarything.com and got into contact with a few people that way, too.

What I found striking is that these networks work best when you fit in well, i.e., they are not that good yet at taking care of people who are in the "long tail" of users. For instance, I grew up and live in France, and I'm 36; my high school (collège), my university, my former work, etc., do not exist in Facebook yet. My "regional" network in Facebook is just "France." Despite the buzz about the long tail, it seems to me there still exists a lot of subjects/people/regions, etc., about which you have trouble finding a way to hook up to other people through online social networks.

Wittmann: I use wikis for professional purposes. I run four wikis for different users, all in the field of libraries. I also use blogs, mostly blogs with library themes; I read and sometimes comment on them, but I don't run my own blog.

Trust and Privacy

We asked our interview subjects for their thoughts on trust and privacy issues in online, networked communities. Some of the perspectives revealed differences in levels of tolerances between generations, willingness to share information and even the definition of privacy.

Houghton-Jan: I think in an environment where Amazon tracks everything you buy and suggests things to you based on that, or even just based on the items that you've

Pascal Krajewski is Manager of Information Technology at his library. He is responsible for the ILS department at the Public Library of Toulouse (France), a position he has held since January 2007. Krajewski has a doctorate in Art Sciences, and an interest in library applications of social networking software.

❝ People have built their social networking without us, and we are knocking at their doors, begging to play with them …❞

viewed recently, I think that people are more willing to give up a certain level of privacy if it means that they will get some kind of service in return. Our catalog has something called "My Reading History" that will track what people read and keep a list of that in their accounts. Not only can they access that, but if the FBI wanted to, they could access it, too, I'm sure. And they love it; they want it. There are very few people who don't want it. Even when you explain, "This is now going to be kept online forever unless you get rid of it, so if law enforcement asks for it, we have to give it over," they say, "Why would I care? I don't do anything wrong. It doesn't matter to me." I don't think there's much thought about individual privacy anymore. It's like privacy's gone out the window for most library users. The staff still cares about it, but nobody else does.

I think the only exception to that would be the use of our public computers. It seems to me that people do care, for whatever reason, and they want to make sure that what they're viewing hasn't been tracked in any way and is being deleted. That one area, perhaps because it's more tangible and has been better publicized, is something people do care about.

The staff still cares about [privacy related to reading], but nobody else does.

Mathews: We're in a highly digitized society now and people have to assume that every e-mail they write, every Web site they visit, and every phone conversation they have is being tracked and stored somewhere by someone. So as far as privacy goes—there is none anymore. That said, social networking Web sites have done a great job of building in privacy features, so that if this is important to you, you have a lot of control. You can limit who views your information and dictate the level of interaction and openness you desire. But speaking generally, the current political administration

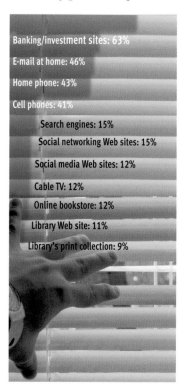

Privacy of Everyday Activities

By Total General Public

Note: *Extremely private* and *very private* responses.

Banking/investment sites: 63%

E-mail at home: 46%

Home phone: 43%

Cell phones: 41%

Search engines: 15%

Social networking Web sites: 15%

Social media Web sites: 12%

Cable TV: 12%

Online bookstore: 12%

Library Web site: 11%

Library's print collection: 9%

Source: *Sharing, Privacy and Trust in Our Networked World*, OCLC, 2007, question 926, "For each of the following, please rate how private, if at all, your activity is while using ...."

Brian Mathews is an information services librarian at the Georgia Institute of Technology. He is the subject liaison for mechanical engineering and computer science, and is the Coordinator for Distance Learning Library Support. Mathews is very involved with service assessment, social marketing and empathetic design. He frequently presents and publishes on social software, advertising and the culture of academic libraries. His blog is *The Ubiquitous Librarian* (http://theubiquitouslibrarian.typepad.com).

66 *Social networking Web sites allowed me to enter unobtrusively into the patron consciousness. To discover how they felt about the library, what services they actually used, and their unfilled needs. It also opened the door for a less formal method of interaction.* 99

Useful Rewards from Affinity Cards

Note: *Extremely private* and *very private* responses.

of the total general public feel that

affinity cards

provide rewards

that are

useful.

Source: *Sharing, Privacy and Trust in Our Networked World,* OCLC, 2007, question 1126, "Considering the reward/loyalty cards you use, please rate the degree to which you agree or disagree they provide rewards that are useful to you." Base: Respondents who have reward/loyalty cards.

has routinely demonstrated that privacy is not a priority, and since there has not been a large-scale outcry or protest, it seems that people just accept and assume that privacy is extinct.

In terms of libraries nationally, it seems that a lot of energy is spent discussing and protecting privacy, and ensuring that patrons follow our policies or learn the proper way to use the library, rather than concentrating on better licensing agreements, better access to information and more intuitive search tools. Perhaps this will balance out over the next decade or so? The rising generation seems more interested in access to information, rather than control of it.

Enright: I will point to a quote that I always found was really interesting on the subject. Bruce Schneier ... wrote a book called *Secrets and Lies*, about security. In his book he says, "People talk as if they don't want megadatabases tracking their every spending move, but they are willing to get a frequent-flyer affinity card and give all that data away for one thousandth of a free flight to Hawaii. If McDonald's offered three free Big Macs for a DNA sample, there would be lines around the block."

With something like libraries, I think that ... the same kind of model exists. If you ask 100 people with respect to the library, "Do you care that we are tracking X, Y and Z about your behavior when you make use of the library?" I would guess that at least 99% of those people would probably give you a very strong and impassioned "Yes, I do care. It's something that I take very seriously." But if you say, "Okay, if you wait in this line five people deep to the left, you can use the anonymous terminal where we won't be tracking what you're doing. Or if you want to sit down right now, we have 15 terminals over here on the right, but your records will be tracked and it will be associated with your name and it will be subject to subpoena by law enforcement," most people then, they're going to say, "Well, I'm not doing anything wrong anyway. I really don't want to wait in that line. I'm going to go ahead and do the thing on the right."

Fox: Our patrons tend to be very savvy about security. They don't give out access to their bank account or credit card information. They know about copyright and music

Nicolas Morin studied history at Bordeaux (France) and Bristol (U.K.), then Philosophy at the Sorbonne (Paris, France). He became a librarian in 2000. He was a systems librarian for Angers University Libraries until July 2007 and, in September 2007, he began teaching automation systems and Web site management at the French National LIS school (www.enssib.fr). Morin was among the very first French libloggers in early 2003. He currently blogs at www.nicolasmorin.com/blog/.

66 *... expectations have been lowered in recent years as far as privacy is concerned;... in a trade-off for better services. I think libraries should take that evolution into account and, while continuing to adhere to strong privacy policies, be less shy in asking for and using personal information from patrons to be able to provide better online services to them.* 99

pirating. But that's all very different from privacy. Our students seem less concerned about privacy—they are willing to sacrifice an element of personal privacy and control in return for the benefits they get or think they get by creating a login or otherwise revealing some of themselves.

I would say that our average patron doesn't care that much about how libraries technically might be able to push privacy boundaries, such as tracking circulation records. They are willing to let the library keep a list of all the books they have ever checked out, because the trade-off of letting go of a bit of privacy is worth it to be able to look back at a comprehensive list of what you checked out when you're trying to remember the author of that book you read two years ago. Our library science students are particularly attentive to this as a potentially controversial issue. The library science students are very well-versed in things like the USA Patriot Act and much more concerned about privacy and personal rights than your average students.

Sauers: [There is] a need for balance. Many say "I don't talk about my personal life on my blog," but then say "Here, go see pictures." I tend to be a very open person. I started my blog so my parents would stop asking me where I am this week. I did actually have the ten-second thought of "do I want to." It is that equation of what are you doing, and in what I do, social networking, at some level I am aware of what I'm giving up to do it. I enjoy it. I'm open on my blog.

Some [young people] don't realize what they're giving up, but should be made aware. Some of them don't realize what they're doing on MySpace. I'm not saying they shouldn't do it, but beware of what you're doing. When you go to look for a job, somebody's going to Google your name and find the pictures of the drunken party you had last Saturday night that you just put up on your MySpace account. Because all of this is archived somewhere. All of this is copied somewhere. And I think there needs to be an education at that level to at least make them aware of the privacy issues.

Vaidhyanathan: I don't sense that there is widespread concern [that certain information about them is being kept] among most users, and I anticipate that there

Internet Privacy
By Total General Public

Source: *Sharing, Privacy and Trust in Our Networked World*, OCLC, 2007, question 930, by total general public, "Generally, do you think that your personal information on the Internet is kept more private than, less private than, or the same as it was two years ago?"

Andy Powell is Head of Development at the Eduserv Foundation where he is responsible for specifying and delivering the Foundation's programme of internal research and standards-making activities and helping to oversee external grants. His primary areas of interest include: metadata, repositories and resource discovery; access and identity management; service architectures and Web 2.0; e-learning, e-portfolios and the use of 3-D virtual worlds such as Second Life in education. Powell was the principal technical architect of the JISC Information Environment. He has been active in the Dublin Core Metadata Initiative for a number of years. He is a member of the DC Advisory Board and was previously a member of the DC Usage Board and chair of the DC Architecture Working Group. Powell jointly authored the DCMI Abstract Model and several other Dublin Core technical specifications. More recently he jointly authored the DC Eprints Application Profile for the JISC. He was also a member of the Open Archives Initiative technical committee. Powell was previously an Assistant Director at UKOLN, University of Bath and before that he worked for the University of Bath Computing Services (BUCS).

66 *... libraries remain as highly trusted public bodies. I think that some patrons care (in the sense of being aware) that libraries keep records of personal information (others probably do not), but that almost all patrons currently trust libraries not to abuse that information.* **99**

won't be widespread concern among users about data retention ... until there is some high-profile event in which such personal information is used against somebody to harm somebody.

I do know that there has been a very helpful conversation over the past year, since MySpace really broke onto the news, about having conversations between parents and children about what is appropriate information to post in social networking spaces. I've participated in radio shows in which concerned parents were talking about what they see as the deep danger of social networking, and I kept trying to emphasize that every time a new communicative technology comes up, we have to have this conversation all over again. You have to tell people ... you have to generate norms. And some of the basic norms, especially when you're dealing with children here, involve limiting access, limiting personal information.

I think that privacy and data retention is the number one issue right now. User confidentiality. I think that that's an issue that's sort of focused by the acquisition of MySpace by News Corporation and focused by the data retention behavior of search engine companies like Google and Yahoo!. It's also a big concern as Microsoft shifts more of its applications to an online environment to mimic Google's position and movement.

Powell: I've had a significant number of spam e-mail sent in my name—as has everyone I should think. This was worrying when it first happened, but is now generally considered to be the "norm." I don't trust e-mail any less because of it— I'm just more wary about what I receive and check a little harder.

Wittmann: No, users do not care if the library keeps their records, as it [the library] does it now already anyway. Furthermore, it is presumably no longer an issue for the majority of users because of the practices of Google, Amazon, eBay and so on.

Farkas: To have a successful blog, you have to walk a fine line between self-disclosure and thinking about privacy and the image you are projecting. I have seen bloggers write things that I think are a little too personal and maybe something that

Michael Sauers is the Technology Innovation Librarian for the Nebraska Library Commission in Lincoln. For nine years prior to moving to Nebraska, he was the Internet Trainer for the Bibliographical Center for Research. He has been a public library trustee and a bookstore manager for a library friends group, and has worked for both the New York State Library and the New York State Assembly. He is also the webmaster for the Greece, New York Historical Society and for the science fiction/fantasy author L. E. Modesitt, Jr. Sauers is the author of eight books on technology for librarians and has written dozens of articles for various journals and magazines. In his spare time he reads about 130 books per year.

66 *I ... think when people go out on MySpace ... the library is probably one of the last things they're thinking of when they're sending messages back and forth or playing on the computer or whatever. But if the library can get into that space, we can change that perception. Yes, we are here.* 99

they'll regret having told thousands of people later on. But it is a personal decision that everyone makes. I know there are some people who won't even mention their spouse or personal life in any way online. I really like my blog to be somewhat personal and human, and really reflective of who I am. At the same time, I don't want it to be so personal that I'm saying things that could get me in trouble or might embarrass me later in life.

Morin: I think [users] care once they understand that we do keep records [on their personal information use]. But I also think there's a high level of trust in the library as an institution. They know, I think, that we won't sell their e-mails to spammers.

At the same time, I'm not quite sure they understand why we keep those records, since we don't seem to be using them (to provide personal recommendations, tailored interfaces, etc.).

I think that privacy and data retention is the number one issue right now.

Kelly: Many [library users] won't care [that the library keeps records of their personal information and reading behaviors]—although back in 1980 I came across one example which illustrated possible dangers. Back then in the U.K., the Yorkshire Ripper was believed to have a Sunderland accent. I worked at Sunderland Borough Council at the time, and the IT and Library staff were worried that police would request information on people who had borrowed books about Jack the Ripper. To avoid this happening, it was decided not to store the identities of people who had borrowed particular books.

Siva Vaidhyanathan, a cultural historian and media scholar, is the author of *Copyrights and Copywrongs: The Rise of Intellectual Property and How it Threatens Creativity* (New York University Press, 2001) and *The Anarchist in the Library: How the Clash between Freedom and Control is Hacking the Real World and Crashing the System* (Basic Books, 2004). Vaidhyanathan has written for many periodicals, including *American Scholar, The Chronicle of Higher Education, The New York Times Magazine, MSNBC.COM, Salon.com, openDemocracy.net* and *The Nation.* After five years as a professional journalist, Vaidhyanathan earned a PhD in American Studies from the University of Texas at Austin. He has taught at Wesleyan University, the University of Wisconsin at Madison, Columbia University and New York University, and was a fellow at the New York Institute for the Humanities. Vaidhyanathan is currently Associate Professor, Media Studies Program, at the University of Virginia Charlottesville.

66 *They really want to make sure that people find this stuff really easy to use. We're at the point where 8-year-olds can post on MySpace without a problem, and 88-year-olds can, too. So that's kind of a nice thing.* 99

Speaking of Policies ...

Some participants provided thoughts on privacy policies, both now and in the future, and the role that librarians and library organizations should and should not play. Different opinions emerged among experts from different countries.

Source: *Sharing, Privacy and Trust in Our Networked World*, OCLC, 2007, question 1051, "In general, when you browse/purchase on Web sites, how often do you: decide not to purchase an item online after reviewing a company's privacy policy?" Base: Respondents who have used a commercial site.

Enright: I think [privacy policies are] necessary right now but not sufficient to protect anyone's real interests in privacy. I think many people recognize that, in many cases, they're no more than cosmetic. When you go back in a brief history of the Internet, you had a long period of time where attorneys were telling their clients, "Don't post a privacy policy, because you're not required to by law and if you do post one, you're creating legal commitments that can then be enforced against you." So that was really the standard legal advice for Web sites. Then the Federal Trade Commission started really saying quite strongly that any entity that was collecting individually identifiable information online should post a privacy policy. So then you had a mass exodus of merchants, and anyone who was collecting PII (personally identifiable information) reputably recognized they needed to post some kind of statement on the Web explaining to visitors what they could and couldn't do with this information.

There's research out there to suggest the consumers actually changed their behaviors based on the language within the privacy policy. The emblems, sometimes called trustmarks, that appear on Web sites like Truste, etc. ... I'm skeptical about all of that data. I'm sure that there is a brand of consumers who are affected by those kinds of things, but I just find it hard to believe that there's a statistically significant number of people that when they're doing their holiday shopping, they're taking the time to read a two- or three-page privacy policy and that's going to influence whether they bother to consummate that transaction or not. I'm not convinced of that.

Mathews: I guess that I would fall in with the anti-policy crowd, however I am not an administrator, so I don't have a global perspective. I definitely think it would be a mistake for libraries or the government to censor social Web sites. These tools are valuable for social development and social learning. If you're going to block

Alfons Wittmann is a librarian in the computer systems department at University Library, Catholic University of Eichstätt-Ingolstadt. Responsible for system/server administration, Wittmann has been engaged in computer technology since 1991 and online services since 1992. He is one who started to think early on about social consequences of the development of computer technologies, especially Internet technology. Wittmann uses the opportunities of Internet-based social networks to practice professional and personal pursuits: photography, music, literature.

❝ It's not currently present in the consciousness of the majority of users that libraries should participate in social networking. Only very few users can see a connection between libraries and future or actual social networks at the moment. ❞

MySpace, you might as well go all in and block Google Mail, Yahoo! and AOL Instant Messenger too.

I really hope that ALA, ACRL or even OCLC do not produce "best practices, guidelines, standards or recommended policies" for online social networks; that would kill creativity and originality. Mediocrity is a big problem for libraries in terms of inventiveness. Most people want to just stay even with the pack and not make waves. Most people just want to copy-and-paste whatever everyone else is doing and call it innovation. It is very unfortunate.

Morin: I'm often amazed to see how willingly people give out private information on the Internet. There's no question that expectations have been lowered in recent years as far as privacy is concerned; not so much through pressure from the big corporations such as Google, but by the people themselves, in a trade-off for better services. I think libraries should take that evolution into account and, while continuing to adhere to strong privacy policies, be less shy in asking for and using personal information from patrons to be able to provide better online services to them.

On the other hand, people should (and will hopefully) better learn how to manage their online identities. One will learn how to keep some things for oneself while being online, how to have several online identities with a wall between some of them so as to prevent some information from being pulled together. I think libraries and librarians have an educational role to play here.

Farkas: I think there are a lot of things that have come with the portability and fluidity of content that fall into a murky area that isn't clearly governed by policy. I would predict that we're going to see a lot more copyright infringement lawsuits where an individual has syndicated someone else's content onto their own Web site. It is so easy now to take other people's text and images and put them on your site. Content that has an RSS feed can easily be placed on another Web site where people can ostensibly make money off of someone else's blog content or even articles from a major newspaper. It's interesting to me that newspapers make other newspapers pay to syndicate their stories, but anyone can take the RSS feed from the *New York Times* and syndicate their stories right onto their Web site for free. I don't know if there's going to be more legislation, but I think people are going to be more explicit whenever they are posting content online about how their content is licensed and how it can be used. The Creative Commons licenses are great tools for explicitly stating this is what you can and cannot do with my content.

Vaidhyanathan: Interestingly, one of the big challenges I face is that university policy … is often shortsighted. We're seeing a proliferation of universities restricting the use of Skype, for instance. Skype is not only a fascinating phenomenon worth researching and worth writing about, it's also an essential tool in information gathering. If you're having a conversation with someone in another part of the world, Skype is often essential. It's an essential way to converse with people so they don't have to use landlines, which are notoriously undependable in much of the world.

University policy on copyright, university policy on network technologies, on bandwidth, all of these things, have been deeply frustrating. It troubles me when a university bans a particular kind of technology. It seems to me to strike at the very heart of academic freedom.

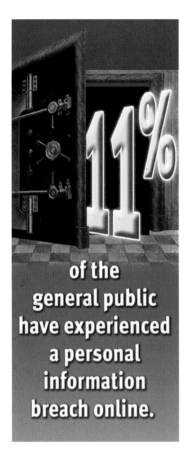

11%

of the general public have experienced a personal information breach online.

Source: *Sharing, Privacy and Trust in Our Networked World*, OCLC, 2007, question 1135, "Have you or has anyone you know ever had personal information used online without consent?'"

Krajewski: In France, the CNIL (Commission Nationale de l'Informatique et des Libertés) is the official institution who looks after that. They have decided that a library couldn't keep any personal behaviors longer than three months, I think. I mean personal information such as names. We have some statistics and can do lots of things, but I cannot say to a patron standing in front of me what he borrowed four months ago. On the other hand, it can be useful [to say] "Those who borrowed this, borrowed that."

So we just have to prove how we use fairly their data, and, at the same time, assure them that we do all that is necessary to protect them and their privacy rights (no sharing with anyone, anonymity when it's possible, etc.).

I have no idea [what policies would look like in three years]. Right now, I cannot figure out why it could change.

Hoffman Gola: I think we need to push the wall more and more to try to get the revisions of our copyright laws. And I think we have to look globally when we think about our copyright laws. Right now, while we have a lot of issues in our state about copyright restrictions, it's not like that in other countries; they don't have the same laws. And so they are accessing some of our copyrighted information and photographs and music and things for free.

How do we control that? I think that's going to be a big question for [the] libraries, music world, entertainment world and government of how do we bring a balance to our copyright laws when other countries don't have the same ideas of about what it means to hold copyright.

Wittmann: I don't think much will change. Not many Internet users have expressed their awareness about the problems related with privacy rights/violations, etc. However, it has been changing slowly as successful efforts are being made to raise awareness among the people about this issue. Therefore, I think there will soon be better and more trustworthy ways of encoding and dealing with personal data. But I don't think this will happen in the next three years.

Powell: I think libraries remain as highly trusted public bodies. I think that some patrons care (in the sense of being aware) that libraries keep records of personal information (others probably do not), but that almost all patrons currently trust libraries not to abuse that information.

I suspect that any loss of this trust would be a significant step towards us losing libraries as we currently know them.

I'm reasonably confident that libraries will retain their position of trust into the future.

I think libraries have to be careful as they grow relationships with commercial services. Public trust in some commercial services is diminishing. One wouldn't want this to 'rub off' on libraries. Ditto other Web 2.0 services such as Facebook.

Similarly, delivering services through 3-D virtual worlds such as Second Life requires foresight and a bit of caution. The trust issues are compounded by the end user needing to trust both the library and the provider of the virtual world (e.g., Linden Lab).

Bankhead: [With respect to policies, we should] allow more personal tailoring of information points, items. Tagging is the biggest thing about social software. Do you allow tagging for your catalog? Policy kind of takes another look. [Related to privacy policies we should] kind of look at what we can do to protect privacy, but allow people to participate in social software, in tagging. Allow tagging in catalogs.

I think [tagging] will benefit us. Even though [they are] not library ... subject headings, tags are the same thing—metadata. People are adding metadata to the catalog. That should be a good thing. Because even though it is not official metadata, metadata is metadata. People call a palm tree a palm tree. They don't call it by its Latin name. Things are common language that we communicate. It can't be a bad thing for [there] to be another access for information.

Kelly: We will all have acceptable use policies [in the future] which address issues such as privacy, acceptable language and behavior, etc. We will do this in order to clarify our policies and manage risks.

Sauers: I actually did an article [on policies in WebJunction called "Don't Doesn't Work"]. [Libraries] make all these rules about what you can't do and what you can do. I took an extreme position, to a certain level I had to. You create these policies about what you can and can't do on the computer. You create these policies that you can't use your cell phone in the library. You can't do this. You can't do that. In response to the technology, we already have policies in most cases that say you have to behave in the library.

[Social networking users] talk to each other, and it brings them together. And it may not be how your parents learned how to do that, definitely not how your grandparents learned how to do that.

Violations of Privacy and Identity

Interviewees' shared their thoughts on and experiences with online deception, identity theft or other problems associated with trust, privacy and personal information.

Mathews: I've had my credit card number stolen. I bought golf shoes from a discount vendor online and they had their customer database compromised. My bank contacted me when they noticed irregularity in purchasing and cleared everything up. This was probably three or four years ago, and afterwards I became more cautious. Now I only purchase from larger companies, like Amazon.

[Concerning online deception.] MySpace really has some problems. It's a spammers' paradise. There is a constant flood of fake profiles, password phishing, identity and endorsement theft, and server downtime. It's like the Wild West. As a result, many people have started to lock down their profiles, limiting who can view their information or who can send them messages or friend requests. This is very unfortunate because the appeal and success of MySpace is the openness, the serendipitous discoveries.

61%
of the total general public agree that they have the **same personalities** online as they do in person when using social networking sites.

Source: *Sharing, Privacy and Trust in Our Networked World*, OCLC, 2007, question 971, "Thinking about the social networking Web sites you use, how strongly do you agree or disagree with the statement, 'I have the same personality online as I do in person.'" Base: Respondents who have used a social networking site.

Enright: There are other ways, I think, that personal information can be compromised [over] the Web. [It] would be very, very easy to track people via Googling or even free Web-based search tools. You can learn an awful lot about people, probably more than many of them would like you to know, and I do have acquaintances who are directly impacted by that. The people that they thought they had left behind in their lives were able to figure out where they lived, even if their phone number was unlisted. That used to be enough—to take yourself ... off the grid and prevent most people from finding you—but now having your phone number unlisted really doesn't mean you won't be found. The Web definitely has created a much larger spotlight for people who want to locate people that might not want to be located.

I don't even know that people consider [creating different online identities] overtly deceptive. It's interesting. I think one of the direct definitions requires that one have the intention of deceiving. But for a female to create an avatar that's male, I think it's just sort of caveat of social networking and [if] people are assuming that's an accurate representation of who the person [is] behind that avatar, then they're probably taking an overly simplistic view of what community is all about.

Hoffman Gola: I think [deception] is well in the back of our minds. I think in any kind of environment there's always going to be that person or that group of people who tries to mislead you. I think [people are] going to be concerned about it, but not let it ... rule them. They're not going to not get involved and do things, because of those people out there that are deceptive.

Deception is just part of the world. It's part of being human ...

Number of aliases, avatars or pseudonyms created for the Web

2-4: 50%
5-9: 8%
10+: 4%
1: 36%   None: 3%

Source: *Sharing, Privacy and Trust in Our Networked World*, OCLC, 2007, question 830, by total general public, "How many aliases, avatars or pseudonyms have you created for the Web?"

Fox: I think people automatically assume that there's a lot of identity masking and misrepresentation online. And while some are doing it for nefarious reasons, much of it is acceptable and expected. In something like Second Life, a total immersion social networking experience, you're encouraged to be something other than what you are in the real world. If you want, you can be a different gender or age or race. Or someone who is wheelchair-bound in real life can choose to be the same in SecondLife or choose to walk or even fly. In Second Life, you can have a bubble over your head identifying the group you belong to—and of course you can belong to many, many groups, and have different identities for each. One of the first times I was in SecondLife, I saw a couple where one had a bubble [that said] "Rachel's Dad," and the other "Rachel's Mom." When I approached, they stopped their conversation, and the label above the man's head changed to "Reference Librarian," and he asked if I had any questions. I loved seeing the instant transformation, and it did establish a level of trust to see this facet of his identity change to fit the situation. I don't think users think most online manifestations are deception so much as it is creativity and interactive exploration of alternatives other than what we might normally have or be on a daily basis.

Houghton-Jan: Someone used my identity to post to a couple of message boards that didn't have a whole lot to do with the types of things I write about (libraries and technologies), but they were definitely posing as me. I got really angry and I wrote to the site owners and said, "This person is posing as me. This is not me who wrote that. Could you please take it down?" And they did so and also, of their own volition, blocked the person who had done that from posting any future items on their message board.

Vaidhyanathan: Deception is just part of the world. It's part of being human. I met my wife through an online dating service. That's a social networking phenomenon that involves a tremendous amount of deception. I think people expect to be deceived to a certain degree and I think that's a healthy expectation. We have been using this stuff long enough that we understand that we are being lied to in many cases by people and by institutions.

Libraries and Social Networking

We asked our panel about the role libraries play—and could play—in online communities and social media. Both the tactics and the strategies of how to use these new social networking tools within the context of libraries varied among the group. A single vision for online social spaces and libraries has not yet been formed.

Powell: I think libraries have two key roles.

Firstly, they have a role to raise understanding of the information literacy aspects of social networking tools—helping users to understand issues like quality, trust, provenance as they relate to social tools.

Secondly, they have a role in the long-term management, preservation and curation of social networking tools. This includes both actively carrying out the preservation and management and advising others about doing it. It also includes supporting aspects of resource discovery across the content of social tools.

There may also be a role for libraries in using social tools to deliver their existing online services—but it is not totally clear to me how library services fit into the typical usage scenario of social tools.

At a slightly more mundane level, it is clear that social tools such as Facebook have a role in disclosing people's personal tastes in books—also in supporting activities such as reading groups. There is a clear potential role for libraries in this space.

It is also possible to see social tools like Facebook supporting the activities of learners and researchers (both of which are essentially social activities). Again, one could expect this to be an area where libraries have a role to play.

"Books, books, books, rows and rows of books, stacks of books, tables filled with books, people holding books, people checking out books. Libraries are all about books. That is what I think and that is what I will always think."

41-year-old from Canada

Source: *Perceptions of Libraries and Information Resources*, OCLC, 2005, question 807, "What is the first thing you think of when you think of a library?"

Kelly: There are three ways that libraries may participate in social networking. By:

1) Using them to engage with their user communities.

2) Educating users on best practices, as part of an information literacy strategy.

3) Providing library information in forms which can be integrated into social networks e.g., providing RSS feeds, blogs, etc., which can be syndicated elsewhere.

Some [of the library's users] will welcome [social networking] involvement in the libraries; others won't care.

Hoffman Gola: I kind of wonder right now whether our users see libraries as a major role in their lives.... It is really funny, a lot of my friends, who are my age, they have absolutely no idea what I do as a librarian.... Because they still see it as a place for books and that place for studying ... I think we have to sort of change the landscape of what we traditionally do as librarians.... So I think if we're going to be using social software tools, we have to learn how to incorporate them into the way students are using our library.

I think, as librarians, we have a choice to make; we can ... continue to exist as we do today or we can choose to play a major role in social software and really learn a lot more about our users than [we've] ever been able to figure out before. I think the biggest things that librarians need to recognize with using these social tools is that the new generations can't necessarily be generalized. But rather each individual is looking for services that are specific to them ... And one of the things we can do [is] find out what ... each one of our users wants or needs. And I think we have the option to start making libraries definitely more individualized with these tools.

> ### *... each individual is looking for services that are specific to them ...*

Houghton-Jan: Most users I don't think understand that libraries even have DVDs, or public access computers, or Internet classes, or give photography classes. I just don't think they have an idea that we're even technically proficient, much less out and about in these spaces. I think most people, if you ask them, would say, "Libraries have a role [in social networking]? Do they even know what it is?"

The phrase the "third place" has been tossed around quite a bit, libraries being one of the possible destinations for people, other than work/school or home, and libraries could, if we put some effort into it, fill this space within our communities.... I think that's where libraries can succeed in social networking. We can provide spaces online in which people can connect one-on-one or in a group environment. We can provide discussion boards on certain topics, things like a local history discussion board, a user group for people who are interested in a certain type of book for your book club, or a space for teens participating in game nights to talk—really just providing a space in which your users, based on their interests and their abilities, can interact.

It also provides an opportunity for us to be present in the space that our users already are present in. [If] users are already using it to communicate with friends and family, and we put ourselves in that space, we can be a resource that they can tap when they need us. I think other examples of that would be a place like Flickr. We could be present there. People could do searches for our local community and find out that, "Wow, the library took photos of all the historical buildings in the area. Isn't that neat?" This is one more reminder that the library has a presence within the community.

> *... we would only improve by raising awareness of what we can do for people by making ourselves more visible on the Web ...*

Bankhead: In a way,... the librarian is still kind of the gatekeeper. We have our online catalog. We have all our stuff on our server,... our Web page and we point to a bunch of different resources that we pay for. Our databases, our e-books and our catalog. And we kind of maintain this little empire within our own network environment, and we let people in based on their library card number authentication or whether they are inside the library.

But more and more, especially database providers like Access My Library, Gale, OCLC [are] also doing this—trying to get information out on ... WorldCat, out on the Web—to point people back to these resources. Analogous to that kind of process, I think what we need to do is try to distribute ourselves more ubiquitously out on the wider Web rather than trying to horde everything within our own server environment. And I see that the whole social software paradigm as kind of being a model for that kind of behavior. So instead of saying, "You guys have to come to the library Web site and do this and that and then look at our catalog." We have to kind of put ourselves and our information out in different places like MySpace or del.icio.us.

My general feeling is that our users know that we are good at doing books. But I think that they would be surprised to know about the other various electronic resources that we have available. So from the user perspective, my anticipation, my conjecture would be that we would only improve by raising awareness of what we can do for people by making ourselves more visible on the Web, in general.

Mathews: I really want to teach a semester-long course on social networks, blending the cultural context with application development, artistic design and problem solving. In academia we aim to teach "information literacy" and using MySpace as a platform to gather, evaluate and shape information is far more interesting than current methods.

have provided information on a library's Web site about books they have read.

Source: *Sharing, Privacy and Trust in Our Networked World,* OCLC, 2007, question 875, "Which of the following types of information have you ever supplied about yourself when using an online library service on a library's Web site?" Base: Respondents who have used an online library.

I think that librarians should avoid playing the parental role, warning patrons about the dangers of online predators or identity theft, or worst devaluing the significance of these Web sites, and instead we should emphasize productivity, self-expression and the communication channels that these tools provide.

As for our role, I think that libraries should strive to embed themselves within their user community—online and in real life. Social networking allows us to form a better connection with our patrons. It can be a great publicity tool, a chance to tell our story and to craft a meaningful, shareable message. Web 2.0 tools enable us to have genuine conversations with patrons, rather than us just babbling on about what we feel is important, what they need to know. Aside from that, social networks are excellent assessment and usability tools, but are we really ready to know what they think? Are we really ready to listen?

> *... libraries should strive to embed themselves within their user community— online and in real life.*

Krajewski: Library 2.0 may be the last attempt to enter the game for grumpy librarians who have been kicked out of the playground by their former users. Library 2.0 may be the last lightning [bolt] of a profession doomed to die, and trying to survive a little bit longer. Do we propose Library 2.0 tools because our patrons need them or because WE need them (to prove that we are alive and useful)?

I think that is quite like The Enlightenment.

During The Enlightenment of the XVIIIth century, European people had been given new powers, new status, new consideration, new missions, new roles, new responsibilities. At that time, thinkers judged that to face this tremendous change, people should be educated. They did need libraries, schools and also mediators (teachers, representatives, etc). Do our patrons really need "Enlightenment 2.0"? Maybe, yes. So far, I haven't seen them in that light, but I could be wrong, or it may come later. People have built their social networking without us, and we are knocking at their doors, begging to play with them ("Please, be my friend ..."). Maybe they do need us. It's a question of faith. It's a gamble.

We can also have a much more pragmatical state of mind. We invade their social network spaces just to make figures (charts) and to put up some signs to bring them back where we are supposed to be good—our core business—maybe knowledge, education, entertainment, public open access, etc. I mean the very missions of libraries. I think that just as there are some signs in the city to show where the library is, we should put some virtual signs on the different social networking Web sites. In that respect, the personal space of a library on a social network is just a sign, with a mere semiotic function.

Wittmann: It's not currently present in the consciousness of the majority of users that libraries should participate in social networking. Only very few users can see a connection between libraries and future or actual social networks at the moment.

I recommend libraries look at the following ways of participating in social networking:

- Make platforms available
- Actively offer and maintain content
- Have a presence in social networks
- Utilize capabilities from social networks (tagging, folksonomies, etc.) for the enhancement/enrichment of certain services (catalogs, etc.)
- Actively support library users in using social networks; but this is also important and true: actively support library users through the use of social networks

... it could be that libraries provide the only mechanism whereby large populations of people ... have the opportunity to interact with social networks ...

Morin: We should provide data in the user's environment. We should provide applications (widgets, etc.) usable in the user's environment. We should help foster online social networks which, while not library-centered, are useful to our patrons and where we might fit in well as a data and service provider. The network might be about a place, it might also have to do with a subject matter about which you have truly useful collections. I don't think libraries should try to have a presence in every social network, but we should definitely make every effort to have a presence where that presence is obviously useful to the public.

I'm not sure [users] give much thought to [the role libraries should play in social networking spaces]. I'm not sure they should. I have a feeling that online social networks are a world of opportunity; as I use them myself, you roam the online space, find stuff, use it or not. But in truth I don't know the answer to this question, and I feel it's too early to tell without proper studies and focus groups, etc.

Enright: I don't have firsthand knowledge of this, but I know that libraries in schools are one mechanism whereby people are trying to address the digital divide. In giving high-speed access to underprivileged communities that otherwise wouldn't have access. So it could be that libraries provide the only mechanism whereby large populations of people would even have the opportunity to interact with social networks—which would otherwise be entirely closed to them.

When you're specializing in privacy and information access, where I do think that gets interesting ... when you're dealing with legislation or policies that would ... mandate any kind of filtering, then I think you have some tricky considerations in terms of determining whether or not those filters might limit people's access to social networks that they would otherwise want to or need to be involved with. I think how those filters are constructed is a very, very real risk that heavy-handed filtering could prevent social networks from being ... [and] accessible in public spaces like libraries.

I think [users] don't know that there's a role for [libraries in social networking] ...

Fox: Social networking is becoming a prime way for college-age students and high-school-age students to communicate. It's how they're talking to their friends and interacting with their peers, how they're talking to complete strangers and making real connections. If they're not doing things like e-mail or restricting e-mail for work purposes only, as so many studies have reported recently, then we need to figure out how else to communicate with them. If they don't use the college e-mail system regularly, how can we integrate the Facebook 'Share' functionality? If librarians want to continue engaging our patrons and helping them to see the possibilities of what's available in the library, then this is another road to do that, another means of making our services open, and keeping patrons aware and involved.

We also have, of course, obligations for information literacy and teaching people how to find the best, most valuable information. And therefore making sure that they understand the limits of the kind of content information they can find in MySpace—knowing that anybody can put anything up, it doesn't necessarily need to be true. Just as we have to teach our users to evaluate a Web page and how to use information responsibly, this applies to content in social networking sites as well.

Unfortunately, I think most users don't naturally think that there is a role for libraries at all here. They are doing personal interactions on these sites, and the appearance of a librarian is still somewhat akin to the telemarketer who calls during dinner or an annoying Web pop-up advertisement—it's out of place and even resented. Even if we are offering a service or product they want, it's at the wrong time and/or through the wrong vehicle. It will take time to change users' perspective so that they do realize librarians can add value in an appropriate way in this environment.

Farkas: I think that libraries play a really important role on two levels. The first is education. A lot of times young people really don't think about the ramifications of the online identity that they are building and how that might affect them in the future when they're looking for a job or even if someone they're dating is looking them up. I think libraries have an important role in making people aware of these issues and

56% of college students and 28% of the total general public use social networking.

Source: *Sharing, Privacy and Trust in Our Networked World,* OCLC, 2007, question 530.

how they could come back and haunt them—years and years later—because it is really hard to completely get rid of online content with caching and the Internet Archive. But I also see us having an important role in going where our patrons are, providing services inside of the tools that our patrons are already using like instant messaging, MySpace and Facebook. I know there are a lot of libraries basically creating portals to their library services inside of MySpace, and I think that's a great way to make the library and its services more visible.

Sauers: At a minimum, I think [libraries] should be participating in the social networking environment. That's the starting point. I don't think you can do anything beyond that, unless you're participating in the first place. The standards of just blogs, Flickr accounts, that sort of thing. I see what some libraries are doing and even just basic items are getting a big response. And when I see what other libraries just aren't doing, I want to say, "Hello," give them a little shake.

I've read OCLC's [*Perceptions of Libraries and Information Resources*] report. I think in most cases, my impression is that [users] don't look at the library in that way [social networking]. Yes, they like the library. Yes, the library is comfortable. Yes, they know they can get books there. But I ... think when people go out on MySpace ... the library is probably one of the last things they're thinking of when they're sending messages back and forth or playing on the computer or whatever. But if the library can get into that space, we can change that perception. Yes, we are here. We are where you are. We're here to help.

Vaidhyanathan: Social networking is a catchall for a variety of communicative forums. If you think about the sites that we classically consider social networking sites—like MySpace, like Facebook—they are essentially simple content management systems. They are easy to use. They are easy to modify. They are user-friendly. Now, as content management systems, you can actually imagine them playing a role not too far away from course management systems, which are, after all, another form of content management system.... I see great potential for using the model of social networking interfaces in community-based conversations in which people are linking to good references. I see the potential for using social networking to generate bibliographies—both within classes and outside of classes. I could see if there is a group of people involved in an environmental activism project in their local community.... They could use social networking to maintain a list of scientific journal articles or journalism articles that they have culled from a library, and update the bibliography as a group, essentially, maintain it as a group.

Prognostication

We asked the experts to predict where they see the social networking scene going in the next few years.

Farkas: I think there are going to be a lot more libraries making better decisions about what social software they implement to provide services to their patrons. I think right now we're still largely in the "me too" stage; the idea that having a MySpace page or a blog makes a library "cool" is quite prevalent. I think that libraries are going to get much smarter about planning these services. Yes, these tools are free to set up, but it takes a real commitment to maintain them on a day-to-day basis. The content has to be updated, the software needs to be maintained and they have to be made appealing to the patron. I think there's often little planning that goes into these online library storefronts. I think there is going to be more of that in the library world in the future—real planning and thinking about the sustainability of the project and how it is meeting the needs of our patrons.

> *... we're going into all these spaces and building services, yet we're not thinking about what their future is.*

Mathews: I think that the battle between MySpace and Facebook will continue to escalate. They are the Coke and Pepsi of the social networking scene. Eventually things will probably break off into niche networks, into segments ... social networks for cat lovers, for book lovers, for marathon runners, for coffee fanatics, for out-of-work actors in Los Angeles. People want to connect with others who share their interests, that's the core benefit and attraction of these Web sites. I think that university portals as well as course management systems, like WebCT, will eventually incorporate social features and profiles. Facebook started as a tool for Harvard students to meet each other.

A current challenge is designing a network that grows with users; MySpace is popular with high school students, Facebook dominates the college market, but what about when they enter the workforce. LinkedIn is a more professional-oriented network, but it's fee-based and sterile. Regardless, current students are going to be so interconnected with their friends and peers that it will result in better career opportunities and social engagement in the long run.

What's interesting is how elements of social networking have started to appear throughout the Web: newspapers allow readers to share opinions and interact with each other, Netflix has built a culture around renting DVDs, fantasy sports bring fans together, and corporate intranets connect employees more efficiently. The Web will increasingly become more social, and networking functionality will help enhance that experience. Before long, I don't think people will use the term "social network." It will just become ubiquitous. People will expect it wherever they go online.

Bankhead: I think that basically now it is kind of a field of innovation.... So the fact that YouTube was bought by Google kind of makes it more of a volatile space, and that gives more incentive for people to create new applications and potentially become millionaires.

Krajewski: I don't know, and in fact, I don't care.

Libraries don't create trends and tendencies, they follow. We are not able to compete with the big actors whose core business is [to create and publicize trends]. We have no choice than to follow and be grafted like plants.

Hoffman Gola: I see more things happening with tools like Second Life ... where we have virtual environments and our real selves. Where in the virtual environment, we know you as five foot six, beautiful supermodel and then in our real life where we have our real friends and where we network in different ways ... I think that the whole concept of Second Life is very interesting. I'm not sure if it will last, but it will be interesting to see what other things come out that are similar in nature to Second Life.

> ## I think that the whole concept of Second Life is very interesting.

Enright: Online generally, I think its current course is fairly apparent. We are kind of limping towards Web 2.0.... The fact of that Google/YouTube acquisition—they clearly fired a shot across the bow letting everybody know that the Web is changing, vis-à-vis the content, and the [Web] traffic ... at least in Google's estimation, is incredibly valuable. That is going to influence the behaviors of other online interests, so you're going to have every future online player, I think, trying to empower their consumers—their visitors, interacting with them in a more dynamic way.

Another interesting observation about social networking sites is that they grew up in scale so quickly that they clearly have infrastructure problems. Some social networking sites are not very reliable—they go down a lot, slow down a lot and have server trouble. I think we're going to see a lot of that stuff mature that hasn't matured. Interfaces are going to get slicker and they're going to continue adding new functionality. One social network's recent privacy fumble where they had introduced some functionality thinking they were adding a feature and it created an unanticipated active backlash across a large portion of their user community to the extent that they ultimately very, very vocally said, "We made a mistake. We are apologizing for what went on here." I think that is a very interesting impact but social networking up to that point hadn't really suffered that kind of slap on the hand for manipulating the data of their membership.

Fox: I think there will be more merging of the different services. So as opposed to having a separate Flickr site and a MySpace site and a YouTube site, more and more of these will be merged, so that you won't have to have multiple identities, multiple URLs, multiple logins or multiple links. Also, I hope we continue to see libraries collaborating more with some of the big social networking sites—for example, recently a couple of libraries have gotten permission from Facebook to make a "search the library catalog" plug-in feature available in Facebook. Reports talk about how much a link in Facebook or MySpace drives traffic to a regular Web site; it would be great to have more prominent library presence.

I've been really impressed with the LibGuides product from SpringShare, which both shows the convergence of several of the social networking tools. It works like a wiki and a blog; can embed IM, video, shared bookmarks; and it also can be integrated right into Facebook. And this is a library-specific, designed-for-libraries tool. We need more innovations like this.

Sauers: I think libraries have to participate in social networking and it will evolve over the years. More people are on MySpace. Which, to me, implies that all the kids are going to go, "We're going to go find something else," because all these adults are here. The moment you tell them, they're going to bail, really quick, and they're going to find something else.

Vaidhyanathan: Social networking sites are merely another level of user-friendly design. I would imagine that those goals will still consume the people who engineer this stuff. We've seen a remarkable level of ... creative democracy as a result of the creation of these sites, and I see no reason for that not to be the goal of these people who design this.... They really want to make sure that people find this stuff really easy to use. We're at the point where eight-year-olds can post on MySpace without a problem, and 88-year-olds can, too. So that's kind of a nice thing.

68%

of those who use a
**library Web site
say it is easy
to use,**
compared to

75%

*for social
networking sites.*

Source: *Sharing, Privacy and Trust in Our Networked World*, OCLC, 2007, questions 956 and 1066. Base: Respondents who have used a library in person or online and/or a social networking site.

> *The hype [about social networking] is over. People will now move on to examine other things that are more realistic, to their advantage.*

Powell: Hmmm, difficult. I'll make some predictions on a tool-by-tool basis.

Facebook: I think usage will continue to grow generally for a while, though I suspect that lots of its more mature users will become bored by its functionality and somewhat frustrated by its limitations. I think that it will expand to better capture the 'researcher' market (as opposed to students) by offering applications that help researchers do their work. In a year's time I think we could easily all be using something similar, but different (and hopefully better).

Twitter: I think usage will grow, as will functionality—particularly in terms of functionality to have 'conversations' with subsets of people.

Flickr and Slideshare: I foresee no major change in the service profiles and I think usage and functionality will continue to grow.

Blogging: I predict there will be continued growth, particularly as researchers use it to share research outcomes. I see a good chance that blogs and social tools like Facebook (e.g., Nature Network) will grow in use by researchers.

Second Life: I'm not sure. I suspect there will be some kind of backlash against Second Life in some way, but that there will be continued growth of usage by educational institutions over the next year. Not sure beyond that. Performance and reliability will improve. We'll also see growth in open-source variants such as Croquet.

LinkedIn: There will be a general demise I think. It does not have enough functionality to grab attention.

Wikis: I can think of no major change in the service profile, but I suspect slow growth in use—certainly within the education sector.

Wittmann: The hype [about social networking] is over. People will now move on to examine things that are more realistic, to their advantage. Many of the sites will disappear, but it will also give way to many services which can be applied to completely normal everyday work and recreational activities. Libraries must take an active role in this process and help shape it.

Summary

The viewpoints expressed from the early pioneers in the field highlight the many ways in which the social Web is still the "Wild West" and much is left to be discovered.

The experts had many unique perspectives and ideas about the roles of social networks and libraries. Yet most also see a frontier that is quickly and, likely permanently, changing the landscape of the Web. There is not a unified vision of the future. What is coming into focus is that librarians are just beginning to experiment with networked communities to reach their users. All agree that we have learning to do and we should get started and get active. It is where our users are living.

A special thanks to all of our participants for their willingness to contribute.

Report Highlights

Our survey results, research and conversations with industry leaders provide a wide body of evidence that what has been anticipated, and hyped, about the next generation Web—the creation of the social Web—is well underway. Users do not currently envision a role for libraries on their new social Web.

... on Using the Web

- **The Internet has come of age, for all ages.** No longer a new technology, the Internet has become a core economic and social infrastructure for the majority of the population surveyed for this report. The vast majority (89%) of the 6,163 general public respondents have been using the Internet for four years or more; half have been using the Internet for seven years or more, a quarter have been online for nearly a decade.

- Web use is not dominated by the young. **The majority of the online population surveyed have moved from "digital immigrant" status to fully naturalized digital citizens.** Nearly two-thirds of the general public respondents over the age of 50 have been online for seven years or more, and nearly a third have been using the Internet for more than 10 years, the highest percentage of any age group.

- The Web is increasingly ubiquitous across geographies. Among respondents in all countries surveyed, **online tenure was consistent across urban, suburban and rural users.**

- The adoption of standard Internet services such as e-mail and search engines has reached near-saturation levels. In the 18 months since the publication of the *Perceptions of Libraries and Information Resources* report in 2005, the number of e-mail users in the same base countries surveyed (Canada, U.K., U.S.) increased from 73% to 97%. **The use of search engines increased from 71% to 90%.**

- The majority of Web users surveyed shop online. **More than three-quarters of the general public respondents (77%) indicated they have browsed for or purchased items online in the past 12 months.** Amazon, eBay and Rakuten are among the most used commercial sites.

- **The Web community has migrated from using the Internet to building it.** In 2005, just 16% of respondents used blogs; today that number approaches 50%. Approximately a quarter of the general public respondents have created Web pages and used chat rooms and social networking sites. **The Internet's readers are rapidly becoming its authors.**

- **Web users read more.** Approximately a quarter of the general public respondents reported that time spent reading, print or digital, has increased over the last 12 months. **In no country surveyed was there an overall decrease in reading time.** And respondents who spend time using social networking sites read more than nonsocial site users.

... on Social Networks

- **The emergence of a new classification of "social" Web sites is changing the construction and culture of the Web.** In these shared spaces, users are not only the audience, but they create content, design pages and architect entirely new social networks. **We have moved from an Internet built by a few thousand authors to one constructed by millions.**

- Wikipedia defines a social network as a social structure made of nodes (generally individuals or organizations) tied together by specific types of relationships, such as values, visions, ideas, financial exchange, friends, kinship, etc. Social sites are classified in the report into two types: **social networking sites designed to allow users to interact and share interests, attitudes and activities (e.g., MySpace, Mixi, Facebook, etc.); and social media sites used predominantly to post, access and exchange content (e.g., YouTube, Snapfish, etc.).**

- On average, **more than a quarter of the general public respondents currently participate on some type of social media or social networking site.** Respondents in the U.S. lead in the number of social networking site users at 37%; respondents in the U.K. lead in use of social media sites at 34%.

- **Over half of college students surveyed (56%) use social networking sites.** (See Appendix A.)

- **MySpace, the number one social networking site used by survey respondents,** was launched in 2003. MySpace is the top social networking site used by our respondents in Canada (60%), the U.S. (75%), France (70%), Germany (54%) and the U.K. (72%). Mixi dominates social networking use in Japan (91%). Alexa ranked MySpace sixth in global traffic in September 2007.

- **YouTube is the top social media site among respondents in all countries surveyed:** Canada (73%), U.S. (73%), Japan (83%), France (76%), Germany (83%) and the U.K. (83%). Alexa ranked YouTube fourth in global traffic in September 2007.

- **The general public respondents are more likely to have used a social networking or social media site (28%) than to have searched for or borrowed items from a library Web site (20%).**

- Social networking site users are active participants. **More than a third of social networking users (39%) log in at least daily,** often several times a day.

- **Frequency of use on Mixi is the highest of any social networking site, with 59% of users logging onto the site at least daily;** 34% log on several times a day.

- Much of what takes place on social spaces is motivated by a desire to increase personal interaction. ***My friends use the same site* (66%) is the top criteria in using a social networking site.** *To network or to meet new people, The Web site is fun* and *to be part of a group or community* are also top social networking site selection criteria.

- **Forty-two percent (42%) of social networking users *agree* these sites *help maintain current relationships*.** An even higher rate, 47%, *agree* that social networking sites *help build new relationships*.

- To date, social networking users stay with their favorite sites. **Just 16% have stopped using a social networking site in the last 24 months.**

- **Cell phones are becoming social networking devices.** The majority of respondents have cell phones and **more than three-quarters are now using their phones for more than just talking.** Over half use text-messaging, while in some countries, usage approaches 80%. Japanese respondents lead other countries surveyed in use of cell phones for searching the Internet. While 15% of the total general public respondents across all countries use cell phones to search the Internet, nearly three times more Japanese respondents do so, at 40%.

... on Sharing on the Web

- **General public respondents are sharing information, including personal information, on a growing number of commercial Web sites.** Approximately three-quarters of users of commercial sites have supplied their given/first name, surname/last name, e-mail and street address; about half have provided a phone number, birthday and credit/debit card information.

- Respondents provide information on commercial sites to be notified about future events or services. **A third of commercial site users have signed up for electronic newsletters and have provided information to receive e-mail alerts; a quarter have created "favorites."**

- **Sharing on social networking sites showed different patterns from sharing on commercial sites.** Users of social networking sites are less likely to have provided contact information (name, address, phone number, etc.) but are much more likely to have shared individual information (birthday) and interest information (books read, subjects of interest, etc.). While 73% have provided a surname/last name on a commercial site, only 46% have shared their surname/last name on a social networking site. Fifty percent (50%) have supplied a phone number on a commercial site; just 12% have done so on a social networking site. **On social networking sites, 39% have shared a book they have read, 57% have shared photos/videos and 14% have shared self-published information.**

- **College student respondents are more likely to share information on social networking sites** than the total general public. (See Appendix A.)

- **Sharing habits on both social networking and commercial sites vary among respondents by country,** but most show a strong willingness to have contributed information on social sites. Social networking users in Canada, the U.S. and the U.K. are more likely to have shared personality or physical attributes on a social networking site than users in Japan, France or Germany.

- When registering on a Web site, general public respondents are willing to provide more than just what is required; **67% *always, often* or *sometimes* complete the entire registration form, not just the required information.**

- The majority of the respondents (54%) are more comfortable sharing their "true personalities" (feelings, attitudes and interests) in person. **Thirty percent (30%) are equally as comfortable online as in person and about 16% are more comfortable sharing their true personalities online.**

... on Privacy

- **Respondents are split on their views about Internet privacy and security.** Twenty-three percent (23%) of the general public respondents feel their personal information is *kept more private* on the Internet than it was two years ago; 27% feel it is *kept less private*. A roughly equal number, 29%, feel there has been *no change* in Internet privacy; 21% are *not sure*.

- **Attitudes on Internet security were similarly split.** Twenty-six percent (26%) of respondents feel their personal information is *kept more secure* on the Internet than it was two years ago and 25% feel it is *kept less secure*. Thirty percent (30%) believe there has been *no change* in Internet security and 19% are *not sure*.

- Our research showed a relationship exists between the views on privacy and security on the Internet. **Respondents who feel their personal information is *kept more private* on the Internet tend to feel it is *kept more secure* as well.** In fact, 74% of those who feel their personal information is *kept more private* also feel it is *kept more secure*.

- **Views on privacy and security vary by country.** Respondents in Canada, the U.S., France and Germany are more likely to feel their personal information on the Internet is *kept more private* than it was two years ago compared to respondents in the U.K. and Japan. Respondents in Canada and France are more likely to feel their personal information is *kept more secure* on the Internet; only 10% of French respondents feel their personal information is *kept less secure*.

- **College student respondents are slightly more likely to feel their personal information is *kept more private* and *kept more secure* on the Internet** than it was two years ago compared to the total general public. (See Appendix A.)

- **Eleven percent (11%) of the general public respondents have had their personal information used without their consent.** This number is consistent across all countries surveyed.

- Privacy matters to respondents. Over 10,000 verbatim comments were analyzed to understand privacy concerns among the general public respondents. ***Advertising/spam, identity theft* and *protecting personal information* were top privacy concerns.** More than 10% indicated they had *no privacy concerns,* 3% expressed concerns about *privacy rights* and 0.5% had concerns related to *library/reading privacy issues*.

- Over 60% of the general public **respondents feel that online banking/investments Web sites are *extremely* or *very private*,** the highest privacy rating of services evaluated. **No other activity came close.** Over 40% feel their use of the telephone, cell phones and e-mail at home is *extremely* or *very private;* 15% feel their activity on search engines is *extremely* or *very private.*

- **Respondents do not distinguish library Web sites as more private than many other sites they are using.** Just 11% of online users surveyed feel that activities done while using a library Web site are *extremely* or *very private*, a rating slightly lower than search engines (15%), social networking sites (15%) and online bookstores (12%).

- While a third or more of users of social, commercial and library sites *agree* they prefer to remain anonymous while using these sites, **most use their real names (65%), real e-mail addresses (80%) and real ages (80%), and over half provide their real telephone numbers when registering at a Web site.**

... on Privacy Rules and Trust

- Respondents feel it is important to have control over how their personal information will be used or shared on the Internet. **Nearly three-quarters of respondents indicated that it is *extremely* or *very important* to be able to specify who can use and who can view their personal information. Less than half,** however, *always* or *often* **actually use those controls** to specify who can view their personal information when using social networking sites (45%), social media sites (36%) or the library (24%), indicating a gap between expectations and actions.

- Although respondents attach a high importance to being informed about how their information will be used on the Internet, just **a third *always* or *often* review a social networking site's privacy policy before registering;** 26% of library users review the privacy policy on a library Web site before registering.

- **Security icons are viewed more often than privacy policies. Over half of respondents *always* or *often* look for security icons while browsing or shopping on Web sites.** Shoppers in Germany and Japan are less likely to look for security icons; while French users are most likely.

- **Online trust increases with usage.** Half of commercial site users *agree* that the longer they use the Web site, the more they trust it. Forty-one percent (41%) of social networking sites users and 37% of social media site users also indicate that trust increases with usage of the respective sites; 32% of library Web site users indicate that trust grows with use.

- **Seventy percent (70%) of social networking users indicate they *always, often* or *sometimes* trust who they communicate with on social networking sites.**

... on Information Privacy and Library Privacy

- **Respondents do not attach a high degree of privacy to searching and browsing information.** Just over a quarter of respondents (28%) feel that the subjects they search on a search engine are *extremely* or *very private*. **Subjects searched while at the library or a bookstore, or while using the library Web site or online bookstore are even less private;** fewer than 20% feel this information is *extremely* or *very private*. Just 16% of respondents indicated that the specific books they read are *extremely* or *very private*.

- **While less than 20% of general public respondents feel library information or books read are *extremely* or *very private*, approximately half feel it is *extremely* or *very important* that the library keep this information and other library activities private.** The desire for library information privacy was consistent across all countries surveyed.

- **While 64% of respondents feel it is *extremely* or very *important* for the library to have a privacy policy, just 26% *always* or *often* review the library Web site privacy policy before registering.**

- Most respondents feel it is *extremely* or *very important* that libraries keep their library information private, yet **less than 15% feel that their activities on library Web sites are *extremely* or *very private*.**

- Libraries are seen as trustworthy institutions; **60% of general public respondents *agree* they trust the library.**

- **Library Web sites, however, are not seen as any more private than commercial or social sites researched.** Commercial bank sites were the only sites evaluated that are differentiated as more private.

... on U.S. Library Directors

A total of 382 U.S. library directors completed the same base survey questions as the online general public. Directors were asked additional questions about their views on user activities and attitudes. A third of U.S. library director respondents (34%) are under the age of 50 and 66% are 50+. Just 4% of respondents were under the age of 30.

- Library directors are Internet pioneers. **U.S. library directors have been using the Internet longer on average than any group surveyed;** 60% reported that they have been online for more than a decade, double the rate of the U.S. general public.

- On average, **library directors are more likely to have used Internet services than the populations they serve.** More directors have browsed or purchased items online, 92% compared to 76%; read someone's blog, 68% compared to 44%; and created a Web page, 37% compared to 18% for the U.S. general public.

- Five years ago, most U.S. library directors were concerned about the validity and credibility of information located using Internet search sites. Concerns continue, but today, **directors are using Internet search engines (97%) at a rate greater than the U.S. general public (86%).**

- **Overall, U.S. library directors feel their personal information is *kept less private* and *kept less secure* on the Internet than it was two years ago.** The U.S. general public feel that, overall, their personal information is kept as private or more private and kept as secure or more secure on the Internet than it was two years ago.

- **The use of social networking sites by U.S. library directors is substantially less than that of the U.S. general public;** 22% of U.S. library directors have used a social networking site, compared to 37% of the U.S. general public. While overall usage lags behind the U.S. general public, library directors ages 22–49 have used social networking sites (38%) at a rate on par with the total U.S. general public.

- **U.S. library directors have the same favorite social sites as the U.S. general public.** MySpace (75%) is the top social networking site for U.S. library directors; YouTube (72%) is the top social media site.

- **Amazon (92%) was the most used browsing/purchasing site among library directors.** A library Web site was second, at 77%.

- While directors share many of the same favorites as the U.S. general public, their motivations for using these services vary. **U.S. library directors are more likely to use social networking sites to use the service in conjunction with their work. The U.S. general public is more likely to utilize these sites for social functions.**

- **Online privacy is more important to U.S. library directors than to the U.S. general public.** Directors are much less likely, and in many instances, significantly less likely to share personal information on social networking and social media sites than the U.S. general public. For all types of personal information evaluated, library directors ages 22–49 are more likely to have shared information on a social networking site than their colleagues age 50+.

- **Top privacy concerns for U.S. library directors surveyed mirror those of the U.S. general public: *advertising/spam, credit and financial theft* and *identity theft.*** Neither the U.S. general public nor U.S. library directors listed *freedom of thought* as a significant privacy concern.

- **Both U.S. library directors and the U.S. general public rely on security icons as a measure of a Web site's security.** Directors check for privacy policies at a higher rate than the U.S. general public.

- **U.S. library directors have an inflated view of the information privacy attitudes among the U.S. general public, particularly related to privacy of library information.** While less than 20% of the U.S. general public indicated that library items checked out online or in person were *extremely* or *very private*, over 50% of library directors estimated users would consider this information to be *extremely* or *very private*. While 16% of the U.S. general public indicated that books they have read are *extremely* or *very private*, nearly half (48%) of library directors estimated users would consider this information *extremely* or *very private*.

- **U.S. library directors feel it is their professional responsibility to keep a user's library information private.**

... on Libraries and Social Networks

- **Thirteen percent (13%) of the total general public and 9% of the U.S. general public respondents feel that it is the role of the library to create a social networking site for their communities;** about a third are not sure. Top reasons provided for why the library should not build a social networking site: *Library is for learning/information* (25%), *Not the role of the library* (16%), *Library is not for socializing* (7%), *Don't care/no opinion* (7%) and *Personal/individual matter* (7%).

- **Fourteen percent (14%) of U.S. library directors believe social networking is a role for libraries;** about 40% of directors are not sure. Top reasons library directors provided for why the library should not build a social networking site: *Not the role of the library* (30%), *Enough social networking sites exist already* (16%), *Library is for learning/information* (14%) and *No time/resources* (9%).

- Both the total general public respondents and library directors indicated that hosting **book clubs was the top social networking service that libraries should consider if they were to build social networking sites.** A small number of the total general public respondents also indicated that homework help, support groups, sharing interests and education services could be useful social networking library services.

- As of September 28, 2007, **MySpace had 197 groups with "book club" in the title.**

... on Countries

The survey findings highlight the reality that the Internet is indeed becoming a World Wide Web; a platform for international sharing, multicultural contribution and global community. Much of what respondents told us about online practices, attitudes and activities on their favorite sites held constant across all countries surveyed. Having shared common Internet services, tools, sites and protocols since the inception of the Web, Internet users have in many ways created a common online culture and community. And yet it was also evident from the findings that the emerging social Web can equally support individualization and cultural expression. We observed both trends in our research.

A unified Web culture

- **All countries surveyed use common Internet services**—e-mail, blogs, IM, commerce sites, social networking sites, library Web sites, etc.—**and use them at strikingly similar rates.**

- All countries use common Web sites, and in most instances, **YouTube, Amazon, eBay and MySpace were the favorites.**

- **Motivations for using social sites are common**—my friends are there.

- Participation in online activities is comparable across all countries—**searching, shopping, blogging and online banking are used at very similar rates.**

- Attitudes about **Internet privacy and security are consistent—users are comfortable.**
- **Views on libraries and information privacy** are alike across geographies—**these activities are not very private.**

Distinctions

- While all countries share the same top Internet sites, **many country-specific commercial and social sites are frequently used by respondents.**
- **Japanese respondents expressed the most distinctive views** about all aspects of life online—commerce, sharing on social sites, privacy and libraries.
- **American respondents are the most indistinguishable** across countries surveyed, with very few "most" or "least" in any area of research.
- **Canadian and American views are largely consistent** across almost every dimension.
- **Germany and France often provide the highest activity levels** in many of the commercial and social online activities.
- **The U.K. reported many of the highest levels of browsing and purchasing activity.**

The following pages contain a "country focus" profile on each of the six countries surveyed. The graphics provide a quick overview of the respondents' online activities, use of social sites, views on Internet privacy and security, and the role of libraries on the social Web.

Country Focus
... on Canada

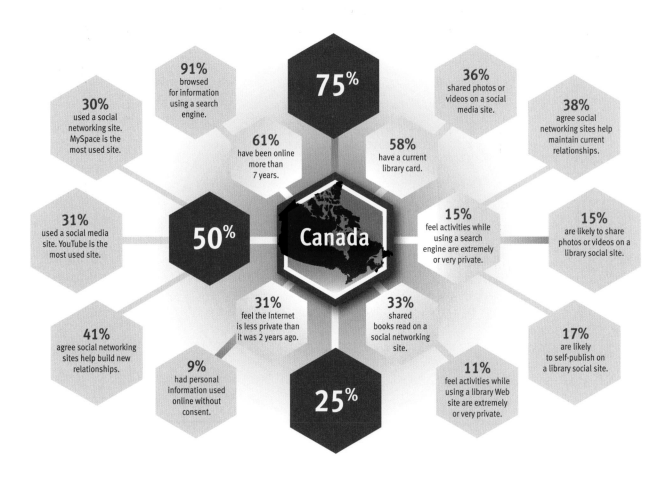

91% browsed for information using a search engine.

30% used a social networking site. MySpace is the most used site.

75%

36% shared photos or videos on a social media site.

38% agree social networking sites help maintain current relationships.

61% have been online more than 7 years.

58% have a current library card.

31% used a social media site. YouTube is the most used site.

50%

Canada

15% feel activities while using a search engine are extremely or very private.

15% are likely to share photos or videos on a library social site.

31% feel the Internet is less private than it was 2 years ago.

33% shared books read on a social networking site.

41% agree social networking sites help build new relationships.

9% had personal information used online without consent.

25%

11% feel activities while using a library Web site are extremely or very private.

17% are likely to self-publish on a library social site.

75% Highest frequency to trust the people they communicate with on social networking sites. (Total general public = 70%)

25% Low percentage who are equally comfortable sharing their true personality online or in person. (Total general public = 30%)

50% Feel the Internet is as private or more private than it was two years ago. (Total general public = 52%)

Country Focus

... on the United States

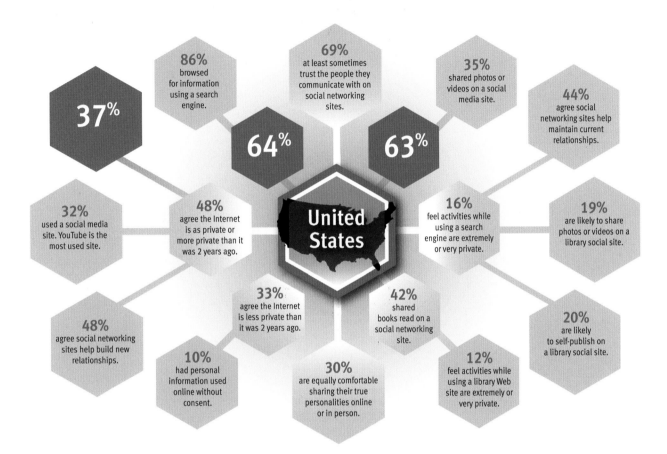

37% Highest usage of a social networking site in the last year. Most used site: MySpace. (Total general public = 28%)

64% Highest percentage to be using the Internet for seven years or more. (Total general public = 58%)

63% Highest propensity to have a current library card. (Total general public = 55%)

Country Focus

... on Japan

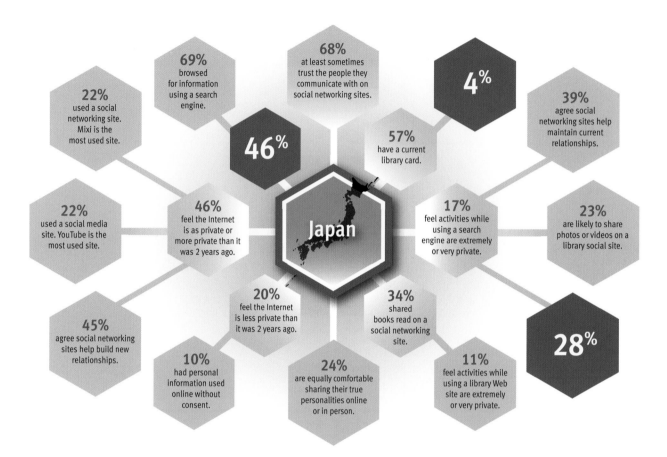

22% used a social networking site. Mixi is the most used site.

69% browsed for information using a search engine.

68% at least sometimes trust the people they communicate with on social networking sites.

4%

39% agree social networking sites help maintain current relationships.

46%

57% have a current library card.

22% used a social media site. YouTube is the most used site.

46% feel the Internet is as private or more private than it was 2 years ago.

Japan

17% feel activities while using a search engine are extremely or very private.

23% are likely to share photos or videos on a library social site.

45% agree social networking sites help build new relationships.

20% feel the Internet is less private than it was 2 years ago.

34% shared books read on a social networking site.

28%

10% had personal information used online without consent.

24% are equally comfortable sharing their true personalities online or in person.

11% feel activities while using a library Web site are extremely or very private.

46% Lowest percentage to be using the Internet for seven years or more. (Total general public = 58%)

28% Among the highest percentage to be likely to supply self-published information on a library social site. (Total general public = 22%)

4% Lowest percentage to have shared photos or videos on a social media site. (Total general public = 30%). However, 51% take/send photos on their cell phone. (Total general public = 39%)

Country Focus

... on France

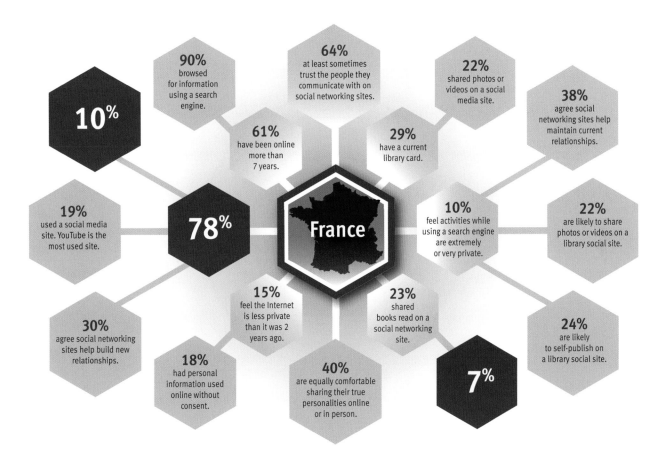

Least likely to have used a social networking site in the last year.
(Total general public = 28%)

Highest confidence in Internet privacy—feel the Internet is as private or more private than it was two years ago. (Total general public = 52%)

Lowest percentage to feel their library Web site activities are extremely or very private. (Total general public = 11%)

Country Focus

... on Germany

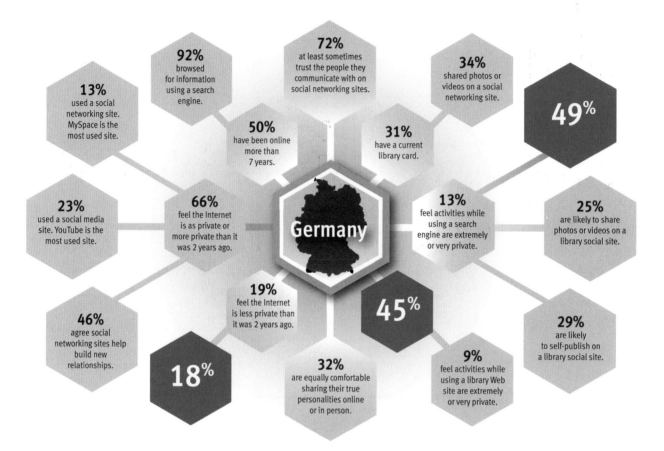

- **13%** used a social networking site. MySpace is the most used site.
- **92%** browsed for information using a search engine.
- **72%** at least sometimes trust the people they communicate with on social networking sites.
- **34%** shared photos or videos on a social networking site.
- **49%**
- **50%** have been online more than 7 years.
- **31%** have a current library card.
- **23%** used a social media site. YouTube is the most used site.
- **66%** feel the Internet is as private or more private than it was 2 years ago.
- **13%** feel activities while using a search engine are extremely or very private.
- **25%** are likely to share photos or videos on a library social site.
- **19%** feel the Internet is less private than it was 2 years ago.
- **45%**
- **46%** agree social networking sites help build new relationships.
- **18%**
- **32%** are equally comfortable sharing their true personalities online or in person.
- **9%** feel activities while using a library Web site are extremely or very private.
- **29%** are likely to self-publish on a library social site.

 45% Highest percentage to have shared books read on a social networking site. (Total general public = 39%)

 49% High percentage of social networking users who agree these sites help maintain current relationships. (Total general public = 42%)

 18% High percentage who have had their personal information used online without their consent. (Total general public = 11%)

Country Focus
... on the **United Kingdom**

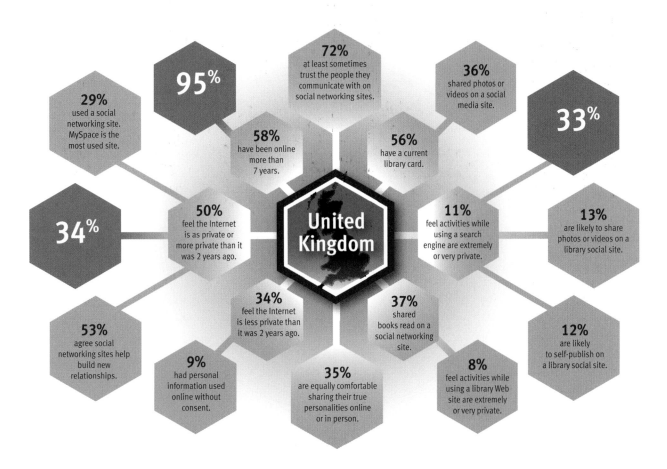

95% Highest propensity to have used a search engine in the last year. (Total general public = 85%)

34% Highest percentage of the general public to have used a social media site in the last year. (Total general public = 28%)

33% Lowest percentage of social networking users who agree these sites help maintain their current relationships. (Total general public = 42%)

Conclusion:

A Few Thoughts on the Findings ... and the Future

"2015—The Web continues to evolve from a world ruled by mass media and mass audiences to one ruled by messy media and messy participation."

—Kevin Kelly, "We are the Web," in *Wired*, August 2005.

The Internet has come of age. It is not only the habitat of the digital natives who grew up with a mouse, a joystick, a laptop, a cell phone, texting and an iPod or two, but for all of us. We are the millions who log onto the Internet every day to do what has become routine—check our e-mail, get driving directions, find a recipe, browse a health care site, do our banking, book a flight, and of course, delete the annoying messages that found their way through our spam filters.

Web users have all become as experienced as digital natives. In the 18 months since the publication of the *Perceptions of Libraries and Information Resources* report, the use of search engines and e-mail has grown by more than 20% over what were already enormous participation levels. User participation in basic Internet services, such as searching and e-mailing, is approaching total participation. More than twice as many respondents are using blogs now as then.

The majority of the respondents are using online banking, purchasing goods on commercial Web sites and using instant messaging. Social Web sites have gone from obscurity to mass use in the last two years. Over a quarter of respondents (28%) use social networking sites. Five social spaces are in the Alexa top ten global Web sites, including MySpace, Wikipedia and YouTube. And use of these social spaces is growing exponentially. YouTube had over 188 million visitors in June 2007, up over 280% in one year according to comScore.

Internet use has not simply increased, it has infiltrated our lives, offering more and more services at more and more service points. Use has grown for almost every Internet service we measured in this survey—well, almost every service.

The percentage of Internet users that have used a library Web site has decreased. Library Web site use declined from 30% of respondents in Canada, the U.K. and the U.S. in 2005 to 20% of the general public in these same countries in 2007, a 33% decrease.

Yet why should such a decline surprise us? It is to be expected that an online population equipped with do-it-yourself discovery tools will continue to expand their reach, as well as their desire to be self-sufficient, looking for information on their own in more and more places. Now experts themselves at search and find techniques, users naturally would move away from last-generation, "expert-based" information systems and gravitate to sites designed for them and by them, sites offering self service, quick access and limited rules. No authentication needed, no ILL forms to fill out, just free content and the tools to share it or create it.

The more intriguing question is—what are the services and incentives that online libraries could offer users to entice them to come back or to visit more often or even devote some of their own time to help create a social library site?

The survey results offer some clues.

Messy Participation

In Kevin Kelly's 2005 *Wired* article, "We are the Web," he paints a future vision of a powerful, universal Web. It is a Web of both technology and people, built not by the few chief architects who created the first generation Web, but a Web built by millions and empowered by the users—users who are now both creators and consumers.

Kelly's 2015 prediction of a user-empowered Web is probably much closer. Every day, tens of millions log on to MySpace, Facebook, Mixi and YouTube and they create. They create content, build profiles, upload videos, share photos—and then they erase their creations and start again. They build messy Web pages. They participate on others' sites. They share with their friends, they share with strangers—they lurk, they interlope and they engage. They create new communities and they join others. They socialize. Today's Internet can be characterized as unruly, close to Kelly's predicted world of "messy" participation.

The drive to participate, to build, to seek out communities is certainly nothing new. "Connect with friends," "be part of group," "have fun" and "express myself" are the top motives for using social networks according to our research. We could as easily be describing the motives behind the rise of the telephone, civic associations or, more recently, the cell phone, or the motivations that drew e-mail from the office into the home. The motives that are driving the rise of social networking are not unique.

And yet, this particular Internet innovation, the social networking craze, feels different. It doesn't seem to be playing out like the digital revolutions that preceded it. Social networking is doing something more than advancing communications between individuals, driving commerce or speeding connectivity. It is redefining roles, muddying the waters between audience and creator, rules and relationships, trust and security, private and public. And the roles are changing, not just for a few but for everyone, and every service, on the Web.

Whether one views this new social landscape as a great opportunity for improved information creation and exchange or as a messy playground to be tidied up to restore order, depends on one's point of view.

Privacy Windows

Users want privacy windows— permanent, impenetrable, but transparent and with the ability to open.

Our study offers a quick snapshot of life on the Internet, just a brief view from the sidelines of a scene that is playing out on millions of individual, but shared, playing fields. Our snapshot provides tens of thousands of unique attitudes, activities and motives, and, in aggregate, we saw a general public whose Internet activities, attitudes and motives were strikingly similar across the countries surveyed. Having shared common Internet services, tools, sites and protocols since the inception of the Web, Internet users have in many ways created a common online culture and community.

The builders of the social Web are comfortable and open. The Internet is now an everyday activity like making a phone call or watching TV. Internet activities are familiar and comfortable and, perhaps as a consequence, are not seen as particularly private. The users feel their personal information is as private and secure on the Internet as it was two years ago, and the more users participate on their favorite social and commercial sites, the more trust develops between the users and the sites.

Survey respondents told us that privacy absolutely matters. But more specifically they told us that what matters is the ability to be in control of their personal information. Users want, and expect, online services to have privacy and security policies. They want services to provide options that limit who can access their personal information, even if they usually choose not to use these options. And users want to know how their data will be used. They are often trusting of the people they communicate with online, and, they believe these social sites help build and maintain relationships.

They don't typically stop and read privacy policies, but they do look for symbols— identifiable marks that convey that the essentials of security and privacy are in place. Users want the freedom to safely share. They are not looking for privacy controls to serve as locked doors or barriers to their online activities. Rather, social Web users want privacy windows, shields of safety glass—permanent, impenetrable, but transparent and with the ability to open.

We observed a different perspective of the social Web from the 382 U.S. library directors we surveyed.

Library directors, like the general public surveyed, are active participants on the Web. In fact, on many services, they are even more active. Library directors have been online longer than the users they serve, and they e-mail, search, purchase online and build Web sites at rates greater than the general public.

But, unlike the general population, library directors see the Internet as a much less carefree environment. They feel their personal information is kept less private on the Internet than it was two years ago. While their personal information was breached at the same rate as the general public, they perceive their personal information on the Internet as less secure. And they predict the public share their same level of concern.

U.S. library directors do not see many everyday activities, such as home e-mail, search engine use and cable TV, as more private than the general public, with one exception. Library directors view the privacy of library activities as substantially more private than the general population does. And the directors feel users share their views. In fact, they anticipated that users would provide even higher privacy ratings than they personally provided for library activities.

These strong privacy concerns were reflected in their online behaviors on social sites. Library directors share less personal information than the general public. While equally willing to provide basic contact information on commercial sites, library directors are less willing to share information about themselves (e.g., personality or physical attributes, photos or videos or marital status) on social sites.

We see a social Web developing in an environment where users and librarians have dissimilar, perhaps conflicting, views on sharing and privacy. There is an imbalance. Librarians view their role as protectors of privacy; it is their professional obligation. They believe their users expect this of them. Users want privacy protection, but not for all services. They want the ability to control the protection, but not at the expense of participation.

A minority of users view library services and books they have read as very private—less than a quarter of respondents. It may be that for most of the population surveyed, books are not perceived as confidential, but, in fact, public. Books are everywhere—in airports, in grocery stores, at Wal-Mart, and of course, online. Over 50% of users surveyed have visited an online bookstore in the last 12 months. They rate the privacy of their activities at bookstores and on online bookstores roughly equal to the library—not very private.

Users and librarians have dissimilar, perhaps conflicting, views on sharing and privacy.

Libraries = Books

Libraries equal books, both offline and online. Our survey respondents told us this in OCLC's 2005 *Perceptions* study. Brand drives expectations. It drives expectations for the users/customers of the brand and it drives expectations for the builders of the brand. Brand creates an important and useful set of expectations of what the organization should deliver, and conversely, brand often puts boundaries around what users believe an organization can deliver.

The library brand has put boundaries around the expectations of libraries on the social Web. Overwhelmingly, neither the general public nor librarians see a role for libraries as providers of social sites.

Offline, libraries are vibrant social spaces. They are hubs of community activities and provide a venue for open exchange and dialogue. Yet, neither users nor librarians can see such a role for libraries online. Less than 15% of the users, or library directors, think libraries should construct or sponsor social networking sites. An equally small percentage of users say they would be very likely to contribute content, view others' collections or become involved in a social site if one was provided by a library.

Of the roughly 15% of both general public and library directors who saw a role for their libraries in social networking, the top suggestion for services their libraries should provide was predictable—"book clubs."

The Socially Networked Library

"Before long, I don't think people will use the term "social network." It will just become ubiquitous. People will expect it wherever they go online.

—Brian Mathews

It is unlikely that online book clubs alone will be the enticement to draw the builders of the social Web back to libraries or to libraries' Web sites. If Mathews is correct, and the survey results suggest that he likely will be, users will not be looking at the Web or the services they use as "social sites"; the distinction will be gone. Such labels will no longer differentiate Web sites. And it is probably no longer important if MySpace or Facebook or YouTube holds a position in the top 10 most used Web sites (except for the owners and financiers of the sites). It probably will not be important or interesting because the social Web will simply become our Web. Today's messy rules of participation will simply become the mode of operation, the expectation for all world-class Internet services. To entice users to the online library, libraries must expand their social activities, allowing users to easily share and create content and collaborate with others. They must build a high-value presence on the Web, a strong enough brand to compete.

As the Comparative Timeline in Appendix F chronicles, librarians have pioneered many of the digital services we now see in broad use on the Web: intranets to share resources, electronic information databases and "ask-an-expert" services. And although it took some librarians awhile to embrace the use of search engines as hubs for information access, librarians are now Googling more frequently than their users and teaching users how to maximize the potential of this powerful tool.

But, unfortunately, librarians are not pioneering the social Web. Whether it is a privacy concern, a lack of resources or the expectations of their users, librarians are lagging, not leading. Even when it comes to the social networking activity most easily associated with the library—book clubs—the digital pioneers are being out-innovated. As of September 2007, MySpace reports 197 online groups with "book club" in the title. And, book-swapping Web sites are becoming increasingly popular. Sites such as Paperback Swap, Book Mooch and Read It Swap It allow users to register and share books with other users, socializing a service that libraries have traditionally provided.

Many U.S. library directors are simply not engaged in the socialization of the Web. In the U.S., 37% of Web users surveyed are participating on social networks, and, across the countries surveyed, 56% of college students now use social networking. Yet, less than a quarter of U.S. library directors are engaged on social networking sites.

Increasing staff engagement on social sites should be included in every library's strategic plan.

To engage library users on social sites, our findings suggest that librarians will not only have to participate more, but they will also have to challenge the traditional approaches to protecting users' information privacy. Since the early 1900s (see Appendix F), U.S. librarians have been privacy pioneers, ensuring that users have freedom of thought. Now, librarians must identify how best to continue to defend privacy, while adapting the traditional privacy principles to the open world. Must information privacy protection remain the sole responsibility of the library, or can users become involved? Is it possible to give the users privacy controls alongside the libraries' privacy rules?

We know that privacy is important to users, and to librarians, but we also know that sharing and open access matter. Privacy matters, but sharing matters more. If the axiom "convenience trumps quality" was the trade-off that gave rise to the search portals as providers of "good enough" information, it might be said of the social Web that "sharing trumps privacy."

But is a trade-off required? Are there methods of providing both sharing and privacy? Is it possible for libraries to pioneer social solutions? Banks provide an interesting case study.

Of the 18 everyday activities that we evaluated, online banking was the single activity that respondents, both the general public and librarians, rated as very private. Across all countries surveyed, online banking was seen as very private by over 60% of users. Online banking has become one of the most widely used online services. Over half of respondents indicated that they have used an online banking site in the last year.

Banks have successfully migrated the privacy and security promise of their physical institutions to their online institutions. Without compromising privacy, banks have increased self-service, established user control and created 24 x 7 service and access. The transition has not been without work. Online banks have done many things to not only build their solutions but to communicate their value and their brand promise. Online banking sites offer both written privacy policies and privacy symbols, or icons, to convey their privacy and security promise. Banks regularly communicate their online security policies with written direct marketing materials. They market privacy in their physical locations, on their banking kiosks and on their bankcards.

"Convenience trumps quality."
−2005

"Sharing trumps privacy."
−2007

Libraries have a similarly high institution trust level. Sixty percent (60%) of survey participants rate their libraries as trustworthy. To date, libraries have been unsuccessful transferring this brand promise online. Online libraries are seen as no more private than commercial sites and social sites. Many users (24%) are not aware that libraries have policies on how their personal information is used.

Most physical libraries have no visual signs or symbols that promote a privacy promise to users, even though over 45% of library directors indicated that it was their professional responsibility to protect users' privacy. Similarly, most library Web sites do not have any visual symbols, or icons, to promote the promise of privacy and security. Does your library card carry a promise of privacy? (The author's library card carries a warning about responsibility for lost items, but no brand promise.)

On the social Web, is it possible to make library privacy a differentiator—a brand promise—not a barrier to access or information sharing?

If convenience does trump quality, then it is the librarians' job to make quality convenient. If sharing will trump privacy on the social Web, it is the librarians' opportunity to make privacy shareable.

Open the Doors

On the social Web, the library brand must go from institutional to personal.

For example, many libraries have initiated broadcast services on their Web sites; RSS feeds and blogs are among the most common. No doubt, these are useful services. But if our goal is to create a social library, focusing on these broadcast services is likely leading us in the wrong direction—perpetuating the traditional concept (brand) of the library as a supplier of information, an institution, not a place for idea generation and exchange. Some very simple techniques are creating a personal brand promise for online commercial sites. A quarter of survey respondents told us they establish a "my favorites or wish list" on commercial sites. No such service exists on most library sites. While this simple application is no doubt a relatively useful service for consumers, it is an invaluable brand endorsement for the vendor. It creates a partnership into the future, a sense of joint ownership of the Web experience and provides users with a personal reason to return. By inviting participation, the connection between the customer and the supplier, or the user and the library, changes. And so do the perceptions.

Our perceptions become our realities, and often, our limitations.

Our perceptions become our realities, and often, also our limitations. This was clearly the case for the authors of this report when we began our research on social networks a year ago. There is no doubt that our initial perceptions of social networks influenced our approach to this study. Handicapped by only limited personal experiences with sites, we began our study as we had every study before it—by looking at social networks as a service or set of services to be studied, learned and implemented. We conceived of a social library as a library of traditional services enhanced by a set of social tools—wikis, blogs, mashups and podcasts. Integrated services, of course, user-friendly for sure and offering superior self-service. We were wrong.

Our view, after living with the data, struggling with the findings, listening to experts and creating our own social spaces, is quite different. Becoming engaged in the social Web is not about learning new services or mastering new technologies. To create a checklist of social tools for librarians to learn or to generate a "top ten" list of services to implement on the current library Web site would be shortsighted. Such lists exist. Resist the urge to use them.

The social Web is not being built by augmenting traditional Web sites with new tools. And a social library will not be created by implementing a list of social software features on our current sites. The social Web is being created by opening the doors to the production of the Web, dismantling the current structures and inviting users in to create their content and establish new rules.

Open the library doors, invite mass participation by users and relax the rules of privacy. It will be messy. The rules of the new social Web are messy. The rules of the new social library will be equally messy. But mass participation and a little chaos often create the most exciting venues for collaboration, creativity, community building—and transformation. It is right on mission.

Our pioneers in "Beyond the Numbers" indicated that they started with a small step into the social world, by blogging, chatting or contributing to wikis—by participating. And discussing what they learned. We want to hear your perspectives and ideas. Share your comments at www.oclc.org/reports/sharing/.

The new Web is a very different thing. Libraries need to be very different, too.

Invite users in to create content and establish new rules.

Appendices

A: College Students in Our Networked World   A-1

B: Glossary   B-1

C: People Consulted   C-1

D: Readings and Other Sources   D-1

E: About OCLC   E-1

F: Comparative Timeline   F-1

Appendix A: College Students in Our Networked World

Time doesn't matter on these networks. You can keep in contact with people you haven't talked to in years and years and years.... It was more difficult before these technologies....

Now it's limitless, almost. You can keep in touch with whomever you want to whatever extent you want.

—Undergraduate student, McMaster University, Hamilton, Ontario, Canada

511 college students across all countries surveyed provided insight into their digital lives, their favorite social sites and their motivations for social networking.

They shared their views on Internet privacy and security and attitudes about trusting people they meet online.

They also expressed their opinions about information privacy and the library's potential role in social networking.

Our Digital Lives—College Students

The participation in many online activities by the college students surveyed outpaced that of the total general public.

Online Activities

What type(s) of online activities have you done or participated in during the last 12 months?

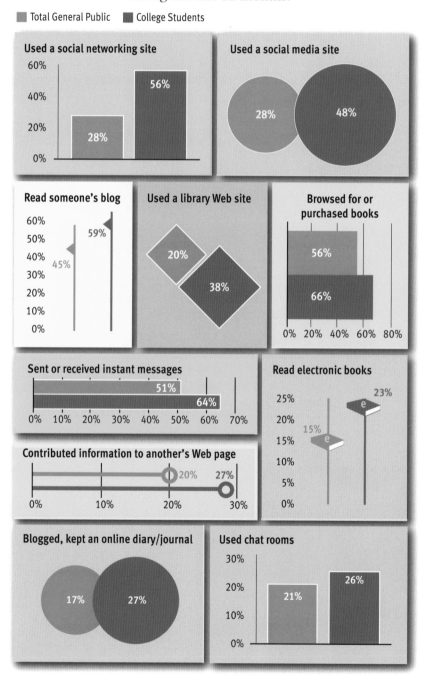

56% *of college students and*

28% *of the total general public* have used a social networking site.

38% *of college students have borrowed items or searched for specific items through the* library Web site *compared to*

20% *of the total general public.*

Source: *Sharing, Privacy and Trust in Our Networked World*, OCLC, 2007, question 530.

Our Social Spaces—College Students

Usage of Social Networking, Social Media and Commercial Sites

Below is a list of [social networking, social media, and/or commercial Web sites]. Please select all the Web sites you have used in the past 12 months.

Base: Respondents who have used a social networking, social media, commercial and/or library Web site.

Of those who use social networking sites:

61%

of college students and

61%

of the total general public use

MySpace.

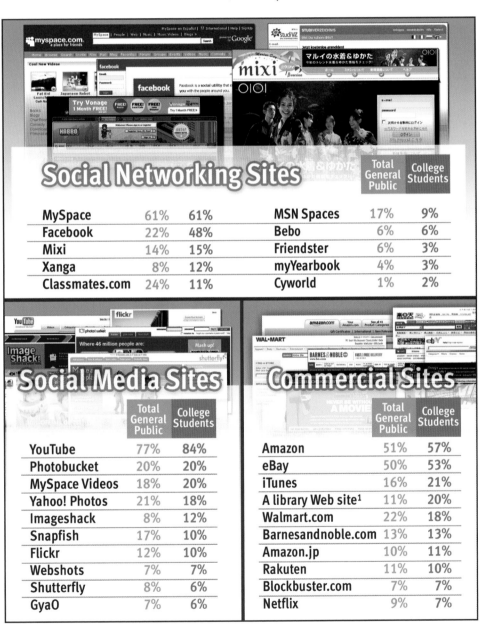

Social Networking Sites

	Total General Public	College Students		Total General Public	College Students
MySpace	61%	61%	MSN Spaces	17%	9%
Facebook	22%	48%	Bebo	6%	6%
Mixi	14%	15%	Friendster	6%	3%
Xanga	8%	12%	myYearbook	4%	3%
Classmates.com	24%	11%	Cyworld	1%	2%

Social Media Sites

	Total General Public	College Students
YouTube	77%	84%
Photobucket	20%	20%
MySpace Videos	18%	20%
Yahoo! Photos	21%	18%
Imageshack	8%	12%
Snapfish	17%	10%
Flickr	12%	10%
Webshots	7%	7%
Shutterfly	8%	6%
GyaO	7%	6%

Commercial Sites

	Total General Public	College Students
Amazon	51%	57%
eBay	50%	53%
iTunes	16%	21%
A library Web site[1]	11%	20%
Walmart.com	22%	18%
Barnesandnoble.com	13%	13%
Amazon.jp	10%	11%
Rakuten	11%	10%
Blockbuster.com	7%	7%
Netflix	9%	7%

Note: The chart shows the top 10 social networking, social media and commercial sites.

[1]Library Web site was grouped with commercial sites to provide a view of relative usage across countries.

Source: *Sharing, Privacy and Trust in Our Networked World,* OCLC, 2007, questions 605, 710 and 770.

Information Shared on Social Networking Sites

Which of the following types of information have you ever supplied about yourself on a social networking Web site?

Base: Respondents who have used a social networking site.

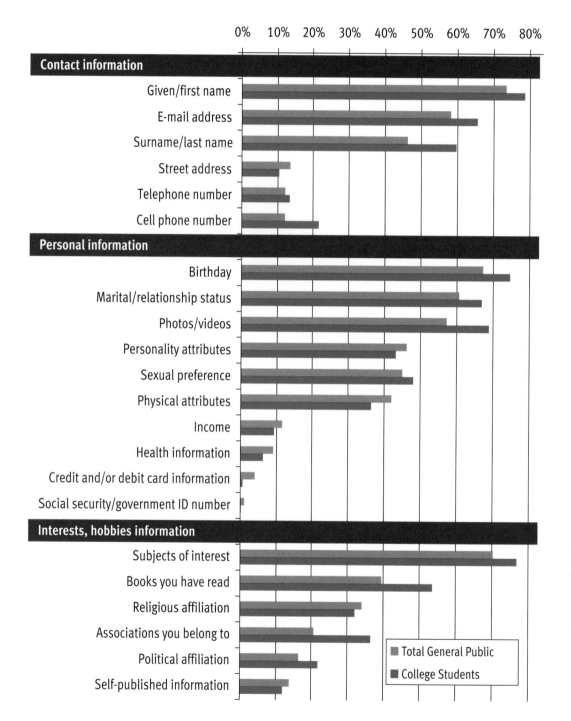

69%
of college student social networking users *have shared photos/videos.*

College students are
more likely
than the total general public to have
shared information
on a social networking site.

Source: *Sharing, Privacy and Trust in Our Networked World*, OCLC, 2007, question 625.

Why Students Use Social Networking Sites

Which of the following describe why you use
your preferred social networking Web site(s)?

Base: Respondents who have used a social networking site.

80%

*of college students who
use a social networking
site do so because their*
friends are there.

*I'm not trying to meet
new people, I'm just*

maintaining
friendships

*with people that I know
in person.*

**25-year-old undergraduate
student from the U.S.**

Source: *Sharing, Privacy and Trust in Our
Networked World*, OCLC, 2007, question
975, "Why do you prefer to remain
anonymous on social networking Web
sites?"

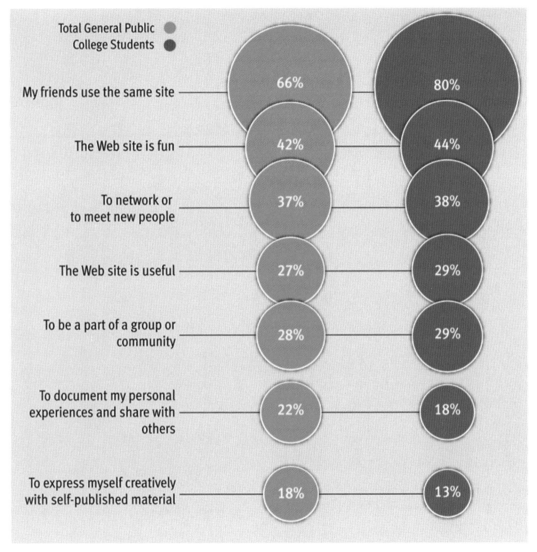

Total General Public
College Students

	Total General Public	College Students
My friends use the same site	66%	80%
The Web site is fun	42%	44%
To network or to meet new people	37%	38%
The Web site is useful	27%	29%
To be a part of a group or community	28%	29%
To document my personal experiences and share with others	22%	18%
To express myself creatively with self-published material	18%	13%

Source: *Sharing, Privacy and Trust in Our Networked World*, OCLC, 2007, question 626.

*It's like economies of scale. When you pick up the
telephone to call, you're only talking to one person, but
when you go online, you can have multiple conversations
in the same amount of time.*

Undergraduate student from Canada
Source: *Sharing, Privacy and Trust in Our Networked World*,
OCLC, 2007, discussion group.

Why Students Use Social Media Sites

Which of the following describe why you use
your preferred social media Web site(s)?

Base: Respondents who have used a social media site.

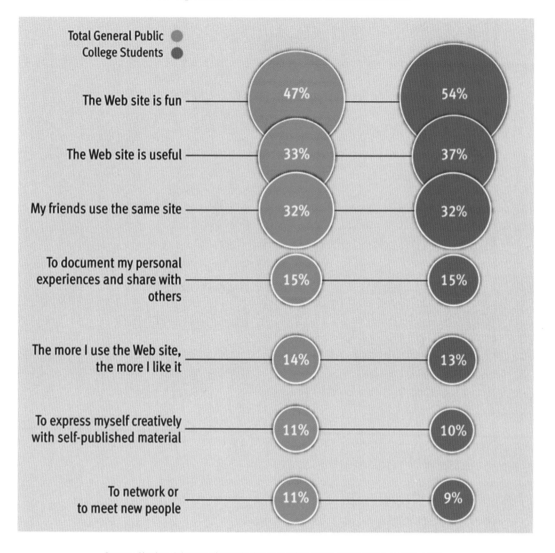

Total General Public ●
College Students ●

The Web site is fun — 47% | 54%

The Web site is useful — 33% | 37%

My friends use the same site — 32% | 32%

To document my personal experiences and share with others — 15% | 15%

The more I use the Web site, the more I like it — 14% | 13%

To express myself creatively with self-published material — 11% | 10%

To network or to meet new people — 11% | 9%

Source: *Sharing, Privacy and Trust in Our Networked World*, OCLC, 2007, question 730.

84%
of college students
***have used
YouTube in the
last 12 months.***

***66% of college students have browsed for
or purchased books online, compared to
56% of the total general public.***

Privacy, Security and Trust—College Students

There's a sort of
fluid scale
(about privacy)
that you have to keep in mind as you fill out online applications. How important is this service or product to me ... they're asking "this much" information from me.
Is it worth it?

Undergraduate student from Canada

Source: *Sharing, Privacy and Trust in Our Networked World*, OCLC, 2007, discussion group.

54%
of college students feel the Internet is
as private or more private
than it was two years ago;
59%
as secure or more secure.

Perception of Internet Privacy

Generally, do you think that your personal information on the Internet is kept more private than, less private than, or the same as it was two years ago?

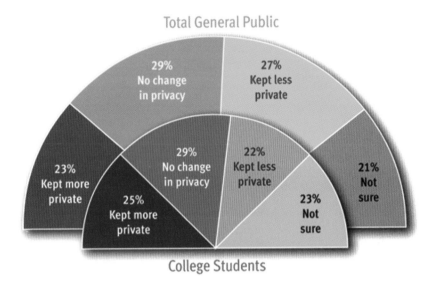

Source: *Sharing, Privacy and Trust in Our Networked World*, OCLC, 2007, question 930.

Perception of Internet Security

Generally, do you think that your personal information on the Internet is kept more secure than, less secure than, or the same as it was two years ago?

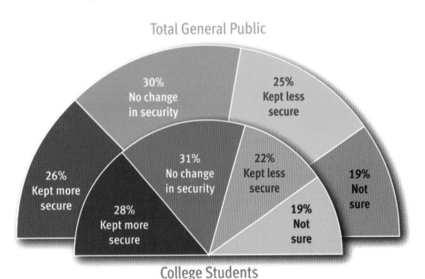

Source: *Sharing, Privacy and Trust in Our Networked World*, OCLC, 2007, question 935.

Privacy of Browsing/Searching Activities

Please rate how private, if at all, the following information is to you.

Note: The chart shows the *extremely private* and *very private* responses.

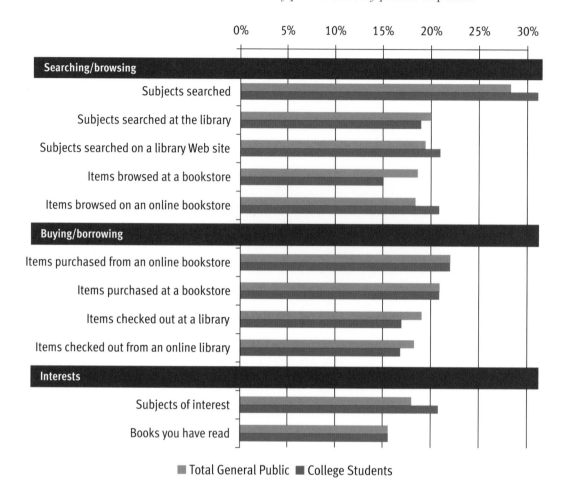

College students feel that items browsed/purchased at a book store or online are

at least as private

as items browsed or checked out at the library or a library Web site.

Source: *Sharing, Privacy and Trust in Our Networked World*, OCLC, 2007, question 911.

Students and Trusting Whom They Meet on the Internet

In general, when using [social networking, social media and/or library Web sites], how frequently do you trust the people you meet?

Base: Respondents who have used a social networking site, social media site and/or the library Web site.

Note: The chart shows the *strongly agree* and *somewhat agree* responses.

College students are
slightly less likely
than the total general public to
trust
those they meet on social networking sites.

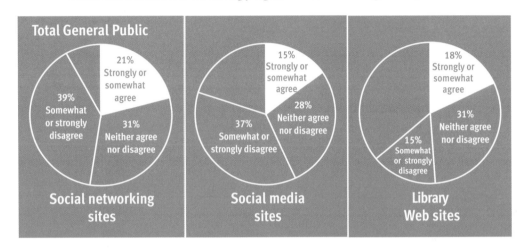

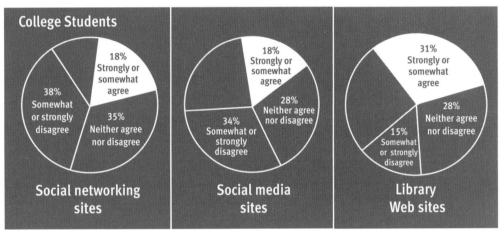

Source: *Sharing, Privacy and Trust in Our Networked World,* OCLC, 2007, questions 971, 1011 and 1086.

そこにいる人たちをまったく信用できないから。他人と交流する必要がないため。

[Because I absolutely do not trust the people in there. Since there is no need to exchange with strangers.]

20-year-old junior college student from Japan

Source: *Sharing, Privacy and Trust in Our Networked World*, OCLC, 2007, question 1015, "Why do you prefer to remain anonymous on social media Web sites?"

I trust (social networking sites) because they give you the option of blocking whoever you want ... you can block specific people. It's totally up to you how much information you want online.

Undergraduate student from Canada

Source: *Sharing, Privacy and Trust in Our Networked World*, OCLC, 2007, discussion group.

Libraries, Students and the Social Web

Importance of Keeping Library Information Private

In thinking about privacy, how important, if at all, is it to you that the library you primarily use would keep ... private?

Base: Respondents who have used the library in person or online.

Note: The chart shows the *extremely important* and *very important* responses.

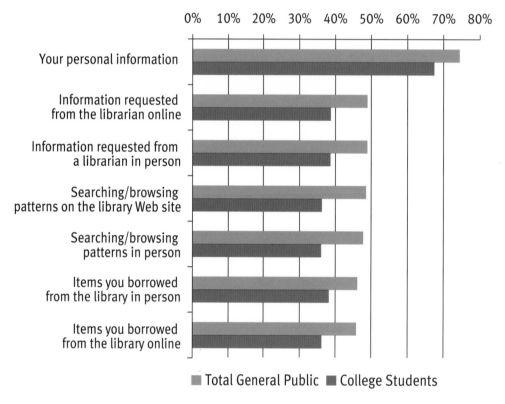

■ Total General Public ■ College Students

Source: *Sharing, Privacy and Trust in Our Networked World*, OCLC, 2007, question 1076.

When you go into (a database) and look for a specific journal (the library system) doesn't let you put it in your favorites, **which is so annoying.**

Graduate student from Canada

Source: *Sharing, Privacy and Trust in Our Networked World*, OCLC, 2007, discussion group.

College students are **less likely** *than the total general public to feel it is very important to keep library information private.*

Library Social Networking Sites

Do you think it should be the role of the library to build
social networking sites for your community?

Base: Respondents who have used the library in person or online.

Just

13%

*of college students think
libraries should build
social networking sites.*

56%

*of college students use
social networking sites.*

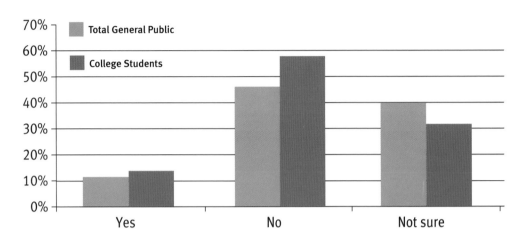

Source: *Sharing, Privacy and Trust in Our Networked World*, OCLC, 2007, question 1100.

Library's have that kind of

opportunity,

*but it does not seem like
it should be something
forced upon the library.
Libraries started as*

places for
books, no?

**18-year-old undergraduate
student from the United States**

Source: *Sharing, Privacy and Trust in Our
Networked World*, OCLC, 2007, question
1113, "Why do you think that it should
not be the library's role to build social
networking sites in your community?"

*That's just not the library's function. It
would definitely be a cool concept, but with
so many underfunded libraries, it should
not be added to their burden.*

**20-year-old undergraduate
student from the United States**

Source: *Sharing, Privacy and Trust in Our Networked World*,
OCLC, 2007, question 1113, "Why do you think that it should
not be the library's role to build social networking sites in your
community?"

Participation in Library-Hosted Social Networking Activities

How likely would you be to participate in each of the following activities on a social networking/community site if built by your library?

Base: Respondents who have used the library in person or online.

Note: The chart show the *extremely likely* and *very likely* responses.

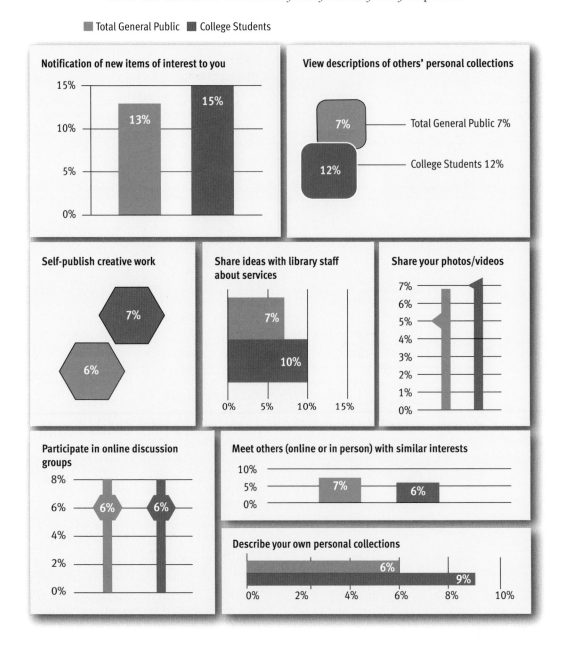

Most college students would be

unlikely

to participate in social networking services offered by a library.

Source: *Sharing, Privacy and Trust in Our Networked World*, OCLC, 2007, question 1096.

College Students' Thoughts on Social Networking

Note: All verbatim comments are presented as entered by survey respondents, including spelling, grammatical and punctuation errors.

I reveal more about myself as I get to know people, but a lot of the time random people are looking at my profile and I don't want them to know too much about me.

20-year-old undergraduate student from the U.S.

Source: *Sharing, Privacy and Trust in Our Networked World*, OCLC, 2007, question 975, "Why do you prefer to remain anonymous on social networking Web sites?"

Meinungsaustausch über bestimmte Themen und Bücher [Exchange of ideas about certain topics and books].

17-year-old undergraduate student from Germany

Source: *Sharing, Privacy and Trust in Our Networked World*, OCLC, 2007, question 1112, "Please describe the top two most interesting activities that could be included in a library's social networking/community site."

One of the best benefits of social networking is that they expose you to more people ... all over the world.

Graduate student from Canada

Source: *Sharing, Privacy and Trust in Our Networked World*, OCLC, 2007, discussion group.

it is really no one else's business. not that we have anything to hide, i just feel it is a breach of our privacy.

18-year-old undergraduate student from the U.S.

Source: *Sharing, Privacy and Trust in Our Networked World*, OCLC, 2007, question 915, "Why do you feel that the subjects that you have searched on the Internet are (private, very private or extremely private)?"

there is too much things on the internet now. let the library be a library and thats that!

19-year-old undergraduate student from Canada

Source: *Sharing, Privacy and Trust in Our Networked World*, OCLC, 2007, question 1113, "Why do you think that it should not be the library's role to build social networking sites in your community?"

インターネットの匿名性を信頼して使用している面があるから。

[Because there is a sense that I am using the Internet while putting faith in the Internet's anonymity.]

22-year-old undergraduate student from Japan

Source: *Sharing, Privacy and Trust in Our Networked World*, OCLC, 2007, question 915, "Why do you feel that the subjects that you have searched on the Internet are (private, very private or extremely private)?"

le rôle de la bibliothèque est de mettre à disposition des livres articles... pas de mettre les individus en relation [The role of the library is to make books and articles available.. not to connect individuals].

26-year-old graduate student from France

Source: *Sharing, Privacy and Trust in Our Networked World*, OCLC, 2007, question 1113, "Why do you think that it should not be the library's role to build social networking sites in your community?"

Appendix B: Glossary

2xMoinsCher—A French e-commerce company that provides a wide variety of consumer goods and services. These include computer hardware and software, DVDs, CDs, video games, telephone and entertainment equipment, books and sporting goods. The site also offers clothes, shoes and accessories. 2xMoinsCher was founded in 2001 and is headquartered in Paris, France. It operates as a subsidiary of Trokers SA. www.2xmoinscher.com

7dream.com—A Japanese e-commerce Web site owned by 7-Eleven Japan Co. Ltd., Japan's largest convenience store. The site launched in mid-2000 and enables its shoppers to browse through more than 100,000 items—including music, flowers and photo supplies—place orders online and pay for the items when picked up at local 7-Eleven stores. www.7dream.com

Aeonshop—An online outlet for Aeon Group (a developer of shopping malls), Aeonshop is a Japanese e-commerce site that offers an extensive variety of consumer goods. www.aeonshop.com

Aggregator—An organization, individual or application that gathers content from multiple sources for presentation elsewhere. Syndication occurs when Web content is gathered and redistributed.

Alapage—A French e-commerce enterprise and subsidiary of France Telecom. Alapage offers a wide variety of goods and services, including computer hardware and software, video and sound equipment, books, music, videos, hobby and crafting supplies, and travel services. Alapage reports a million visitors to its site each day. www.alapage.com

Alexa.com—A subsidiary company of Amazon.com. Based in California, Alexa Internet, Inc. is best known for operating a Web site that gives users information on Web traffic to other Web sites. Alexa collects information from people who have installed an "Alexa Toolbar," allowing Alexa to provide statistics on Web site traffic, as well as lists of related links. www.alexa.com

Amazon and Amazon.jp—An American e-commerce company based in Seattle, Washington, U.S., it was one of the first major companies to sell goods over the Internet. Founded in 1994 and launched in 1995, Amazon.com began as an online bookstore, though it soon diversified its product lines, adding VHS, DVDs, music CDs, computer software, video games, electronics, apparel, furniture, food, toys and more. Amazon has established separate Web sites in Canada, the United Kingdom, Germany, Austria, France, China and Japan and ships globally on selected products. www.amazon.com and www.amazon.jp

Application sharing—A feature of many videoconferencing applications that enables the conference participants to simultaneously run the same application. The application itself resides on only one of the machines connected to the conference.

Architecture of Participation—Tim O'Reilly, founder of O'Reilly Media, uses this term to describe systems that are designed for user contribution. O'Reilly first used this term during a presentation at the Warburg Pincus Annual Technology Conference, May 2003.

Ask.jp video—A Japanese video-sharing site operated by Ask.jp Co., Ltd. of the transcosmos group and founded in 2000. http://video.ask.jp

Authentication—The process of confirming that the user accessing a site is authentic and a registered user. Also, in computer security, the process of verifying the digital identity of the communication sender.

Baidu.com—China's leading search engine. Baidu searches audio files, images and Web sites. It features an interface that is similar to Google's and has discussion forums that are searchable by keyword, and an online Wikipedia-like encyclopedia (Baidu Baike). It was ranked eighth in Alexa's Internet rankings, as of September 7, 2007. Baidu indexes more than 740 million Web pages, 80 million images and 10 million multimedia files. www.baidu.com

Bandwidth—A measure of capacity in a channel for electronic communication. Bandwidth is often expressed by users as a measurement of speed. The higher the bandwidth, the less time it takes to transmit information.

Barnesandnoble.com—Barnes & Noble.com is a wholly-owned subsidiary of Barnes & Noble, Inc., that began operation in 1997. It offers online customers books, music, DVD, video games, and related products and services. Barnes & Noble originated in 1873 when Charles M. Barnes opened a book-printing business in Wheaton, Illinois, U.S. www.barnesandnoble.com

BBC Newsline—The BBC's regional television news service for Northern Ireland. On the air in its current format since 1996, BBC Newsline broadcasts brief five-to-ten-minute bulletins seven days a week and a 30-minute news program on Monday through Friday evenings.

Bebo—A social networking Web site founded in 2005. Bebo allows friends to communicate by posting pictures, writing blogs and sending messages to one another. Bebo's format is similar to Xanga, MySpace, and Yahoo! 360. www.bebo.com

Berners-Lee, Tim—Inventor of the World Wide Web in 1989. Director of the World Wide Web Consortium, Senior Researcher at Massachusetts Institute of Technology's Computer Science and Artificial Intelligence Laboratory, and Professor of Computer Science at Southampton Electronics and Computer Science.

Blockbuster.com—Blockbuster began in Dallas, Texas, U.S. in 1985 as a movie rental operation and in 2004 introduced an online DVD rental service in the U.S. Its online operation includes 36 warehouses and 1,400+ stores. At the end of the third quarter of 2006, it had 1.5 million subscribers. www.blockbuster.com

Blog (or Web log)—A Web-based journal of short, dated entries in reverse chronological order. Most blogs focus on one subject area and are updated daily. Entries typically consist of links to external Web pages with summaries of or commentary on the content. *See also "Corporate blogging."*

Blogosphere—A term used to describe the total number of blogs.

Blogroll—A list of links to other blogs found on a blog.

BookMooch—An online group of around 40,000 members that specializes in book exchange. A user registers a book list online and may request books. Points are awarded for each book listed and exchanged, and the points are used to obtain the books. BookMooch was started by John Buckman. http://bookmooch.com

Broadband—High-speed Internet access. In the United States, Internet access over 200 kbit/s is classified as broadband.

buch.de—A German-based Internet trade enterprise offering books, e-books, video, software and floral products. Nearly 80% of buch.de's 2006 sales were for its book products. Most of its 80 employees are based at the Münster headquarters. www.buch.de/shop/home/show/

buecher.de—A German-based Internet trade enterprise offering books, music, videos, software and video games. www.buecher.de

Bulletin board—A bulletin board functions very much like a newsgroup with the users of the board posting messages; these messages are then displayed to all those who access the bulletin board. It is a low-tech solution for providing a forum for users whose numbers are too small or whose focus of interest is too specialized to be supported by a newsgroup.

Cafesta—A Japanese communication portal site begun in 2002 that offers e-mail service, online gaming and real estate information. Cafesta has a membership of over 14.4 million. Free and open to anyone, membership ranges from elementary and junior high school students to parents and other adults. www.cafesta.com

Camtasia—Screen recorder and editing software offered by TechSmith Corporation. www.techsmith.com/camtasia.asp

Cdiscount—A leading French e-commerce site that offers 15 online stores. Items and services available for purchase include CDs, DVDs, books, videos and video games, household electronics, photography services, mobile phones, music, home décor and travel. Founded in 1998 and headquartered in Bordeaux, France, Cdiscount has a staff of 650. www.cdiscount.com

CD WOW!—An online retailer of music CDs, DVDs and video games. Launched in 2000, CD WOW! is based in Hong Kong and maintains Web sites in a number of primarily European countries. It is known for its discounted prices, and has been legally challenged by the British Phonographic Industry for its business practices. www.cd-wow.com

Chapters.Indigo.ca—A leading Canadian online bookseller for books, games, DVDs, toys and music CDs. Chapters.Indigo was formed in 2001 from the merger of Indigo Books and Music and Chapters, Inc., then the largest book retailer in Canada. Its online shopping service, Chapters.Indigo.ca, operates one of the leading Internet affiliate programs for Web site owners. www.chapters.indigo.ca

Chat—The process of communicating with other Internet users in real time.

Classmates.com—The first social networking Web site, created in 1995. The site is owned by Classmates Online, Inc., a subsidiary of United Online. Classmates Online, Inc. also owns Classmates International, which operates similar sites in Germany and Sweden. Classmates.com is used by members in the U.S. and Canada to find and connect with friends from school, work and the military. Over 40 million users are registered on the site and the site is ranked by Alexa.com as the 938th most used Web site globally. In the U.S. and Canada, the site is ranked 179th and 289th, respectively. www.classmates.com

Collaboration—Sharing and viewing a document or computer application simultaneously with both parties having the ability to make modifications. *See also "Mass collaboration."*

Commercial sites—Web sites used for browsing and purchasing goods and services.

comScore—An Internet information provider that measures Web site use. According to the comScore, over two million consumers allow comScore to capture their browsing and transactions on the Web. comScore aggregates this data to provide analysis of Web site use and traffic.

Connotea—Free online reference management system for clinicians and scientists. www.connotea.org

Consumer digital rights management—Consumer-oriented protection from misuse of copyright of intellectual property, distributed in digital form.

Consumer privacy—Laws that protect individuals from loss of privacy due to interactions with corporations.

Content aggregation and syndication—Aggregation allows content from multiple sources to be consolidated into one repository or Web site. Syndication allows desired content to be distributed between servers efficiently.

Content aggregator—An individual or organization that amasses or collects information for resale.

Content integration—Tools to link the content that is dispersed throughout the enterprise in diverse applications and databases.

Copains d'avant—A French social networking site that focuses on helping users locate friends, conduct genealogical searches, plan social events and pursue professional networking opportunities. www.copainsdavant.fr/

Corporate blogging—The application of personal online publishing "Web log" styles—that is, online publishing in a daily or frequently updated "log" format—to corporate objectives. *See also "Blog (or Web log)."*

Craigslist—An American Web site that hosts 100 topical forums and local classified advertisements for 450 cities worldwide. Incorporated in 1999, Craigslist strives to remain relatively uncommercial while connecting site users with a vast array of consumer goods and services available from third parties. Headquartered in San Francisco, California, U.S. Craigslist reports a monthly user base of 25 million customers who view more than 8 billion pages per month. www.craigslist.org

Creative Commons—A nonprofit organization founded in 2001. Copyright holders may use free Creative Commons licenses to share their information over the Web. With the Creative Commons license copyright holders indicate how others may use their information. http://creativecommons.org

CURURU—A Japanese social networking Web site. www.cururu.jp

Cyberlaw—The body of law related to the use of communication technology, including the Internet.

Cyberspace—The electronic medium of computer networks, in which online communication takes place.

Cyworld—An online community for trusted friendships and creative communication. Launched in 1999 in South Korea, Cyworld recently expanded to China, Japan, Taiwan and the U.S. Cyworld is owned by SK Communications, a subsidiary of SK Telecom, the number-one provider of mobile telecommunications in Asia. http://us.cyworld.com

Dailymotion—The leading independent provider of online video content in France, headquarted in Paris and founded in 2005. Dailymotion's objective is "to propose the best possible content to its users while offering the largest possible audience to its partners." In June 2007, it reported having 37.6 million unique users worldwide and 715 million video viewings. It is ranked among the top 60 most visited Web sites worldwide. www.dailymotion.com

del.icio.us—A social bookmarking Web site that allows users to store bookmarks online. del.icio.us users have access to the same bookmarks from any computer, and they can organize their bookmarks by tagging them. Users may also share links to their bookmarks. http://del.icio.us

Digg—A social networking site that helps discover and share content from across the World Wide Web. Launched in 2004, Digg focuses primarily on technology and science articles, but has added categories such as politics and entertainment, recently. Digg features social bookmarking, blogging and syndication with a distributed, decentralized editorial control. Users submit news stories and Web sites, which may be voted on and then be sent to the front page through a unique user-oriented ranking system. www.digg.com

Digital asset management—Provides a repository for data types such as images, audio and video. Functionality should include search and manipulation of these objects.

Digital divide—A metaphorical description of the boundary between people affluent enough to have a personal computer regularly at their disposal and those who cannot.

Digital Immigrant—A term used to describe people who were not born into the digital world, but who have become interested in, learned and adopted many of the new technologies that characterize the digital world. *See also "Digital Native."*

Digital Native—A term used to describe people, born in the late 1970s through early 1980s, who have grown up immersed in technology and who are said to speak the digital language enabled by new technologies such as the Internet, cell phones, videos and computers. *See also "Digital Immigrant."*

Digital Rights Management (DRM)—Technology or technologies that enable the secure distribution, promotion and sale of digital media content.

Disintermediation—Occurs when simplifications in technology, economic forces or other causes displace someone, usually an intermediary, from a customary role in a process. This term is also used as a verb to describe how this displacement process happens; for example, computerized typesetting systems in the newspaper companies disintermediated the linotype machines; operators who were their predecessors a few generations earlier disintermediated manual typesetters.

Disruptive technologies—New products or distribution processes superior to the ones they replace. They characteristically simplify those processes, improve the product and reduce costs so much that they change the basis of competition in an entire industry. Disruptive technologies typically destroy companies and even whole industries. The eventual disruption of the integrated steel-producing companies by the mini-mills is the historical process that gave rise to this concept.

DivX Stage6—An online platform for video sharing. Stage6, a division of DivX (headquartered in San Diego, California, U.S.) launched in 2006 and enables users to upload, download, view and share videos. http://stage6.divx.com

Document exchange—The sharing of documents over the Internet.

Document imaging—A mature technology for rendering paper documents as electronic images.

DOI (Digital Object Identifiers)—System for identifying and exchanging intellectual property in the digital environment. It allows for the construction of automated services and transactions for e-commerce. www.doi.org

eBay—An American Internet company that manages eBay.com, an online auction and shopping Web site where people and businesses buy and sell goods and services worldwide. In addition to its original U.S. Web site, eBay has established localized Web sites in several other countries. eBay also owns PayPal, Skype and other businesses. The online auction Web site was founded in San Jose, California, U.S. in 1995 by computer programmer Pierre Omidyar as AuctionWeb. Millions of collectibles, appliances, computers, furniture, equipment, vehicles and other miscellaneous items are listed, bought and sold daily. www.ebay.com

eHarmony—A U.S.-based personal relationship service that promotes its use of a scientific approach for matching single adults. The company was founded in 2000 by author and clinical psychologist Dr. Neil Clark Warren. According to press releases and news articles, eHarmony has more than 13 million users (as of August 2005) and reports more than 6,000 marriages between members (as of August 2004). www.eharmony.com

E-mail—A form of electronic messaging where a user creates a text message (that may have a number of attachments) and sends it to a recipient.

Facebook—Created by a Harvard student in 2004, Facebook began as a digital version of a printed photo guide of incoming college freshmen and quickly expanded to include the student bodies of more than 2,100 colleges. In 2005, high schools were invited to join. In September 2006, Facebook changed the registration policy so that anyone with a valid e-mail address could become a Facebook user. Facebook now has more than 24 million members (about half are current college students) and is ranked by alexa.com as the 18th most used Web site globally. www.facebook.com

Faceparty—A community social networking Web site created in the U.K. in 2000. Faceparty allows users to create online profiles and interact with each other using instant chat and messaging facilities. As of June 2006 the site claimed 6 million 'audited' subscribers with an additional 35,000 new members every week. www.faceparty.com

FC2—An online site for nontraditional fiction. FC2 is an author-run, not-for-profit publisher, with its executive offices at Florida State University (FSU) in Tallahassee. Founded by six authors in 1973 as the Fiction Collective, FC2 is partially supported by FSU, the Florida Arts Council, Illinois State University, the Illinois Arts Council, the National Endowment for the Arts and private contributors. www.fc2.org

Flickr—Launched as a utility for an online game in 2004 and acquired by Yahoo! in 2005. Flickr's creators discovered it would work better as a way for people to share digital photos with each other. Today it is a social media Web site for photo sharing and management. Users can provide keyword tags for the photos, allowing searchers to quickly find appropriate images. Flickr has over 4 million registered users and, as of June 2, 2007, was ranked by Alexa.com as the 47th most used Web site globally. www.flickr.com

Fnac—The largest French retailer of products such as computer software and hardware, televisions, cameras, video games, books, CDs and DVDs. Founded in 1954 as Fédération Nationale d'Achats pour Cadres, Fnac is headquartered in a Paris suburb and has operations in Europe, Brazil and Taiwan. www.fnac.com

Folksonomy—The aggregation of tags developed by the user community rather than taxonomy professionals.

Free—A Paris, France-based Web enterprise, Free.fr is an Internet provider started in April 1999 by the Iliad Group. Free offers access to a broad array of online news, information and shopping services. In 2003 it began offering television access over its DSL lines. www.free.fr

FriendsReunited—A British social networking site launched in July 2000, originally aimed at helping old friends and schoolmates reconnect, and then expanded to involve coworkers and others. The site was acquired by British TV station ITV in late 2005 and now has 12 million registered users. www.friendsreunited.co.uk

Friendster—A leading global, online social network founded in Mountain View, California, U.S. in 2002. Over 48 million members use Friendster as of September 2007. Friendster focuses on helping adults stay connected to friends and discover new people and topics of interest to them. www.friendster.com

Future Shop—A Canadian electronics and home appliance retailer founded in 1982 and owned by Best Buy since 2001. Future Shop operates more than 125 retail stores across British Columbia (where it is headquartered in Burnaby), Alberta, Manitoba and Ontario. www.futureshop.ca

Google—A public corporation specializing in Internet search and advertising that indexes billions of Web sites. Based in Mountain View, California, U.S., Google was cofounded in 1998 by two Stanford University students. Its offerings have broadened from the initial search and advertising business into products including free, Web-based e-mail, online mapping, office productivity and video sharing. In December 2006, Google was the most used search engine. www.google.com

Goo.ne.jp—Goo is a Japanese search engine and portal service. Often compared to Yahoo!, the site offers Web search, news, maps, shopping information and other services. www.goo.ne.jp

GREE—A Japanese social networking site launched in 2004, GREE has some features in common with Facebook, such as friend designations, picture posting and the ability to create a diary (blog). A mobile version of the service, EZ GREE, is also available. www.gree.jp

GyaO—A Japanese enterprise for broadband communications and related interests. GyaO was established in 1961 and now provides online access to a wide variety of cultural interests including movies, music, sports, news and business. www.gyao.jp

Habbo Hotel—A virtual community owned and operated by Sulake Corporation. Habbo Hotel launched in Finland in 2000 and then in the U.K. in 2001, and now reaches over 30 countries on five continents. Designed primarily for teenage users, Habbo Hotel is an online game centered around visual representations of its members (Habbos) that incorporates chat room functionality (virtual Hotels). As of mid-2007, there were 7 million unique visitors to the virtual hotels each month. www.habbo.com

Hi5—A social networking site headquartered in San Francisco, California, U.S. since its founding in 2003. Hi5 has over 60 million registered users and provides a localized experience for them that enables them to connect with others based on language or other relevant shared interests. www.hi5networks.com

HMV—A music retailer formed in 1998 with over 680 stores and 11,200 full-time employees in the U.K., Canada and Asia. HMV's products include recorded music, videos, DVDs, books and computer games. The acronym HMV stands for "His Master's Voice," the title of a famous 1899 painting by Francis Barraud of a dog listening to his master's voice on a gramophone. www.hmv.com

Hollywood.com—An online entertainment destination owned by Hollywood Media Corporation that generates revenue by selling advertising on its Web site, and also receives commission revenue for advertising sold by the Hollywood.com ad sales team on MovieTickets.com. Hollywood.com features in-depth movie information, including movie previews, descriptions and reviews, movie showtime listings, entertainment news, celebrity fan sites, celebrity photo galleries and an extensive multimedia library. Hollywood.com's features also include audio podcasts and blogging. www.hollywood.com

Identity Management—A broad administrative area that deals with identifying individuals in a system (a network, a country, an enterprise) and controlling their access to resources within that system by associating user rights and restrictions with the established identity.

Identity Theft—A crime in which an imposter obtains key pieces of personal information, such as a government ID, in order to impersonate someone else. The imposter may use the information to purchase goods or services or as false credentials.

iFilm—A leading online video network, serving user-uploaded and professional content to over ten million viewers monthly. IFilm's extensive library includes movie clips, music videos, short films, TV clips, video game trailers, action sports and its popular 'viral videos' collection. IFilm is one of the leading streaming media networks on the internet. In October 2005, IFilm was acquired by Viacom International, Inc., and is now part of the MTV Networks family of brands that includes MTV itself, VH1, Nickelodeon, Comedy Central, TV Land, CMT, Spike and Logo. www.ifilm.com

ImageShack—An image-sharing social media Web site that can be used to share images with friends or post photos on blogs. Users can directly link photos from ImageShack to Web sites and online auctions. ImageShack, owned by ImageShack Corp., was launched in 2003 and, on June 2, 2007, was ranked by Alexa.com as the 50th most used Web site globally. www.imageshack.us

Information literacy—The skills required to use the search-and-find technologies to locate and sift through information as well as the skills needed to use that information effectively.

Instant messaging (IM)—The generic name of a technology that enables private chat to take place. With IM, messages are exchanged in real-time between two or more people. When IM users log in, they are notified of which IM correspondents are online.

Internet—A worldwide system of computer networks accessed by hundreds of millions of people. *See also "World Wide Web."*

Internet Relay Chat (IRC)—A system that enables online users to join live discussions, allowing people to engage in real-time, online chat.

iSMS—A mobile messaging gateway used to implement SMS-based Web services.

iTunes—A digital media player application, introduced by Apple on January 10, 2001 at the Macworld Expo in San Francisco, for playing and organizing digital music and video files. The program is also an interface to manage the contents on Apple's popular iPod digital media players as well as the recently introduced iPhone. Additionally, iTunes can connect to the iTunes Store (provided an Internet connection is present) in order to purchase and download digital music, music videos, television shows, iPod games, audiobooks, various podcasts and feature length films. www.apple.com/itunes/

J2EE (Java 2, Enterprise Edition)—Widely used platform for building, deploying and managing Web services.

Kodak Easy Share Gallery—A photo storing and printing and social media Web site. Kodak Easy Share Gallery offers free photo editing and creative tools for users. The site was launched in 1999 as Ofoto, purchased by Kodak in 2001 and renamed Kodak Easy Share Gallery in 2005. On June 2, 2007, the site was ranked by Alexa.com as the 964th most used Web site globally. www.kodakgallery.com

Kotopara—A Japanese e-commerce and information site with links to a variety of popular media and consumer goods including music, movies, sports, games and animation. http://kotopara.jp

Library 2.0—"Library 2.0 simply means making your library's space (virtual and physical) more interactive, collaborative and driven by community needs. Examples of where to start include blogs, gaming nights for teens and collaborative photo sites. The basic drive is to get people back into the library by making the library relevant to what they want and need in their daily lives ... to make the library a destination and not an afterthought." —Sarah Houghton-Jan www.librarystuff.net/2006/01/library-20-questions-and-commentary.html

LinkedIn—A U.S.-based social networking site used primarily for business/professional networking. Headquartered in Mountain View, California, U.S., LinkedIn had more than 14 million registered users in 150 countries as of September 2007. www.linkedin.com

Listserv—An electronic mailing list software application developed in the 1980s and a trademark licensed to L-Soft International, Inc. The term is often used generically to mean any mailing list application.

Livedoor—A Tokyo, Japan-based Internet service provider that runs a Web portal and other businesses. Livedoor was launched in 1995 as a Web consultancy called "Livin' on the Edge" and renamed Livedoor in 2004. www.livedoor.com

Mashup—A mixture of content or elements. For example, an application that was built from routines from multiple sources or a Web site that combines content and/or scripts from multiple sources to provide a whole new service is said to be a mashup. An example is an Illinois library using CommunityWalk to map interlibrary lending and borrowing using data from its ILS.

Mass collaboration—Collaboration that occurs when multiple people work individually on a single project, such as an Internet-based project using social software. Wikis are examples of mass collaboration projects.

Meatspace—The physical world, the alternative to cyberspace. After originating in science fiction writing, it has become increasingly common in general usage to refer to face-to-face interactions. "Real Life" can be a synonym, sometimes abbreviated as "RL" or "IRL" (In Real Life) in text conversations, e.g., "I'll tell you tonite IRL."

Meebo—A Web site launched in 2005 offering instant messaging from any computer. Over 80 million instant messages are sent daily using Meebo. Meebo launched the Meebo Me widget in 2006 to allow users to add Meebo to their personal Web sites. www.meebo.com

Meetup—A U.S.-based social networking site, founded in 2002. Meetup helps people identify others who share common interests of many kinds, including hobbies, politics, financial issues, music and much more. As of September 2007, it offered more than 3,500 topics and more than 33,000 groups who meet online to discuss these topics. www.meetup.com

Microsoft—A computer technology company, founded in 1975 and headquartered in Redmond, Washington, U.S. Microsoft Corporation develops, manufactures, licenses and supports a wide range of computing software products. The Microsoft Windows and Microsoft Office products have highly-visible positions in the desktop computer market, with an estimated 90% market share. On September 12, 2007, Microsoft's Web site was ranked by Alexa.com as the 18th most used Web site globally. www.microsoft.com

Mixi—The largest social networking site in Japan. Launched in February 2004, Mixi is growing rapidly and had more than 8 million users by January 2007; 70 percent of those users are "active" (logged in within the last 3 days). Prospective members must be invited to become members of Mixi by an existing member. Available only in Japanese, Mixi includes user reviews for books, CDs, DVDs, games, etc., and the reviewed items are linked to Amazon Japan for purchase. On June 2, 2007, the site was ranked by Alexa.com as the 56th most used Web site globally. www.mixi.jp

MOO—MUD Object-Oriented, a type of MUD. A MOO is a text-based online virtual reality system.

MSN Messenger—A freeware instant messaging client. Developed by Microsoft Corporation, MSN Messenger was first distributed in 1999 and 2005 was targeted toward individual consumers. In February 2006 the MSN Messenger name was changed to Windows Live.

MUD—Multi-User Dungeon or multiplayer computer game.

MySpace—Launched in late 2003 as a site to promote new, budding rock stars and connect fans and friends. MySpace is now a social networking site with unique user profiles that are linked together through networks of friends. Registered users submit personal profiles, blogs, groups, photos, music and videos. MySpace is owned by Fox Interactive Media, a subsidiary of News Corporation (newscorp.com). On average, 230,000 accounts are created daily. On June 2, 2007, MySpace had more than 181.5 million registered users and was ranked by Alexa.com as the sixth most used Web site globally. www.myspace.com

myYearbook—One of the largest U.S. social networks, reaching 4.6 million unique visitors each month. myYearbook has experienced 500% growth in page views and members since early 2007; has grown from a single high school to more than 3 million members; and is now adding 1 million new members every three months. Founded by brother-and-sister teen entrepreneurs Dave and Catherine Cook, myYearbook hosts viral features like Battles, myMag, Match and Video Battles. www.myyearbook.com

Natural-language-based searching—Allows users to phrase their search strings as normal sentences.

Netflix—The world's largest online movie rental service, offering more than 6.7 million subscribers access to 85,000 DVD titles plus a growing library of over 4,000 full-length movies and television episodes that are available for instant watching on their PCs. Established in 1998 and headquartered in Los Gatos, California, U.S., it has amassed a collection of 80,000 titles and over 6.8 million subscribers. Netflix has over 55 million discs and ships 1.6 million a day, on average. www.netflix.com

Nicovideo—A Japanese video streaming site with more than 3 million users (as of September, 2007). The site offers both free and paid memberships, and allows users to upload, view and rate videos. www.nicovideo.jp

OAI (Open Archives Initiative)—An organization dedicated to developing interoperability standards to facilitate the dissemination of content. www.openarchives.org

OneMake—A Japanese social networking site with features such as friend networks, a diary (blog), virtual pets (and pet fighting), chat and group questions. http://one-make.jp

Open-source software—A program in which the source code is available to the general public for use and/or modification from its original design, free of charge.

Orkut—A social networking service run by Google and named after its creator and former Google employee, Orkut Büyükkökten. It has many features similar to MySpace and Facebook, including photo and video sharing, lists, communities (groups) and Instant Messaging through Google Talk. According to Google, as of August 2007, Orkut had more than 65 million worldwide members. www.orkut.com

OUTeverywhere—A U.K.-based social networking site for the gay, lesbian, bisexual and transgender communities. Created in 1995 as a way to stay connected to friends prior to the introduction of instant messaging, OUTeverywhere relaunched under its current name (aimed at men and women) in 2005. The site offers member profiles, discussion boards, online chat and private messages. www.outeverywhere.com

Paperback Swap—An online book club, based in the U.S., dedicated to book exchanges. Paperback Swap users register books they are willing to swap online and, when the books are requested, they are sent to the requestor by mail. The service is free; the sender pays the price of shipping. www.paperbackswap.com

Personalization (general)—Gears a system's activities (a Web site, call center or the entire enterprise) toward a user's specific information needs and preferences.

Personally Identifying Information (PII)—Also called Personally Identifiable Information or Personal Information. Information that can be used to uniquely identify an individual.

Photobucket—A photo, image and video hosting and sharing social media Web site that delivers 3 billion media clips daily. Founded in 2003, Photobucket is also used heavily for linking to images and videos from other social networking sites, such as MySpace. In May 2007, it announced it had accepted an offer to be acquired by Fox Interactive Media, a division of News Corporation, which owns MySpace. The site has 39 million registered users and is ranked by Alexa.com as the 48th most used Web site globally. www.photobucket.com

Play.com—A British e-commerce site that offers a wide variety of consumer goods, including DVDs, music, video games, books, electronics, mobile phones, clothing and accessories. One of the first online retailers in the U.K., Play.com was founded in 1998 and has its headquarters in Jersey, Channel Islands, U.K. According to traffic monitor Hitwise, Play.com is the third largest online retailer in the U.K. and the 50th largest globally. www.play.com

Podcast—Distribution of streaming or downloadable audio content over the Internet via RSS feed. PCMag.com lists the term as an abbreviation for iPod broad*cast*.

Presence management—The ability to detect whether other users are online and whether they are available.

Price Minister—A French e-commerce site that offers a broad range of consumer goods, including electronics, video games, books, music, sporting goods and much more. It reported 6.5 million members as of September, 2007. www.priceminister.com

Privacy—Depending on the context (legal, cultural, personal), the term has different denotations and connotations. One that is relevant in the arena of social networking is people's ability to control information that is released about them. Individuals may voluntarily waive their privacy as a trade-off for goods or services.

Privacy Agreement—A legal document that establishes access, use and ownership rights between visitors to a Web site or portal and the entity that owns the site, or between subscribers/registrants and the owner/manufacturer. Such documents lay out privacy expectations, the terms and conditions of service and also include disclaimers.

Privacy Policy—A privacy policy is the formal statement of a business entity's position on information-gathering, storage, use and disclosure.

QQ—A Chinese instant messaging service that also provides social networking services such as real-time chat, photo sharing and site-specific virtual money. Though exact numbers are elusive, estimates put the membership of QQ at over 150 million users, mostly in China. www.qq.com

Rakuten—One of the biggest online shopping malls in Japan. Rakuten was founded in 1997 and by 2004 was the second most visited Web site in Japan (following Yahoo!) as measured by unique audience. Its online shopping business, Rakuten Ichiba, offers more than 18 million products from more than 18,000 merchants. www.rakuten.co.jp

Read It Swap It—An online book swap group, based in the U.K., that allows users to obtain free secondhand books for ones they have read. Read It Swap It users register their book lists and then select a book they would like from another user. The owner of the book reviews the requestor's book list and chooses a book for the swap. www.readitswapit.co.uk/TheLibrary.aspx

Real Simple Syndication (RSS)—A Web format that allows users to receive the latest content from specified Web sites, downloaded directly to their computers.

Real-time collaboration—Interaction between participants in real time, using a meeting or presentation format. Includes application and whiteboard sharing.

Rhapsody—A U.S.-based membership music service that provides members with unlimited access to a catalog of full-length music tracks. Launched in 2001, Rhapsody was the first service to offer streaming access to its extensive digital music library. It is considered a prime example of "The Long Tail" theory published by Chris Anderson in his 2006 book of the same title. www.rhapsody.com

Search engine—A service that scans content on the Internet using a computer program that searches for specific keywords and returns a list of content in which they were found.

Second Life—3-D virtual world founded in 2003. Second Life is built and owned by its residents. Over 7.6 million people worldwide inhabit this virtual world. www.secondlife.com

Secure Web services—Implementations of Web services that resist hacking or damage through computer attack.

Security—Free from danger. The term can be used with reference to crime or accidents, for example.

Security Icon—A symbol or graphic attached to a Web site to indicate that information is authentic and/or authoritative. The emblem also verifies to users that services received or transactions conducted on it are secure, and in some cases, private. Examples of this symbol include the Trustmark, Truste and VeriSign seals.

Semantic Web—Extends the Web through semantic markup languages, such as Resource Description Framework, Web Ontology Language and Topic Maps that describe entities and their relationships in the underlying document. www.w3.org/2001/sw

Shifted Librarian—Someone who works to make libraries more portable to meet users' information needs in their world. This term was coined by Jenny Levine, Internet Development Specialist and Strategy Guide for the American Library Association (ALA). www.theshiftedlibrarian.com

Shutterfly—A U.S.-based social media Web site launched in 1999 by the founder of Netscape. Shutterfly calls itself a "social expression and personal publishing service" that helps its users "share, print and preserve their memories" using its broad range of digital photography products and services. www.shutterfly.com

Skype—An Internet telephony service founded in 2003 and acquired by eBay in 2005. www.skype.com

Skyrock and Skyblog—A French FM radio station that has approximately 3.7 million listeners, primarily in the 13–24 age range. Skyrock owns Skyblog, a large social networking platform that launched in 2002 and hosts 5.4 million blogs. Skyblog is sometimes referred to as the "French MySpace." www.skyrock.fm/front/

Slope of Enlightenment (Gartner, Inc. term)—This phase of a Hype Cycle is characterized by focused experimentation and solid hard work by an increasingly diverse range of organizations that lead to a true understanding of the technology's applicability, risks and benefits. Commercial, off-the-shelf methodologies and tools ease the development process.

Smart card—A plastic card, about the size of a credit card, that provides tamper-resistant storage of such personal information as passwords or digital signatures.

Smart enterprise suites—The convergence of portals, content management and collaboration functionality into a single product.

SMS—Acronym for Short Message Service, another name for text messaging.

Snapfish—A photo sharing and printing social media Web site. Snapfish was launched in 2000 and acquired as a division of Hewlett-Packard in 2005. The site has more than 40 million registered users and is ranked by Alexa.com as the 2738th most used Web site globally. www.snapfish.com

Social bookmarking—A system that allows users to store links to their favorite sites and share those links with other users.

Social computing—The use of social software.

Social media sites—Web sites that allow individuals to share content they have created, such as YouTube (video sharing) and Flickr (photo sharing). While interaction occurs on social media sites, the primary purpose of the site is to publish and share content.

Social network—A map of the relationships between individuals, showing the ways they are connected. The term was first used in 1954 by sociologist J.A. Barnes.

Social networking sites—Web sites primarily designed to facilitate interaction between users who share interests, attitudes and activities. Examples include Facebook, Mixi and MySpace.

Social software (also known as collaborative software)—The software that supports the ability to collaborate online.

Social Web—An open worldwide data-sharing network that links people, organizations and concepts.

Spam (or Spamming)—Spam is unsolicited electronic mail that is sent indiscriminately to mailing list members or other large groups of email recipients. Spam may also refer to other questionable methods used to direct Web traffic and bolster search engine results, such as "comment spam," "trackback spam" and "forum spam."

StayFriends—A German social networking site that launched in 2002 to help users locate and contact former schoolmates. It includes links to similar sites in Sweden and France, as well as Classmates.com sites in Canada and the U.S. www.stayfriends.de

StudiVZ—A social networking platform for students, primarily college and university students in Europe. Based in Berlin, Germany, StudiVZ (full name: Studentenverzeichnis, which means "students' directory") reports about 4 million users as of August 2007, mainly in Germany, Austria and Switzerland. Launched in 2005 by two students, it is considered comparable to the U.S.-based Facebook Web site. www.studivz.net

StumbleUpon—A Web browser plug-in that allows its users to discover and rate Web pages, photos, videos, and news articles. Founded in Calgary, Alberta, Canada, in 2002 and now located in San Francisco, California, U.S., StumbleUpon is a recommendation system that displays new Web pages based on peer-review/comment and social networking tenets. The StumbleUpon system works by a user's ratings of previous pages, ratings by his/her friends, and by the ratings of users with similar interests. In May 2007, eBay acquired StumbleUpon. www.stumbleupon.com

Syndication—A process by which content is taken from one place and reused in another. The content may be used in a different way in the new location.

Tag cloud—A visual display of tags that show, by size of the words, the popularity of each tag, with the largest being the most popular.

Tags—Keywords that describe the content of a Web site, bookmark, photo or blog post. A tag is metadata describing an object.

Team collaboration support—Team-oriented collaboration tools that bring together real-time communications and asynchronous collaboration for team activities and tasks.

Technorati—An Internet search engine for searching blogs. Headquartered in San Francisco, California, U.S., Technorati currently tracks more than 100 million blogs and 250 million pieces of tagged social media. It has an active software developer community and offers a public developer's wiki for collaboration among developers and contributors. www.technorati.com

Transparency—An intermediate step in a production or distribution process that is invisible to those who use or work in the process.

Trust—Confidence in or reliance on the honesty, goodness or character of someone or something.

TRUSTe—An independent nonprofit organization founded in 1997 by the Electronic Frontier Foundation. Headquartered in San Francisco, California, U.S., TRUSTe concentrates on by helping businesses and other online organizations manage privacy concerns through self-regulation. It is best know for its Web Privacy Seal and operates the world's largest privacy seal program that includes more than 2,000 certified sites. www.truste.com

TSUTAYA Online—A Japanese online retailer of DVDs, music, video games, books and other media. www.tsutaya-ltd.co.jp

USA PATRIOT Act—U.S. law signed in 2001 and reauthorized in 2006. The acronym stands for The Uniting and Strengthening America by Providing Appropriate Tools Required to Intercept and Obstruct Terrorism Act of 2001. Under the act, law enforcement has expanded ability to search communications (telephone and e-mail), as well as medical, financial and other records. www.lifeandliberty.gov/highlights.htm

Virgin—A leading U.K. venture capital organization with one of the world's most recognized brands. Conceived in 1970, Virgin operates a range of businesses including mobile telephony, transportation, travel, financial services, leisure, music and publishing. Its 200+ branded companies employ more than 50,000 across 29 countries.

Virtual community—A self-selecting, peer-to-peer group that connects people by interest, skills and practices. Virtual communities complement, but do not supersede, teams and reporting structures.

Virtual teams—A project-oriented group of knowledge workers who are not required to work in the same location or time zone.

Wall—A term used to denote a place for posting comments, sharing photos, etc. Popularized by users of the social networking site, MySpace.

Walmart.com—A subsidiary of Wal-Mart Stores, Walmart.com was founded in 2000 and is headquartered in California, near San Francisco. The parent company was founded in 1962 by Sam Walton in Bentonville, Arkansas, U.S., and has expanded into a worldwide enterprise that includes discount stores, groceries and hypermarkets. It also offers optical, pharmacy and portrait studio services. More than 1 million of its products are available online through Walmart.com, including music downloads and one-hour photo services. www.walmart.com

Web 2.0—A term first used by Dale Dougherty, vice president at O'Reilly Media, to indicate the transition of the World Wide Web from a collection of Web sites to a computing platform providing Web applications to end users.

Webshots—A photo and video sharing social media Web site. Webshots began in 1996 and began offering photo sharing in 1999. The site was acquired by CNET Networks in 2004. Webshots has 7.2 million visits per month and is ranked by Alexa.com as the 250th most used Web site globally. www.webshots.com

The WELL—The Whole Earth 'Lectronic Link, founded in 1985 and one of the first virtual communities. www.well.com

Weltbild—A major German media retailer and publisher (ranked number 2 among online book retailers) that is owned by the dioceses of the Roman Catholic Church in Germany and based in Augsburg. Weltbild reports that some 5.5 million customers in German-speaking countries buy books it sells by mail order, either in one of its 330 retail stores or over the Internet. Rooted in a magazine publishing business founded in Germany in 1948, Weltbild's Internet business began operating in 1997. www.weltbild.de

Whiteboard—An area on a display screen on which multiple users can write or draw. Whiteboards are a principal component of teleconferencing applications because they enable visual as well as audio communication.

Wi-Fi—Wireless fidelity refers to wireless local area networks that use one of the three 802.11 standards (802.11a, 802.11g, 802.11b).

Wiki—A Web site designed for collaborative use, allowing multiple users to contribute to the creation of documents or applications. Wikipedia is an example of a wiki.

Wikipedia—A free, online encyclopedia written and edited by its members. On August 1, 2007, Wikipedia reported 7.9 million articles in 253 languages, 1.9 million of which are in English. As of August 2007, it ranks among the ten most visited Web sites globally according to Alexa.com. www.wikipedia.org

Windows Live Spaces—Microsoft's social networking platform. The site was released in 2004 with the name MSN Spaces, a name users still frequently use. In August 2006, MSN Spaces became part of the Windows Live Services platform. In April 2007, Windows Live Spaces had 120 million registered users. www.spaces.live.com

Workflow—The process whereby items of work move from one person or process to another in an organization.

Xanga—A free, Web-based service based in New York City, New York, U.S., that hosts social network profiles, weblogs, photoblogs, audioblogs and videoblogs. Xanga began in 1998 as a site for users to share music and book reviews and has an estimated 40 million users worldwide. Xanga typically attracts teenage users, who frequently use Xanga sites for personal journaling. www.xanga.com

XML—eXtensible Markup Language—A way to create common information formats and to share these formats on the Web.

Yahoo! Auction, Yahoo! Shopping, Yahoo! Days and Yahoo! Video—E-commerce and video sites that are part of the Yahoo! Internet services company. Yahoo! Auction closed in June 2007. Yahoo! Days is a Japanese site. The parent company, Yahoo!, is headquartered in Sunnyvale, California, U.S., and launched in 1995. Its vast enterprise includes a Web portal, a search engine, an e-mail service and many other online business pursuits. www.yahoo.com

Yahoo!—A public corporation and global Internet services company. Founded in 1994, Yahoo! Inc. provides a Web portal, a search engine, the Yahoo! Directory, Yahoo! Mail, news and posting, among other services. Yahoo! has been one of the most consistently visited Web sites, with more than 412 million unique users, according to comScore, Alexa Internet and Netcraft. In August 2007, Yahoo! released an updated version of Yahoo! Mail that allows users to send instant messages to the largest combined instant messaging (IM) community including users of Yahoo! Messenger and Windows Live Messenger. The new version of Yahoo! Mail also allows users to send free text messages to mobile phones in the United States, Canada, India and the Philippines. www.yahoo.com

Yahoo! Photos—A photo sharing social media Web site launched in 2000 and designed for Yahoo! users. Yahoo! As Yahoo! also owns Flickr, the company announced in May 2007 that it would be shutting down Yahoo! Photos later in 2007. Yahoo! Photos is part of the Yahoo.com site, which is ranked by Alexa.com as the number one most used Web site globally.

YouTube—A popular video sharing Web site where users can upload, view and share video clips. YouTube was created in 2005 (and acquired by Google in 2006) when the founders (former PayPal employees) streamlined the clunky experience of watching video on the Net, in which users often had to choose which media player they wanted to use and then download a bulky clip. Users can rate the YouTube videos, and the site publishes both the average rating and the number of times a video has been watched. On June 2, 2007, YouTube was ranked by alexa.com as the fourth most used Web site globally. Each day, YouTube users view over 100 million video clips and create 65,000 new videos. www.youtube.com

Appendix C: People Consulted

Henry Bankhead
Principal Librarian
Los Gatos Public Library
Los Gatos, California, U.S.

danah boyd
PhD candidate, School of Information (SIMS)
University of California, Berkeley
Berkeley, California, U.S.

Keith Enright, Esq., CIPP/G
Senior Attorney
Director, Enterprise Information Policy
Limited Brands
Columbus, Ohio, U.S.

Meredith Farkas
Distance Learning Librarian
Norwich University
Northfield, Vermont, U.S.

Megan Fox
Web & Electronic Resources Librarian
Simmons College Library
Boston, Massachusetts, U.S.

Christina Hoffman Gola
Coordinator
Undergraduate Instruction and Outreach
Texas A&M University
College Station, Texas, U.S.

Sarah Houghton-Jan
Information and Web Services Manager
San Mateo County Library
San Mateo, California, U.S.

Paul Jones
Director
ibiblio.org

Brian Kelly
National Web Advisor, UKOLN
University of Bath
Bath, U.K.

Pascal Krajewski
Manager, Information Technology
Public Library of Toulouse
Toulouse, France

Cliff Landis
Facilitator of Reference Services
Valdosta State University
Valdosta, Georgia, U.S.

Kwan Min Lee
Assistant Professor
Annenberg School for Communication
University of Southern California
Los Angeles, California, U.S.

Brian Mathews
Information Services Librarian
Georgia Institute of Technology
Atlanta, Georgia, U.S.

Mary Eleanor Miller
Librarian
University of Illinois at Urbana–Champaign
Urbana, Illinois, U.S.

Mary Minow
Librarian and Contributing Author
Library Law Blog
California, U.S.

Nicolas Morin
Librarian and Instructor for Automation Systems
and Web Site Management
L'enssib, Ecole Nationale Supérieure des Sciences
de l'information et des Bibliothèques
Villeurbanne, France

Karen Muller
Librarian and Knowledge Management Specialist
American Library Association
Chicago, Illinois, U.S.

June Pinnell-Stephens
Collection Services Manager, Retired
Fairbanks North Star Borough Public Library
Fairbanks, Alaska, U.S.

Andy Powell
Head of Development
Eduserv Foundation
Bath, U.K.

Howard Rheingold
Nonresident Fellow
Annenberg Center for Communication
University of Southern California
Los Angeles, California, U.S.

Marc Rotenberg
Executive Director
EPIC (Electronic Privacy Information Center)
Washington, D.C., U.S.

Melissa Salrin
Archivist
University of Illinois at Urbana–Champaign
Urbana, Illinois, U.S.

Michael Sauers
Technology Innovation Librarian
Nebraska Library Commission
Lincoln, Nebraska, U.S.

Marc Smith
Senior Research Sociologist
Community Technologies Group
Microsoft Research
Redmond, Washington, U.S.

Michael Stephens
Instructor, Graduate School of Library and
Information Science
Dominican University
River Forest, Illinois, U.S.

Fred Stutzman
PhD student, University of North Carolina School
of Information and Library Science
Chapel Hill, North Carolina, U.S.

Siva Vaidhyanathan
Associate Professor
Media Studies Program
University of Virginia
Charlottesville, Virginia, U.S.

Jessamyn West
Community Technology Librarian and
Moderator, MetaFilter.com
Vermont, U.S.

Alane Wilson
Former OCLC Senior Library Market Consultant
Vancouver, British Columbia, Canada

Alfons Wittmann
Librarian
University Library Eichstätt
UB Eichstätt-Ingolstadt
Eichstätt, Germany

Appendix D: Readings and Other Sources

Readings

About.com: Inventors. *The History of Communication.*
http://inventors.about.com/library/inventors/bl_history_of_communication.htm.

Adams, Helen R., et al. *Privacy in the 21st Century: Issues for Public, School, and Academic Libraries.* Westport, Connecticut: Libraries Unlimited, 2005.

Agre, Philip E. and Marc Rotenberg. *Technology and Privacy: The New Landscape.* Cambridge, MA: MIT Press, 1997.

Alderman, Ellen. *The Right to Privacy.* New York: Knopf, 1995.

Alexander, Bryan. "Web 2.0: A New Wave of Innovation for Teaching and Learning?" *EDUCAUSE Review* 41(2) (March/April 2006): 33–44. www.educause.edu/apps/er/erm06/erm0621.asp.

American Library Association. *Code of Ethics.* 1995.
www.ala.org/ala/oif/statementspols/codeofethics/codeethics.htm.

American Library Association. *Library Bill of Rights.* 1996.
www.ala.org/ala/oif/statementspols/statementsif/librarybillrights.htm.

American Library Association. *Privacy: An Interpretation of the Library Bill of Rights.* 2002.
www.ala.org/Template.cfm?Section=interpretations&Template.

American Library Association. *Task Force on Privacy and Confidentiality in the Electronic Environment. Final Report.* 7 July 2000. [The full report is no longer accessible at this site.]
www.ala.org/ala/lita/litaresources/alataskforce.cfm.

Anderson, Chris. *The Long Tail: Why the Future of Business Is Selling Less of More.* New York: Hyperion, 2006.

Anderson, Janna Quitney. *Imagining the Internet: Personalities, Predictions, Perspectives.* Lanham, MD: Rowman & Littlefield Publishers, 2005.

Angel, Colleen. "The Right to Privacy." *Journal of Information Ethics.* 9(2) (Fall 2000): 11–25.

Arnold, Kenneth. "The Electronic Librarian Is a Verb / The Electronic Library Is Not a Sentence." A lecture delivered at the New York Public Library. *The Gilbert A. Cam Memorial Lecture Series,* October 14, 1994.
www.press.umich.edu/jep/works/arnold.eleclib.html.

Association des Bibliothécaires Français. *The Librarians' Code of Ethics.* [Translated]
www.ifla.org/faife/ethics/frcode-e.htm.

Bachelard, Gaston. *The Poetics of Space.* [Translator, Maria Jolas] Boston, MA: Beacon Press, 1994. (First published in French in 1958 as *La poétique de l'espace.*)

Barabasi, Albert-Laszlo. *Linked: The New Science of Networks.* New York: Penguin, 2003.

Barlow, John Perry. "The Economy of Ideas." *Wired News.* 2.03 (March 1994). www.wired.com/wired/archive/2.03/economy.ideas.html.

———. "The Next Economy of Ideas." *Wired News.* 8.10 (October 2000). www.wired.com/wired/archive/8.10/download_pr.html.

Basandra, Suresh. "Historical Perspective." *Computer Systems Today.* http://books.basandra.com/cst/cst-chap-02-com-history.pdf.

Benkler, Yochai. "Coase's Penguin, or, Linux and The Nature of the Firm." *Yale Law Review* 112(3) (December 2002): 369–446. www.yalelawjournal.org/pdf/112-3/BenklerFINAL.pdf.

———. "Sharing Nicely: On Shareable Goods and the Emergence of Sharing as a Modality of Economic Production." *The Yale Law Journal* 114(2) (November 2004): 273–358. www.yalelawjournal.org/pdf/114-2/Benkler_114-2.pdf.

Bennett, Colin J. and Charles D. Raab. *The Governance of Privacy: Policy Instruments in Global Perspective.* Aldershot, VT: Ashgate, 2003.

Berelson, Bernard. *The Library's Public: A Report of the Public Library Inquiry.* New York: Columbia University Press, 1949.

Bermann, Sol. *Privacy and Access to Public Records in the Information Age.* A working paper prepared for Battelle Policy Day cosponsored by Battelle Memorial Institute and the John Glenn Institute for Public Service and Public Policy, The Ohio State University, Columbus, Ohio, February 7, 2006. http://glennschool.osu.edu/research/papers/Bermann.pdf.

Bigge, Ryan. "The Cost of (Anti-)social Networks: Identity, Agency and Neo-Luddites." *First Monday* 11(12) (December 4, 2006): n.p. www.firstmonday.org/issues/issue11_12/bigge/index.html.

Birchmeier, Zachary, Adam N. Joinson and Beth Dietz-Uhler. "Storming and Forming a Normative Response to a Deception Revealed Online." *Social Science Computer Review* 23 (2005): 108–21.

Blyberg, John. "AADL.org Goes Social." [Blog post] *Blyberg.net*, January 21, 2007. www.blyberg.net/2007/01/21/aadlorg-goes-social/.

boyd, danah. "Blogging Out Loud: Shifts in Public Voice." Presentation at the *LITA National Forum,* San Jose, CA, October 1, 2005. www.danah.org/papers/LITA.html.

———. "Friends, Friendsters, and Top 8: Writing Community into Being on Social Network Sites." *First Monday* 11(12) (December 4, 2006): n.p. www.firstmonday.org/issues/issue11_12/boyd/index.html.

———. "Friendster and Publicly Articulated Social Networking." *Conference on Human Factors and Computing Systems (CHI 2004).* Vienna: ACM, April 24–29, 2004. www.danah.org/papers/CHI2004Friendster.pdf.

Boyle, Michael and Saul Greenberg. "The Language of Privacy: Learning from Video Media Space Analysis and Design." *ACM Transactions on Computer-Human Interaction* 12 (2005): 328–70.

Brin, David. *The Transparent Society.* New York: Addison-Wesley, 1999.

British Library. *From Bones to Bytes* [YouTube video]. www.youtube.com/watch?v=7O_oyuAY2tE.

Caplan, Scott E. "Preference for Online Social Interaction: A Theory of Problematic Internet Use and Psychosocial Well-being." *Communication Research* 30 (2003): 625–48.

Caruth, Nicole J. and Shelley Bernstein. "Building an Online Community at the Brooklyn Museum: A Timeline." Paper presented at Museums and the Web 2007 conference, San Francisco, CA, April 11–14, 2007. www.archimuse.com/mw2007/papers/caruth/caruth.html.

Casson, Herbert Newton. *The History of the Telephone.* Chicago: A.C. McClurg & Co, 1910.

Castells, Manuel et al. *Mobile Communication and Society: A Global Perspective.* "A project of the Annenberg Research Network on International Communication." Cambridge, MA: MIT Press, 2007.

———. *The Rise of the Network Society.* Cambridge, MA: Blackwell, 1996.

Cicognani, Anna. "On the Linguistic Nature of Cyberspace and Virtual Communities." *Virtual Reality* 3(1) (March 1998): 25–33.

CILIP. *Police Access to Library User Records.* October 28, 2005. www.cilip.org.uk/professionalguidance/rightsofaccess?cssversion=printable.

Clayton, Antony. *London's Coffee Houses: A Stimulating Story.* London: Historical Publications, 2003.

Coates, Tom. "Is the Pace of Change Really Such a Shock?" [Blog post] *Plasticbag.org,* April 26, 2006. www.plasticbag.org/archives/2006/04/is_the_pace_of_change_really_such_a_shock/.

Coburn, Pip. *The Change Function: Why Some Technologies Take Off and Others Crash and Burn.* New York: Portfolio, 2006.

Cohill, Andrew Michael. "Thinking Chaordically: The Future of Communities and Technology." Plenary speech delivered at the 10th Annual CTCNet conference, San Diego, CA, June 2001. www.bev.net/about/research/digital_library/docs/chaordic.pdf.

comScore Networks. "More than half of MySpace visitors are now age 35 or older, as the site's demographic composition continues to shift." [Press release] comScore Networks, October 5, 2006. www.comscore.com/press/release.asp?press=1019.

Conhaim, Wally W. "Getting to Know You Online." *Information Today,* 22(7) (Jul/Aug 2005): 31–32.

———. "Social Networks: The Internet Continues to Evolve." *Information Today,* 22(9) (Oct 2005): 35–36.

Corradini, Elena. "Teenagers Analyse their Public Library." *New Library World* 107 (2006): 481–498.

Cottrell, Janet R. "Ethics in an Age of Changing Technology: Familiar Territory or New Frontiers?" *Library Hi Tech* 17(1) (1999): 107–113.

Dawson, Ross. *Living Networks: Leading your Company, Customers and Partners in the Hyper-Connected Economy.* Upper Saddle River, NJ: Prentice Hall, 2002.

De Rosa, Cathy. *Perceptions of Libraries and Information Resources: A Report to the OCLC Membership.* Dublin, OH: OCLC Online Computer Library Center, Inc., 2005.

De Rosa, Cathy, Lorcan Dempsey and Alane Wilson. *The 2003 OCLC Environmental Scan: Pattern Recognition: A Report to the OCLC Membership.* Dublin, OH: OCLC Online Computer Library Center, Inc., 2003.

DigiBarn Computer Museum. *"Xerox Museum" in El Segundo, California.* www.digibarn.com/collections/locations/xerox-museum-el-segundo/index.html.

Dourish, Paul and Ken Anderson. "Collective Information Practice: Exploring Privacy and Security as Social and Cultural Phenomena." *Human-Computer Interaction* 21, no. 3 (2006): 319–342.

EDUCAUSE Learning Initiative. *7 Things You Should Know about...Facebook.* Boulder, CO: August 2006. http://educause.edu/LibraryDetailPage/666?ID=ELI7017.

EDUCAUSE Learning Initiative. *7 Things You Should Know about...YouTube.* Boulder, CO: EDUCAUSE, September 2006. http://educause.edu/LibraryDetailPage/666?ID=ELI7018 .

EDUCAUSE Learning Initiative. *The Learning Grid, University of Warwick.* Boulder, CO: EDUCAUSE, 2006. http://educause.edu/LibraryDetailPage/666?ID=ELI5017.

Eisenstein, Elizabeth L. *The Printing Press as an Agent of Change: Communications and Cultural Transformation in Early-Modern Europe. Volumes I and II.* New York: Cambridge University Press, [1979], 2005.

Elon University/Pew Internet Project. "1870s–1940s Telephone Timeline." *Imagining the Internet: A History and Forecast.* www.elon.edu/e-web/predictions/150/1870.xhtml.

Ernst, Morris L. and Alan U. Schwartz. *Privacy: The Right to Be Let Alone.* New York: Macmillan, 1962.

Estabrook, Leigh. "Public Libraries and Civil Liberties: A Profession Divided." Library Research Center, The Graduate School of Library and Information Science, University of Illinois at Urbana–Champaign, n.d. http://lrc.lis.uiuc.edu/web/PLCL.html.

Fallis, Don. "Information Ethics for Twenty-first Century Library Professionals." *Library Hi Tech* 25(1) (2007): 23–36. www.emeraldinsight.com/0737-8831.htm.

Farkas, Meredith. *Social Software in Libraries: Building Collaboration, Communication and Community Online.* Medford, NJ: Information Today, Inc., 2007.

Federman, Mark. "The Ephemeral Artefact: Visions of Cultural Experience." Keynote presentation at eCulture Horizons: From Digitisation to Creating Cultural Experience(s), *Salzburg Research Symposium 2004,* Salzburg, Austria, September 27, 2004. http://eculture.salzburgresearch.at/2004/presentation_federman.pdf.

Finks, Lee W. "Librarianship Needs a New Code of Professional Ethics." *American Libraries* (January 1991): 84–92.

Foerstel, Herbert N. *Surveillance in the Stacks: The FBI's Library Awareness Program.* Westport, CT: Greenwood, 1991.

Gandy, Jr., Oscar H. *The Panoptic Sort: A Political Economy of Personal Information.* Boulder, CO: Westview Press, 1993.

Gardner, Carrie. "Fact or Fiction: Privacy in American Libraries." *Proceedings of the 12th Annual Conference on Computers, Freedom & Privacy.* San Francisco, CA, April 16–19, 2002. www.cfp2002.org/proceedings/proceedings/gardner.pdf.

Gauder, Brad. "Social Networking Encourages Teen Library Usage at Denver Public." *NextSpace 7* (Sept. 2007): 12–13. www.oclc.org/nextspace/007/advocacy.htm.

Givens, Beth. "Public Records on the Internet: The Privacy Dilemma." *Proceedings of the 12th Annual Conference on Computers, Freedom and Privacy.* San Francisco, CA, April 16–19, 2002. www.cfp2002.org/proceedings/proceedings/givens.pdf.

Goldberg, Ian. "Privacy and Anonymity on the Internet." *Panopticon, The 15th Annual Conference on Computers, Freedom & Privacy, Keeping an Eye on the Panopticon: Workshop on Vanishing Anonymity,* Seattle, WA, April 12, 2005. www.idtrail.org/files/Goldberg_Privacy_Anonymity_Internet.pdf.

Goodall, George. "Shelving the Code of Ethics: Bend it Like Bentham." *Facetation* [Web site], June 14, 2003. www.deregulo.com/facetation/pdfs/shelvingCodeOfEthics.pdf.

Gorbis, Marina and Rod Falcon. "The New Spatial Landscape: Artifacts from the Future." The Institute for the Future, 2004. www.iftf.org/docs/SR-834_New_Spatial_Landsc_Artifacts.pdf.

Greenwell, Stacey and Beth Kraemer. "Internet Reviews: Social Networking Software: Facebook and MySpace." *Kentucky Libraries* 70(4) (Fall 2006): 12–16.

Grossman, Lev. "Time's Person of the Year: You." *Time.* (2006) [online version: December 13, 2006] www.time.com/time/magazine/article/0,9171,1569514,00.html?ref=msn-ara.info.

Habermas, Jurgen. *The Structural Transformation of the Public Sphere: An Inquiry into a Category of Bourgeois Society.* [Translation of *Strukturwandel der Offentlichkeit*] Cambridge, MA: MIT Press, 1989.

Hancock, Jeffrey T. and Philip J. Dunham. "Impression Formation in Computer-mediated Communication Revisited: An Analysis of the Breadth and Intensity of Impressions." *Communication Research* 28 (2001): 325–47.

Henderson, Samantha and Michael Gilding. "'I've Never Clicked this Much with Anyone in My Life': Trust and Hyperpersonal Communication in Online Friendships." *New Media & Society* 6(4) (2004): 487–506. http://nms.sagepub.com/cgi/reprint/6/4/487.

Herring, Susan C. "Slouching Toward the Ordinary: Current Trends in Computer-Mediated Communication." *New Media & Society* 6(1) (2004): 26–36. http://nms.sagepub.com/cgi/reprint/6/1/26.

Hess, Charlotte and Elinor Ostrom, eds. *Understanding Knowledge as a Commons: From Theory to Practice.* Cambridge, MA: MIT Press, 2007.

High-Tech Productions. *The History of Film & Television.* www.high-techproductions.com/historyoftelevision.htm.

Hiller, Harry H. and Tara M. Franz. "New Ties, Old Ties and Lost Ties: The Use of the Internet in Diaspora." *New Media & Society* 6(6) (2004): 731–52. http://nms.sagepub.com/cgi/reprint/6/6/731.pdf.

Himma, Kenneth Einar. "Foundational Issues in Information Ethics." *Library Hi Tech* 25(1) (2007): 79–94. www.emeraldinsight.com/0737-8831.htm.

Hirschey, Mark. "Libraries are Limited, Obsolete." *Lawrence Journal World,* October 2, 2006. www2.ljworld.com/news/2006/oct/02/libraries_are_limited_obsolete/.

Hlebec, Valentina, Katja Lozar Manfreda and Vasja Vehovar. "The Social Support Networks of Internet Users." *New Media & Society* 8(1) (2006): 9–32. http://nms.sagepub.com/cgi/reprint/8/1/9.pdf.

Hodge, Anthony and Bastiaan F. Zwaan. *Risen: Why Libraries are Here to Stay.* [ALA special edition] Amsterdam: Medialab Solutions, 2006.

Hoffman, Kathy. "Professional Ethics and Librarianship." *Texas Library Journal* (Fall 2005): 7–11.

Hooff, Bart van den, Jasper Groot and Sander de Jonge. "Situational Influences on the Use of Communication Technologies: A Meta-Analysis and Exploratory Study." *Journal of Business Communication* 41(2) (2005): 4–27.

Höök, Kristina. "Social Navigation: From the Web to the Mobile." In Ziegler & G. Szwillus (eds.), Mensch & Computer 2003: Interaktion in Bewegung, B G Teubner. S.17–20. http://mc.informatik.uni-hamburg.de/konferenzbaende/mc2003/konferenzband/muc2003-01-hoeoek.pdf.

Horrigan, John and Lee Rainie. Findings: The Internet's Growing Role in Life's Major Moments. *Pew Internet & American Life Project,* April 19, 2006. www.pewinternet.org/.

Howe, Denis. *Free On-Line Dictionary of Computing.* http://foldoc.org/.

Information Please. *Internet Timeline.* 2000–2007 Pearson Education. www.infoplease.com/ipa/A0193167.html.

Innis, Harold A. *The Bias of Communication.* Toronto: University of Toronto Press, 1951.

Ito, Mizuko, Diasuke Okabe and Misa Matsuda, eds., *Personal, Portable, Pedestrian: Mobile Phones in Japanese Life.* Cambridge, MA: The MIT Press, 2005.

Japan Library Association. *Code of Ethics for Librarians.* [Translated] www.ifla.org/faife/ethics/jlacode.htm.

Jenkins, Henry et al. *Confronting the Challenges of Participatory Culture: Media Education for the 21st Century.* The MacArthur Foundation. 2006. www.projectnml.org/files/working/NMLWhitePaper.pdf.

———. *Convergence Culture: Where Old and New Media Collide.* New York: New York University Press, 2006.

Joinson, Adam. *Understanding the Psychology of Internet Behaviour: Virtual Worlds, Real Lives.* New York: Palgrave MacMillan, 2003.

Keen, Andrew. "Web 2.0 is Reminiscent of Marx." *CBSNews.com,* February 15, 2006. www.cbsnews.com/stories/2006/02/15/opinion/printable1320641.shtml.

Kelly, Kevin. "We Are the Web." *Wired,* 13.08, August 2005. www.wired.com/wired/archive/13.08/tech.html.

———. "What Would McLuhan Say?" [Interview with Derrick de Kerckhove] *Wired,* 4.10, October 1996. www.wired.com/wired/archive/4.10/dekerckhove_pr.html.

Kemp, Randy and Adam D. Moore. "Privacy." *Library Hi Tech* 25(1) (2007): 58–78. www.emeraldinsight.com/0730-8831.htm.

Kennedy, Bruce M. "A Confidentiality of Library Records: A Survey of Problems, Policies, and Laws." *Law Library Journal* 81 (Fall 1989): 733–767.

Kerckhove, Derrick de. *The Architecture of Intelligence.* Boston: Birkhauser, 2001.

———. "The Internet Enters Television, a Trojan Horse in the Public Mind." *The McLuhan Program in Culture and Technology.* 2002. www.utoronto.ca/mcluhan/article_internettelevision.htm.

Kilgour, Frederick G. "Evolving, Computerizing, Personalizing." *American Libraries* v. 3 (February 1972) p. 141–7.

Klosek, Jacqueline. *The War on Privacy.* Westport, CT: Praeger, 2007.

Knowledge@Wharton (http://knowledge.wharton.upenn.edu/) Wharton School at The University of Pennsylvania.

Krug, Judith. *The Intellectual Freedom Manual,* 5th ed. Chicago: ALA, 1995.

Lamerichs, Joyce, and Hedwig F.M. Te Molder. "Computer-Mediated Communication: From a Cognitive to a Discursive Model." *New Media & Society* 5(4) (2003): 451–73.

Landsbergen, David. *Human Error, Trust and Trustworthiness.* A working paper prepared for Battelle Policy Day, cosponsored by Battelle Memorial Institute and the John Glenn Institute for Public Service and Public Policy, The Ohio State University, Columbus, Ohio, February 7, 2006. http://glennschool.osu.edu/research/papers/Landsbergen.pdf.

Lankes, R. David, Joanne Silverstein and Scott Nicholson. *Participatory Networks: The Library as Conversation*. "Produced for the American Library Association's Office for Information Technology Policy." Information Institute of Syracuse, Syracuse University's School of Information Studies. 2006. http://iis.syr.edu/projects/PNOpen/ParticipatoryNetworks.pdf.

LaRose, Robert and Nora Rifon. "Your Privacy is Assured—of Being Disturbed: Websites With and Without Privacy Seals." *New Media & Society* 18(6) (2006): 1009–1029. http://nms.sagepub.com/cgi/reprint/8/6/1009.

Lefebvre, Henri. *The Production of Space*. [Translator, Donald Nicholson-Smith] Malden, MA: Blackwell Publishing, 1991. (First published in 1974 as *La production de l'espace*.)

Lenhart, Amanda and Mary Madden. *Social Networking Websites and Teens: An Overview*. Washington, DC: Pew Internet & American Life Project, January 7, 2007. www.pewinternet.org/PPF/r/198/report_display.asp.

——. *Teens, Privacy and Online Social Networks*. Washington, DC: Pew Internet & American Life Project, April 18, 2007. www.pewinternet.org/PPF/r/211/report_display.asp.

Lessig, Lawrence. "The Architecture of Privacy." Draft 2. Essay presented at the Taiwan Net '98 conference, in Taipei, March 1998. www.lessig.org/content/articles/works/architecture_priv.pdf.

——. *Code Version 2.0*. New York: Basic Books, 2006.

Liao, Ziqi and Michael Tow Cheung. "Internet-based E-banking and Consumer Attitudes: An Empirical Study." *Information & Management* 39(4) (2002): 283–95.

Liebhold, Michael. "Infrastructure for the New Geography." Technology Horizons Program, Institute for the Future, SR-869, August 2004. www.iftf.org/docs/SR_869_Infrastructure_New_Geog.pdf.

Lindsey, Jonathan A. and Ann E. Prentice. *Professional Ethics and Librarians*. Phoenix, Arizona: The Oryx Press, 1985.

Long, Sarah Ann. "Digital Natives: If You Aren't One, Get to Know One." *New Library World* 106(1210/1211) (2005): 187–189.

Lorenzo, George, Diane Oblinger and Charles Dziuban. "How Choice, Co-Creation, and Culture Are Changing What It Means to Be Net Savvy." *EDUCAUSE Quarterly* 30(1) (2007): 6–12. www.educause.edu/apps/eq/eqm07/eqm0711.asp.

Los Angeles Times/Bloomberg. "Tracking the MySpace Generation: A Five-part Series." *The Entertainment Poll*. Los Angeles Times, August 2006. www.latimes.com/entertainment/news/la-entertainmentpoll-special,0,5031928.special?coll=la-home-headlines.

Machill, Marcel, Christoph Neuberger, Wolfgang Schweiger and Werner Wirth. "Navigating the Internet: A Study of German-Language Search Engines." *European Journal of Communication* 19(3) (2004): 321–47. http://ejc.sagepub.com/cgi/reprint/19/3/321.

Madden, Mary. "Young and Wired: How Today's Young Tech Elite Will Influence the Libraries of Tomorrow." Paper presented at the annual meeting for the Tampa Bay Library Consortium, November 3, 2006. Tampa Bay, Florida. www.slideshare.net/zbdigitaal/young-and-wired-how-todays-young-tech-elite-will-influence-the-libraries-of-tomorrow/.

Madden, Mary and Susannah Fox. "Riding the Waves of 'Web 2.0': More than a Buzzword, But Still Not Easily Defined." Washington, DC: Pew Internet & American Life Project, October 5, 2006. www.pewinternet.org/.

Mangu-Ward, Katherine. "Is Privacy Overrated?" *Reason Online,* January 9, 2007. http://reason.com/news/show/117748.html.

Mason, Moya K. "The Ethics of Librarianship: Dilemmas Surrounding Libraries, Intellectual Freedom, and Censorship in the Face of Colossal Technological Progression." [Author's Web site] www.moyak.com/researcher/resume/papers/ethics.html.

Mason, Richard O. "A Tapestry of Privacy: A Meta-Discussion." Prepared for *Privacy: Looking Ahead, Looking Back.* Connolly Program in Business Ethics. Georgetown School of Business. http://cyberethics.cbi.msstate.edu/mason2/.

McConnell, Ben and Jackie Huba. *Citizen Marketers: When People Are the Message.* Chicago: Kaplan Publishing, 2007.

McDonald, Robert H. and Chuck Thomas. "Disconnects Between Library Culture and Millennial Generation Values." *EDUCAUSE Quarterly* 29(4) (2006): 4–6. www.educause.edu/apps/eq/eqm06/eqm0640.asp.

McLuhan, Eric. *Electric Language: Understanding the Message.* New York: A Buzz Book for St. Martin's Press, 1998.

McLuhan, Marshall. *The Gutenberg Galaxy: The Making of Typographic Man.* Toronto: University of Toronto Press, 1962, 2002.

McLuhan, Marshall. *Understanding Media: The Extensions of Man.* New York: McGraw-Hill, 1964.

McMillen, David. "Privacy, Confidentiality, and Data Sharing: Issues and Distinctions." *Government Information Quarterly* 21 (2004): 359–382.

Media Awareness Network. *Young Canadians in a Wired World: Student Survey.* Ottawa, ON: Media Awareness Network, 2005. www.media-awareness.ca/english/research/YCWW/ phaseII/students.cfm.

Meyrowitz, Joshua. *No Sense of Place: The Impact of Electronic Media on Social Behavior.* New York: Oxford University Press, 1985.

Minow, Mary and Tomas Lipinski. *Library's Legal Answer Book.* Chicago: American Library Association, 2003.

Mitrano, Tracy. "A Wider World: Youth, Privacy, and Social Networking Technologies." *EDUCAUSE Review* 41(6) (November/December 2006): 16–29. www.educause.edu/apps/er/erm06/erm0660.asp.

Morello, Diane and Betsy Burton. "Future Worker 2015: Extreme Individualization." Research report, G00138172. Stanford, CT: Gartner, Inc., March 27, 2006.

Moschovitis, Chris, Erica Pearson, Hilary W. Poole, Tami Schuler, Theresa Senft and Mary Sisson. *The Internet: A Historical Encyclopedia, Volume 3, Chronology.* Santa Barbara, CA: MTM Publishing, Inc., 2005.

Murray, Peter E. *Library Patron Privacy: SPEC kit.* SPEC kit, 278. Washington, D.C.: Association of Research Libraries, Office of Leadership and Management Services, 2003.

Negroponte, Nicholas. *Being Digital.* New York: Vintage Books, 1996.

Neuhaus, Paul J. "Privacy and Confidentiality in Digital Reference." *Reference & User Services Quarterly* 43(1) (Fall 2003). www.library.cmu.edu/People/neuhaus/privacy.html.

Nunberg, Geoffrey. "The Places of Books in the Age of Electronic Reproduction." [Personal Web site] Published first in *Representations 24* (Spring 1993). www.ischool.berkeley.edu/~nunberg/places3.html.

Nussbaum, Emily. "Kids, the Internet and the End of Privacy: The New Generation Gap." *New York Magazine* [online version], February 12, 2007. http://nymag.com/news/features/27341/index.html?imw=Y.

Oblinger, Diana G. and Brian L. Hawkins. "The Myth about Putting Information Online." *EDUCAUSE Review* 41(5) (September/October 2006): 14–15. www.educause.edu/apps/er/erm06/erm065.asp.

Office for Intellectual Freedom of the American Library Association. *Intellectual Freedom Manual.* Chicago and London: American Library Association, 2002.

Okabe, Daisuke, Mizuko Ito, Jan Chipchase and Aico Shimizu. *The Social Uses of Purikura: Photographing, Modding, Archiving, and Sharing.* Paper presented at the eighth International Conference on Ubiquitous Computing (UBICOMP), Orange County, CA, September 17–21, 2006. www.itofisher.com/mito/okabe.purikura.pdf.

O'Reilly, Tim. "What is Web 2.0: Design Patterns and Business Models for the Next Generation of Software." *O'Reillynet.com,* September 30, 2005. www.oreillynet.com/lpt/a/6228.

Palen, Leysia and Paul Dourish. 2003. "Unpacking 'Privacy' for a Networked World." Paper presented at CHI (Conference on Human Factors in Computing Systems), Fort Lauderdale, FL, April 5–10, 2003. www.ics.uci.edu/~jpd/publications/2003/chi2003-privacy.pdf.

Palmer, Suzy Szasz. "Reference Service: What Makes it Good? What Makes it Ethical?" *Journal of Information Ethics* 8(2) (1999): 46–58.

Perrin, Stephanie. "RFID and Global Privacy Policy." In Simson Garfinkel and Beth Rosenberg (eds.), *RFID: Applications, Security, and Privacy,* Upper Saddle River, NJ: Addison-Wesley Professional, 2005. www.idtrail.org/files/Perrin%20-%20RFID%20and%20Global%20Privacy%20Policy.pdf.

Peslak, Alan R. "Internet Privacy Policies of the Largest International Companies: The Forbes International 100." *Journal of Electronic Commerce in Organizations* 4(3) (2006): 46–63.

Peter, Jochen and Patti M. Valkenburg. "Research Note: Individual Differences in Perceptions of Internet Communication." *European Journal of Communication* 21(2) (2006): 213–226. www.sagepublications.com.

Piñero, Verónica B. "On Panopticism, Criminal Records and Sex Offender Registries." *First Monday* 11(12) (December 2006). www.firstmonday.org/issues/issue11_12/pinero/index.html.

Podcasting News. "iTunes Hits Two Billion Sold Milestone." www.podcastingnews.com/news/07_01/iTunes-Store-Two-Billion-.html.

Prensky, Marc. "Digital Natives, Digital Immigrants." From *On the Horizon* 9(5) (2001). www.marcprensky.com/writing/Prensky%20-%20Digital%20Natives, %20Digital%20Immigrants%20-%20Part1.pdf.

———. "Digital Natives, Digital Immigrants, Part II: Do They Really Think Differently?" From *On the Horizon* 9(6) (2001). www.marcprensky.com/writing/Prensky%20-%20Digital%20Natives,%20Digital%20Immigrants%20-%20Part2.pdf.

———. "Listen to the Natives." Educational Leadership 63(4) (December 2005/January 2006): 8–13. www.ascd.org/authors/ed_lead/el200512_prensky.html.

Quindlen, Anna. "How We Gave Away Our Own Privacy." *Newsweek* [online version]. June 12, 2006: n.p.

Rainie, Lee. "The State of Blogging." Washington, DC: Pew Internet & American Life Project, January 2, 2005. www.pewinternet.org/PPF/r/144/report_display.asp.

———. "Tagging." Washington, DC: Pew Internet & American Life Project, January 31, 2007. www.pewinternet.org/PPF/r/201/report_display.asp.

Ranganathan, Shiyali Ramamrita. *The Five Laws of Library Science.* London: Edward Goldston, 1931.

Raymond, Eric S. *The Cathedral & the Bazaar: Musings on Linux and Open Source By an Accidental Revolutionary.* Sebastopol, CA: O'Reilly & Associates, Inc., [1999], 2001.

Rheingold, Howard. *Smart Mobs: The Next Social Revolution.* New York: Basic Books, 2002.

———. *The Virtual Community: Homesteading on the Electronic Frontier.* Reading, MA: Addison-Wesley, 1993.

Richards, Pamela S. "Cold War Librarianship: Soviet and American Library Activities in Support of National Foreign Policy, 1946–1991." *Libraries & Culture,* 36(1) (2001): 183–203.

Roberto, Katia and Jessamyn West, eds. *Revolting Librarians Redux: Radical Librarians Speak Out.* Jefferson, NC: McFarland & Company, 2003.

Sanchez, Julian. "How We Got to Caballes: The Cases That Shaped Fourth Amendment Law." *Reason Magazine* [print edition] January 2007. www.reason.com/news/show/117075.html.

Saveri, Andrea. "The Cybernomadic Network." Technology Horizons Program, Institute for the Future, SR-843, March 2004. www.iftf.org/docs/SR-843_Cybernomadic_Framework.pdf.

Scheeres, Julia. "Librarians Split on Sharing Info." *Wired News,* January 16, 2003. www.wired.com/news/privacy/1,57256-0.html.

Schneier, Bruce. *Secrets and Lies: Digital Security in a Networked World.* New York: John Wiley, 2000.

Schweiger, Wolfgang. "Media Credibility—Experience or Image?: A Survey on the Credibility of the World Wide Web in Germany in Comparison to Other Media." *European Journal of Communication* 15(1) (2000): 37–59. http://ejc.sagepub.com/cgi/reprint/15/1/37.

Scott, John P. *Social Network Analysis: A Handbook.* Thousand Oaks, CA: Sage Publications, 2000.

Seaman, Scott. "Confidentiality of Library Records." Presentation at the Annual Meeting, Colorado Library Association, Colorado Springs, CO, October 27, 2001. http://ucblibraries.colorado.edu/adminservices/seaman/Confidentialitylaws.pdf.

Seely Brown, John and Paul Duguid. *The Social Life of Information.* Boston, MA: HBS Publishing, 2002.

Seidelin, Susanne and Stuart Hamilton, eds. *Libraries, National Security, Freedom of Information Laws and Social Responsibilities.* IFLA/FAIFE World Series Report Series vol. V: IFLA/FAIFE World Report Series, Copenhagen, Denmark: 2005.

Selwyn, Neil, Stephen Gorard and John Furlong. "Whose Internet Is It Anyway? Exploring Adults' (Non)Use of the Internet in Everyday Life." *European Journal of Communication* 20 (2005): 5–26.

Shannon, Meg McGinity. "Private Lives: Laws Governing Surveillance Must Keep Pace with Technology." *Communications of the ACM* 49 (2006): 23–26.

Shoesmith, Brian and Mark Balnaves. "Mapping the Digital Divide." Euricom Colloquium: Electronic Networks & Democracy, Nijmegen, Netherlands, October 9–12, 2002. http://baserv.uci.kun.nl/~jankow/Euricom/papers/Shoesmith%20&%20Balnaves.pdf.

Soja, Edward W. *Postmodern Geographies: The Assertion of Space in Critical Social Theory.* New York: Verso, 1989.

Solove, Daniel J. "A Taxonomy of Privacy." *University of Pennsylvania Law Review* 154(3) (2006): 477–564. http://papers.ssrn.com/sol3/papers.cfm?abstract_id=667622#PaperDownload.

Spivack, Nova. "The Third-Generation Web is Coming." *KurzweilAI.net,* December 17, 2006. www.kurzweilai.net/articles/art0689.html.

St. Joseph County Public Library. *Ray of Light: St. Joseph County Public Library* [YouTube video]. http://youtube.com/watch?v=vrtYdFV_Eak.

Staples, William G., ed. *Encyclopedia of Privacy.* Westport, CT: Greenwood Press, 2007.

Starr, Joan. "Libraries and National Security: An Historical View." *First Monday,* 9(12) (2004): n.p. www.firstmonday.org/issues/issue9_12/starr/index.html.

Strahilevitz, Lior J. "A Social Networks Theory of Privacy." University of Chicago Law & Economics, Olin Working Paper No. 230; University of Chicago, Public Law Working Paper No. 79, December 2004. http://papers.ssrn.com/sol3/papers.cfm?abstract_id=629283.

Strauss, Howard J. "The Future of the Web, Intelligent Devices and Education." *EDUCAUSE Review* 42(1) (January/February 2007): 33–46. [Originally published in *Educom Review* 34 (4) (July/August 1999)] www.educause.edu/apps/er/erm07/erm0711.asp.

Swinth, Kimberly R., Shelly D. Farnham and John P. Davis. "Sharing Personal Information in Online Community Member Profiles." Redmond, WA: Microsoft Corporation, 2002. http://research.microsoft.com/scg/papers/sharing%20personal%20information%20in%20online%20 community%20member%20profiles%20-%20with%20names.pdf.

Tapscott, Don and Anthony D. Williams. *Wikinomics: How Mass Collaboration Changes Everything.* New York: Portfolio, 2006.

Tenner, Edward. *Why Things Bite Back: Technology and the Revenge of Unintended Consequences.* New York: Vintage Books, 1997.

Turkle, Sherry. *Life on the Screen: Identity in the Age of the Internet.* New York: Simon and Schuster, 1995.

———. *The Second Self: Computers and the Human Spirit.* Cambridge, MA: MIT Press, [1984] 2005.

University of Minnesota. "Timeline." *Media History Project.* www.mediahistory.umn.edu/timeline/.

Vaagan, Robert W. *The Ethics of Librarianship: An International Survey.* International Federation of Library Associations and Institutions. München: Sauer, 2002.

Vaidhyanathan, Siva. *The Anarchist in the Library: How the Clash between Freedom and Control Is Hacking the Real World and Crashing the System.* New York: Basic Books, 2004.

———. *Copyrights and Copywrongs: The Rise of Intellectual Property and How it Threatens Creativity.* New York: New York University Press, 2001.

Valkenburg, Patti M., Alexander P. Schouten and Jochen Peter. "Adolescents' Identity Experiments on the Internet." *New Media & Society* 7(3) (2005): 383–402. http://nms.sagepub.com/cgi/reprint/7/3/383.

VanSlyke, Timothy. "Digital Natives, Digital Immigrants: Some Thoughts from the Generation Gap." *The Technology Source* Archives, University of North Carolina (May/June 2003). http://technologysource.org/article/digital_natives_digital_immigrants/.

Varnelis, Kazys and Anne Friedberg. "Networked Place." Networked Publics [blog], June 19, 2006. http://netpublics.annenberg.edu/about_netpublics/networked_place.

Viégas, Fernanda B. "Bloggers' Expectations of Privacy and Accountability: An Initial Survey." *Journal of Computer-Mediated Communication* 110(3) (2005): n.p. http://jcmc.indiana.edu/vol10/issue3/viegas.html.

Vishwanath, Arun. "Manifestations of Interpersonal Trust in Online Interaction: A Cross-Cultural Study Comparing the Differential Utilization of Seller Ratings by eBay Participants in Canada, France, and Germany." *New Media & Society* 6(2) (2004): 219–34. http://nms.sagepub.com/cgi/reprint/6/2/219.

Walther, Joseph B., Tracy Loh and Laura Granka. "Let Me Count the Ways: The Interchange of Verbal and Nonverbal Cues in Computer-Mediated and Face-to-Face Affinity." *Journal of Language and Social Psychology* 24(1) (2005): 36–65. http://jls.sagepub.com/cgi/content/abstract/24/1/36.

Wang, Youcheng and Daniel R. Fesenmaier. "Modeling Participation in an Online Travel Community." *Journal of Travel Research* 42 (2004): 261–270.

Weber, John. "Thinking Spatially: New Literacy, Museums and the Academy." *EDUCAUSE Review* 42(1) (January/February 2007): 68–69. www.educause.edu/ir/library/pdf/erm0716.pdf.

Wells, Robert A. "Mobilizing Public Support for War: An Analysis of American Propaganda During World War I." Paper delivered at the Annual Meeting of the International Studies Association, New Orleans, LA, March 24–27, 2002. http://isanet.ccit.arizona.edu/noarchive/robertwells.html.

Wengert, Robert G. "Some Ethical Aspects of Being an Information Professional." *Library Trends* 49(3) (2001): 486–509. http://findarticles.com/p/articles/mi_m1387/is_3_49/ai_75278309/print.

Wertheim, Margaret. *The Pearly Gates of Cyberspace: A History of Space from Dante to the Internet.* New York: W.W. Norton, 1999.

West, Jessamyn, ed. *Digital Versus Non-Digital Reference: Ask a Librarian Online and Offline.* Binghamton, NY: Haworth Information Press, 2004.

Wiegand, Wayne A. *An Active Instrument for Propaganda: The American Public Library During World War I.* New York: Greenwood Press, 1989.

Williams, Dimitri, Nicolas Ducheneaut, Li Xiong, Yuanyuan Zhang, Nick Yee and Eric Nickell. "From Tree House to Barracks: The Social Life of Guilds in World of Warcraft." *Games and Culture* 1(4) (2006): 338–361. http://gac.sagepub.com/cgi/content/abstract/1/4/338.

Williamson, Oliver E., and Sidney G. Winter, eds. *The Nature of the Firm: Origins, Evolution, and Development.* New York: Oxford University Press, 1993.

Wilson, Craig. "Internet Privacy for Sale: A Viable Option When Legislation, Litigation, and Business Self-Regulation Are Ineffective in Curbing the Abuses of Online Consumers' Privacy." *Journal of Information Ethics* 14 (2005): 29–43.

Wilson, Samuel M. and Leighton C. Peterson. "The Anthropology of Online Communities." *Annual Review of Anthropology* 31 (2002): 449–67.

Woo, Jisuk. "The Right Not to be Identified: Privacy and Anonymity in the Interactive Media Environment." *New Media & Society* 8(6) (2006): 949–967. http://nms.sagepub.com/cgi/content/abstract/8/6/949.

Yousafzai, Shumaila Y., John G. Pallister and Gordon R. Foxall. "Strategies for Building and Communicating Trust in Electronic Banking: A Field Experiment." *Psychology & Marketing* 22(2) (2005): 181–201.

———. "A Proposed Model of e-Trust for Electronic Banking. *Technovation* 23(11) (2003): 847–860.

Zakon, Robert H'obbes'. *Hobbes' Internet Timeline v8.2.* www.zakon.org/robert/internet/timeline/.

Zuboff, Shoshana. *In the Age of the Smart Machine: The Future of Work and Power.* New York: Basic Books, 1988.

Internet Sources

Social Networking and Social Media Sites:

Bebo (www.bebo.com)

Classmates.com (www.classmates.com)

del.icio.us (http://del.icio.us)

Facebook (www.facebook.com)

Flickr (www.flickr.com)

Freshmeat (http://freshmeat.net)

ImageShack (www.imageshack.com)

Kodak Easy Share Gallery (www.kodakgallery.com)

Library 2.0 Groups on Ning (http://library20.ning.com/)

Mixi (www.mixi.jp)

MySpace (www.myspace.com)

N-O-T-L Public Library (Niagara-on-the-Lake, Ontario, Canada) MySpace Page (www.myspace.com/notlpl)

Photobucket (www.photobucket.com)

Second Life Library 2.0 (http://infoisland.org/)

Snapfish (www.snapfish.com)

Vancouver Public Library MySpace Page
(http://profile.myspace.com/index.cfm?fuseaction=user.viewprofile&friendid=87728948)

Webshots (www.webshots.com)

Windows Live Spaces (http://home.services.spaces.live.com)

Yahoo! (www.yahoo.com)

YouTube (www.youtube.com)

Blogs:

artsplace SL (http://artfossett.blogspot.com/)

Blog2Song (http://blog2song.blogspot.com/)

Blonde2.0 (www.blonde2dot0.com)

Des Bibliothèques 2.0 (http://bibliotheque20.wordpress.com/)

eduserv's eFoundations (http://efoundations.typepad.com/)

Information Wants to Be Free (http://meredith.wolfwater.com/wordpress/index.php)

Jessamyn.com (www.jessamyn.com/)

LibrarianInBlack.net (http://librarianinblack.typepad.com)

Librarian.net (www.librarian.net/)

MetaFilter.com (www.metafilter.com/)

nicolas morin-notes (www.nicolasmorin.com/blog/)

O'Reilly Radar (http://radar.oreilly.com)

The Ubiquitous Librarian (http://theubiquitouslibrarian.typepad.com)

UK Web Focus (http://ukwebfocus.wordpress.com/)

Wikis:

DCMI (Dublin Core Metadata Initiative) (http://dublincore.org/)

Library Success: A Best Practices Wiki (www.libsuccess.org/index.php?title=Main_Page)

Second Life Education (www.simteach.com/wiki/index.php?title=Second_Life_Education_Wiki)

UKOLN (www.ukoln.ac.uk/)

Wikipedia (www.wikipedia.org)

Other Web sites consulted

About.com (www.about.com/)

Alexa.com (www.alexa.com/)

American Library Association (www.ala.org/)

BBC News Online (http://news.bbc.co.uk/)

Compete.com (www.compete.com)

comScore (www.comscore.com)

Dictionary.com (http://dictionary.reference.com/)

DigiBarn Computer Museum (www.digibarn.com/)

Hitwise (www.hitwise.com)

Google (www.google.com/)

Intel Corporation, Inc. (www.intel.com/)

Internet Usage World Stats (www.internetworldstats.com/)

Intel (www.intel.com/pressroom/kits/quickreffam.htm)

ITU – International Telecommunication Union (www.itu.int/net/home/index.aspx)

Merriam-Webster's Dictionary (www.m-w.com)

MSN (www.msn.com/)

Ohio Historical Society (www.ohiohistory.org)

PC Magazine Encyclopedia (www.pcmag.com)

Popular Inventions (Timeline) (http://qqq.douglas-e.com/home/techistory.html)

Skype (www.skype.com)

Whatis.com (http://whatis.techtarget.com/)

Appendix E: About OCLC

OCLC is a nonprofit membership organization that promotes cooperation among libraries worldwide. More than 60,000 libraries in 112 countries have used OCLC services to locate, acquire, catalog, lend and preserve print and electronic library materials.

OCLC serves

60,000

libraries in

112

countries

OCLC was established in Ohio in 1967 by a small group of libraries whose leaders believed that working together they could find practical solutions to some of the day's most challenging issues. What began as a way to automate the traditional library card catalog rapidly became a collaborative revolution that involved thousands of libraries around the world. Working together, OCLC and its member libraries cooperatively produce and maintain WorldCat, which now contains over 85 million bibliographic records and more than 1.1 billion library holdings.

Collaboration among librarians and OCLC solved the practical problem of automated cataloging. Ongoing collaboration led to additional OCLC services, including services that help libraries build e-content collections and provide online access to special library collections like maps, newspapers, photographs and local histories.

The OCLC membership jointly created the largest interlibrary loan system in the world. Recent expansions and new partnerships in Europe now enable the OCLC collaborative to exchange more than 9.7 million items annually to information consumers and scholars around the world.

WorldCat.org continues OCLC's efforts—begun with the Open WorldCat program— to make library resources more visible to Web users and to increase awareness of libraries as a primary source of reliable information and helpful personal assistance. Where Open WorldCat inserts "Find in a Library" results within regular search engine results, WorldCat.org provides a permanent destination page and search box that lets a broader range of people discover the riches of library-held materials cataloged in the WorldCat database. Both services open up the assets of the OCLC cooperative to the searchers of the world.

In addition to the many services offered, OCLC funds library research programs, library advocacy efforts, scholarships, market research and professional development opportunities.

OCLC Programs and Research incubates new technologies, sponsors the work of library scientists and represents libraries on a range of international standards bodies. OCLC Programs and Research is also actively engaged with the world's information community to further the science of librarianship.

OCLC library advocacy programs are part of a long-term initiative to champion libraries to increase their visibility and viability within their communities. Programs include advertising and marketing materials to reinforce the idea of the library as relevant, and market research reports that identify and communicate trends of importance to the library profession. Several of the reports are noted in the introduction to this report and on the following page.

OCLC provides financial support for those beginning their library careers and for established professionals who excel in their endeavors through a series of annual awards and scholarships. Of note is the IFLA/OCLC Early Career Development Fellowship Program, jointly sponsored by the International Federation of Library Associations and Institutions (IFLA), OCLC and the American Theological Library Association (ATLA). The program provides early career development and continuing education for library and information science professionals from countries with developing economies.

OCLC participates in WebJunction, which is an online community of libraries and other agencies that share knowledge and experience to provide the broadest public access to information technology. A service created by the Bill & Melinda Gates Foundation's U.S. Library Program, OCLC and other partners, WebJunction features articles, handouts, courses and forum discussions that are practical, down-to-earth and friendly. WebJunction addresses the real issues that librarians and library staff face every day.

OCLC's vision is to be the leading global library cooperative, helping libraries serve people by providing economical access to knowledge through innovation and collaboration. OCLC is headquartered in Dublin, Ohio, U.S. and has offices throughout the world.

Australia
Suite 5, 131 Paisley Street
Footscray, Victoria 3011
Australia
T +61-3-9362 8500
F +61-3-9362 8501
E australia@oclc.org

Canada
701 Salaberry Street, Suite 200
Chambly, QC J3L 1R2 Canada
T +1-450-658-6583
   888-658-6583
F +1-450-658-6231
E canada@oclc.org

China
Room 1207, 12th Floor
China Electronics Plaza,
Building B
No. 3, Dan Ling Road
Hai Dian District, Beijing 100080 China
T +86-10-8260-7538
F +86-10-8260-7539
E china@oclc.org

France
14, Place des Victoires
92600 Asnières sur Seine, France
T +33-1-55-02-14-80
F +33-1-47-93-50-13
E france@oclc.org

Germany
Grünwalder Weg 28g
82041 Oberhaching, Deutschland
T +49-89-613-08-300
F +49-89-613-08-399
E deutschland@oclc.org

Mexico
Av. Amores 707 Desp. 401
Col. Del Valle
México 03100, D.F.
T +52-55-5687-3307
F +52-55-5523-9212
E mexico@oclc.org

Netherlands
Schipholweg 99, 2316 XA
P.O. Box 876, 2300 AW
Leiden, Nederland
T +31-71-524-65-00
F +31-71-522-31-19
E nederland@oclc.org

Switzerland
St. Jakobs-Strasse 96
4052 Basel, Schweiz
T +41-61-378-80-70
F +41-61-378-80-79
E schweiz@oclc.org

United Kingdom
7th Floor, Tricorn House
51-53 Hagley Road, Edgbaston
Birmingham B16 8TP, UK
T +44-121-456-46-56
F +44-121-456-46-80
E uk@oclc.org

United States
6565 Kilgour Place
Dublin, OH 43017-3395 USA
T +1-614-764-6000
   800-848-5878
   (US + Canada only)
F +1-614-764-6096
E usa@oclc.org

Related OCLC Research and Reports

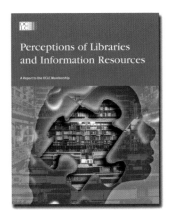

The *Perceptions of Libraries and Information Resources* (2005) report to the OCLC membership summarizes findings of an international study on information-seeking habits and preferences. The study was conducted to help us learn more about: library use; awareness and use of library electronic resources and Internet search engines; use of free vs. for-fee information; and the "Library" brand. The report was based on the survey results from 3,348 respondents from six countries: Australia, Canada, India, Singapore, the U.K. and the U.S. To access the report, visit the OCLC Web site at: **www.oclc.org/reports/2005perceptions.htm.**

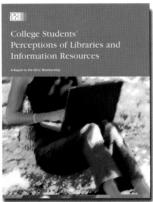

The *College Students' Perceptions of Libraries and Information Resources* (2006) report to the OCLC membership, presents a subset of the *Perceptions of Libraries and Information Resources* report, and focuses on the perceptions and behaviors of 396 undergraduate or graduate students ranging in age from 15 to 57. The study was conducted to help us learn more about: library use; awareness and use of library electronic resources and Internet search engines; use of free vs. for-fee information; and the "Library" brand. To access the report, visit the OCLC Web site at: **www.oclc.org/reports/perceptionscollege.htm.**

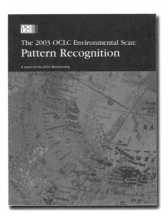

The 2003 OCLC Environmental Scan: Pattern Recognition report was published in January 2004 for OCLC's worldwide membership to examine the significant issues and trends impacting OCLC, libraries, museums, archives and other allied organizations, both now and in the future. The *Scan* provides a high-level view of the information landscape, intended both to inform and stimulate discussion about future strategic directions. To access the *Scan*, visit the OCLC Web site at: **www.oclc.org/reports/2003escan.htm.**

Appendix F: Comparative Timeline

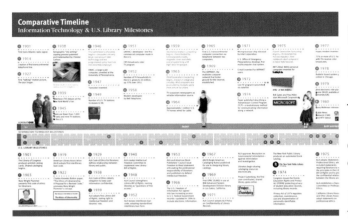

Library and Information Technology

Today's virtual communities and social networking software represent the natural progression of communication and community-building technology that started more than a century ago with the telegraph and telephone.

Libraries have been at the forefront of adopting collaborative technology and delivering content and services on emerging community platforms to better serve users and streamline operations. Below are a few U.S. highlights. For more information, see the "Comparative Timeline on Information Technology and U.S. Library Milestones" insert.

1901   The U.S. Library of Congress produces printed catalog cards. Shared cataloging begins.

1919   American Library Association (ALA) adopts its first resource sharing code.

1952   ALA revises interlibrary loan code, adopting standardized interlibrary loan form.

1969   The first online public access catalog is in use at the IBM Advanced System Development Division library.

1971   Libraries begin sharing cataloging resources electronically.

1979   Libraries begin lending and borrowing resources using a computer-driven interlibrary loan system.

1992   Librarian Jean Armour Polly coins the phrase "surfing the Internet."

1994   Library Web sites launch at Virginia Tech University, the University of Michigan and the U.S. Naval Research library.

1995   Jenny Levine creates the first library technology blog.

1998   Bill Drew at the State University of New York at Morrisville offers real-time reference service using instant messaging (IM).

2006   Libraries start providing services in Second Life, an online, 3D virtual world.

2006   Launch of WorldCat.org—sharing the library holdings of more than 10,000 libraries on the Web.

2007   More than 25,000 videos on YouTube tagged or described with the term "library" or "librarian" as of September 2007.